CULT OF GT-R

A TRUE STORY OF CRIME, OBSESSION AND THE WORLD'S MOST COVETED CAR

RYAN K. ZUMMALLEN

CONTENTS

Chapter 1	1
Chapter 2	11
Chapter 3	25
Chapter 4	50
Chapter 5	71
Chapter 6	89
Chapter 7	101
Chapter 8	121
Chapter 9	143
Chapter 10	166
Chapter 11	183
Chapter 12	198
Chapter 13	208
Chapter 14	225
Chapter 15	245
Acknowledgments	255
Notes	259
About the Author	279

For Nikol.

CHAPTER 1

Follow the man with the keys, I was told. He pushed a small metal dolly, the size of a mini-fridge, with tiny grocery cart wheels that rattled over bumps and cracks in the pavement. I skipped nonchalantly to keep pace, but inside my stomach was leaping with excitement. The cart's bottom shelf held oil jugs, jumper cables, and tackle boxes. Bright blue tackle boxes, full of keys. With each tiny crack along the way the keys clanked and jangled around inside. I had traveled thousands of miles to see what they could unlock.

My hosts asked me, politely, not to photograph the man. Or his cart. Or the building. Not that the building itself is that interesting—located twenty miles outside of Tokyo, it's nondescript, gray, made of corrugated sheet metal. Every day the structure goes completely unnoticed by the thousands who walk or drive past it. But inside, it held treasures. To some, those treasures are worth spending a life pursuing. My guide and I followed closely as the man and his cart moved noisily across the lot. It was a slightly awkward, low-tech parade toward something so hallowed. I had to laugh.

When we reached the structure, the man with the cart stopped by a large roll-up door. He removed the massive padlock holding the door in place, then pressed a button on the wall.

As the door lifted, midday sunlight inched across the ground, creeping into the room and exploring all its corners and walls. My guide and I ducked underneath the door and stepped into the cavernous space beyond, eyes slowly adjusting to the darkness and the hoard within.

Rows and rows of forbidden Japanese sports cars. Everywhere the eye could see.

I HAD COME to Japan to chase a ghost. At least, that's what I thought at first.

Japan has its own world of quirky, cute, and exclusive cars. Compared with typical American cars, the ones on Japanese roads have dimensions and proportions that seem to be from outer space. Often they're incredibly small, or bizarrely skinny and tall. Others have bubbly headlights, or curves and creases that smile at you from all directions. Even the angry-looking ones are at least a little adorable. Each reflects pieces of Japanese culture, which treasures humble principles like politeness, gratitude, and pride in a shared common identity. And when it comes to sports cars, no single model unites people like the golden child of the Japanese auto industry: the Nissan GT-R.

The first GT-R, boxy but shockingly quick, appeared in 1969. But the versions that came later, those that would be immortalized in films and video games and street racing lore, were the third-generation "Skyline GT-Rs." Nissan made them from 1989 to 2002, in three different versions that captured the attention of the world. Enthusiasts refer to those models by their code names: The first, the R32 GT-R, arrived in 1989, followed by the R33 GT-R of 1994 and the R34 GT-R of 1999. Each version achieved global fame on its own terms, and each has a fervent fanbase. In recent years, each has become hugely valuable.

None of these GT-Rs were originally sold in the United States.

You couldn't walk into a Nissan dealership and buy one new, and for the most part, you couldn't find one overseas and bring it to America yourself, either. The Skyline GT-R was as close to banned as any car could get. This was due to an obscure U.S. law, passed in 1988, that expressly prohibited any vehicle not originally certified for American sale from entering the country. Instead, you had to wait until the vehicle turned 25 years old before you could bring it in. As a result, insiders call this the "25-year rule." The law's history is long and complicated, its enforcement shared by dozens of state and federal agencies, but its core edict is clear: If a vehicle is less than a quarter-century old, and wasn't sold here when new, then you're going to have to wait.

Over the last three decades, the third-gen GT-R has steadily built a legend in the United States. Once, simply knowing the car existed made you part of a small, select group. These days, the R32, R33, and R34 GT-Rs are cherished icons. Yet most Americans have never seen one, and have come to accept that they may never see an example in person, much less park one in their driveway—to them the Skyline GT-R exists as more of an idea than a real, physical car you can drive on the road. For professional vehicle importers and sellers, the GT-R was once the equivalent of the Italian black truffle, or a rare and exotic jewel—essentially, worth its weight in gold. And ever since, for U.S. authorities and regulators, the GT-R has been nothing less than a huge pain in the ass.

All this led me to that secret warehouse on the outskirts of Tokyo. I was trying to get to know a phantom. Once I got there, though, it became clear I was on the tail of something much more difficult to pin down: a dream.

I STOOD FROZEN. Inside the hangar-sized space, with its gray walls and aged steel support beams, the building could easily have passed for a Soviet-era bomb shelter. The cars consumed it. There were at least 60 of them, parked side-by-side in rows of 10, with scarcely enough room to squeeze sideways between them. Stranglers nestled neatly in the corners, or wedged into whatever small pockets of open space could be managed.

Nearly all of them were Skyline GT-Rs—the R34 version, to be exact. Today, it's the rarest and most coveted of the trio. Built for the Japanese market, each one was right-hand-drive with a manual transmission. The R34 GT-R is unmistakable with its boxy body, gaping bumper intakes, and enormous rear spoiler. Stare at it from the rear and a pair of comically large, perfect-circle dual taillights will stare right back.

The first two versions of the Skyline GT-R, the R32 and R33, are now more than 25 years old. As a result, they've been eligible to legally import into the U.S. for years. But when I visited the secret storage warehouse, that time had not yet come for the R34. It's incredibly rare to see one in America. They are the forbidden fruit of the car world. There, laid at my feet and basking in the Japanese dusk, were dozens.

"It's a jaw-dropping moment," my host whispered. "You know how much these cars cost."

It takes a special car that will appreciate in value over time. But the appreciation of the R34 GT-R is frankly unprecedented. Adjusting for inflation and converting from Japanese yen, the R34 Skyline GT-R sold for roughly $70,000 USD at the time of its 1999 launch. Two decades later, good examples cost twice that. On the day I stood in that warehouse, many of the cars I saw were valued at $150,000 USD and up, even as the mileage on their odometers surpassed 100,000 kilometers. Some particularly rare editions, or cars with specialty parts, were worth more. Much more.

My guide, a welcoming 26-year-old with floppy bangs named Masaki, or Masa for short, worked at the facility. He pointed out a car whose rare paint color helped elevate its value to more than $200,000. Then he smiled and nodded at another car, stuffed with upgrades, that had recently sold for $300,000.

All told, the warehouse probably held $10 million in GT-Rs.

Every one of them had already been bought and paid for, the vast majority by American customers. Since they were unable to take delivery at home, due to the 25-year rule—at the time of my visit, the closest R34s were still almost a year from that milestone—the cars' owners had paid to keep them stored safely in Japan. Then they waited. One GT-R had been kept in that building for seven years. Technicians started it up occasionally, in order to keep its battery from dying. Some buyers made special trips across the Pacific to "visit" their cars, journeying to the warehouse as if it were the Louvre. Others had been waiting years to bring home a six-figure object they had only seen in photographs. All of them were paying hundreds of dollars in rent each month to store a vehicle an ocean away, and when those machines eventually came of age and got shipped off to America, there were more parked outside, waiting to take their place.

GT-R owners aren't turned off by the fact that the car they love is difficult to acquire and own. On the contrary, they live for it. They are consumed by it. The lengths to which they will go, I would come to learn, are often fanatical. The rewards they seek can appear meager, the risk astronomical. This is, after all, a Nissan. People have smuggled GT-Rs into the U.S. by gambling their careers, their life savings, and even their freedom. The criminal aspect and those it drew in helped make the cars irresistible. People wanted to own one, and movies, TV shows, and video games wanted to showcase one. Maybe you saw a GT-R racing through the streets in *The Fast & the Furious*. Maybe you drove a digital version on PlayStation or Xbox, in *Gran Turismo* or *Forza Motorsport*.

That small taste, a brief screen glimpse or a virtual recreation, was enough for some. The rest became obsessed.

This was the world I wanted to explore. The journey would take me from the gray and black markets of Los Angeles to 19th-century Japan, the roots of illegal street racing in Tokyo, and back to L.A. again. Over ten months of research, interviews, and travel, I examined hundreds of GT-Rs and met countless owners. Each of those people had a version of the dream that was different and unique.

More often than not, those dreams had just one thing in common—the dreamer was determined to make them come true.

And when it comes to making your GT-R dream a reality, and doing it the right way, most everyone agrees that there's only one person to call.

I MET Sean Morris by accident. We're both dads, and our kids periodically attended the same summer camps and swim lessons. But it wasn't until we began running into each other at car shows—me snapping pictures and interviewing owners, Morris exhibiting cars and promoting his business—that the dots connected.

Morris is the director at Toprank International Vehicle Importers, a registered importer and dealer with its U.S. headquarters in Cypress, California, a quiet suburb of Los Angeles. Tucked away in an innocent-looking business park, the company's office gives no outside clues to its status as a pillar of modern car culture. Except, of course, for the spotless Skyline GT-Rs that are usually parked out front.

In the murky underworld of privately imported cars, the Toprank name carries a rare air of sophistication. As one owner told me, "It's almost like you can have a GT-R, or you can have a Toprank GT-R." The firm does more than just imports and sales—it conducts in-depth vehicle inspections, offers service and repairs, and can help customers track down hard-to-find parts or specific models upon request. Toprank has also helped build a cottage industry around Japanese Domestic Market (JDM) machinery, vehicles built specifically for sale in Japan, with extravagant services and practices that many outside the car world might find hard to believe.

"I don't know everything," the 48-year-old Morris told me, "but I know a lot."

The evidence speaks for itself. On a gloomy December Saturday, wearing his trademark unzipped hoodie and a pair of loosely tied sneakers, his short blond hair pushed over and cropped close at the sides, Morris welcomed me into Toprank's waiting room. After a quick hello he led me through the office and down a darkened hallway to a heavy metal door that opened with a creak.

When he flipped on the lights in the next room, dozens of the most desirable cars on the planet appeared, packed together like turbocharged sardines. There was a rare Porsche 911, a dramatic Mitsubishi Evo with fog lights like goldfish eyes, a Lancia Delta hatchback in iconic Martini racing colors. Mostly, however, there were Skylines. Maybe 20 in total, across a wide range of years, and potentially millions of dollars in inventory. Some sat uncovered, others were wrapped tenderly in protective plastic, parked on the floor or hoisted high on hydraulic lifts.

These were not barn finds or forsaken rejects, some forgotten trove rotting after decades of neglect. They were among the best of the best. Cars imported and sold by Toprank are cared for and meticulously prepped by a team of mechanics and technicians that sometimes includes Morris himself. Their batteries are charged, their engines are verified as running well or repaired until they do, and they are not missing parts unless the team has determined it can find and fit a better replacement. If a car in the building isn't already sold, it's being prepped for sale to a hungry customer lying in wait.

This approach has undoubtedly boosted the company's repute. Toprank sells roughly 200 cars per year in the United States, a figure that may sound impressive, but remains a relatively small churn for a business that employs dozens and is subject to steep California taxes. But hard-to-get JDM cars attract a premium, and Skylines make up around 75-percent of sales.

Toprank is a Skyline treasure trove. And the company is particularly adept at dealing with the rarest, meanest, fastest of all—the Skyline GT-R.

Morris can come off as gruff. He is known for chewing people out, and famously has no problem telling someone if he thinks they're wrong. He once described a positive friendship to me with the words, "I think I only threatened to punch him in the face once."

But I have seen moments of sweetness. Once, when I set up a table at a local meet to sell copies of my first book, it came with a space to park a show car. I called Morris, who pulled up in a goofy-looking, imported Australian car-slash-pickup called the Holden Commodore. We threw my books into the open rear bed and sped off. The Holden was the smash hit of the show; people would beeline from across the lawn to see it, and Morris visibly enjoyed answering questions and sharing their memories. He helped me fashion makeshift cardboard book stands. On the drive home, he regaled me with stories, rumors, and myths from his world and its seemingly endless cast of characters—colorful language included.

Morris is an import himself. Born in New Zealand, his family emigrated to America when he was a child. His grandfather bought a gas station; his father became a car dealer. After high school, Morris enlisted in the Navy, where he was assigned to maintain the engines of frigate ships. He carries the self-assured, weathered, seen-it-all look of someone who has spent significant time at sea. After his discharge in the mid-1990s, he entered the family business, which had grown to include the importing and exporting of vehicles.

Morris spent years listening to industry friends tell him that Skylines were illegal to import. He began to wonder why. After acquaintances helped explore the various routes for bringing a car into the United States, he dove into a rabbit hole of restrictions and requirements, one that ended with him becoming the country's de facto authority on GT-R importation. Many of the others who could have vied for that title, at one point or another, have ended up in handcuffs. Morris, however, has managed to stay clean. One of the first GT-Rs he ever imported is a rare R32 Nismo model he owns and drives to this day.

From the outside, Morris doesn't scream "international arbitrage expert." His preferred wardrobe is best described as a cross between San Diego skater and warehouse stocker at your local Best Buy. But he speaks with conviction, and in a drawl that often seems intentionally drawn out to give you time to catch up. Conversations with him can weave through a thick jungle of acronyms, shorthand for everything from laws to government agencies, in a tone that can read as arrogance. It all suggests he knows more than you do—and with importing in general and Skylines in particular, he almost always does. One of Morris's favorite stories to tell is the time he offered to lecture a local branch of U.S. Immigration and Customs Enforcement officers on the various ways they commonly misunderstand their own importing laws.

Confusion abounds in the Skyline community. Lying and cheating are rampant. People regularly come to Morris when they want something done the right way, or to fix their mistakes after they've ventured too far down the wrong path. His straightforward style isn't always gentle, but he likes to think it helps people make informed decisions. One person with more than 20 years in this world told me that Morris is, in his experience, "the only guy to truly be straight-up."

If you're new to the JDM game, the regulatory complexity can make your head spin. Plenty of unscrupulous dealers promise easy solutions that leave customers high and dry. For every company like Toprank, there are many others that will bungle the process, resulting in the government seizing your vehicle or even sending it to the crusher. Some of those firms demand nonrefundable cash down payments, then fail to deliver a car at all. In a business where passionate customers often hand over deposits of $20,000 or $30,000 for an unseen car an ocean away, trust is everything. "You can't afford to do it wrong," Morris said.

Soon after I began researching and reporting this book, I was hanging out at the Toprank office all the time. I was there during Christmas break when employees brought their kids to the office, and I dodged Nerf-gun fights while flipping through archived GT-R books and magazines. I was there when an associate walked through the front door and handed Morris the elusive California environmental certification for an older model of Honda Civic Type R, a document he had waited on for nearly a year. This piece of paper meant the importing process was complete, and the car that had been taking up prime real estate in his lot could finally be shipped to its owner. Morris hugged it tightly to his chest, and smiled mockingly, then danced around the room with it.

If anyone could help me find a true understanding of the GT-R dream, I thought, it was this guy.

CHAPTER 2

In that first visit to the Toprank garage, Morris walked me through some of the more notable cars in the room. Over here, an R32 GT-R, upgraded by a legendary Japanese shop called Mine's with expensive and lightweight carbon-fiber parts. Over there, an R33 in a stunning shade, Midnight Purple, a rare Nissan color that GT-R hunters lust over. And up there, on that lift, an R34, still not legal for ordinary importation. That particular car was brought in through a specific exemption that allows it here ahead of schedule. Another R34 nearby was once raced professionally, by Morris as team boss, its eye-catching red livery bearing the scars of battles long ago.

Nissan built roughly 60,000 examples of the third-gen Skyline GT-Rs, across the R32, R33, and R34 models. Only a tiny fraction of that number now lives in America. Spotting a true GT-R on U.S. roads is unfathomable to most car nuts. If they were dropped into that garage with me, next to Morris, many fans of the badge would simply struggle to speak.

This is the most worshipped car Nissan makes. The very first GT-R coupe, an angular little two-door, dominated Japanese motorsports almost immediately in 1969. The model's official name, 2000 GT-R, was quickly supplanted by a nickname, *Hakosuka*, pronounced "Hah-koe-ska," and rooted in the Japanese slang for "boxy."

The legend was off and running, but it was soon cut off at the knees. The global oil crisis of the 1970s led to restrictions that left the second GT-R, nicknamed *Kenmeri,* listless and without a market. (Depending on who you believe, the name is either a punny salute to the model's Detroitish looks—ken-meri, meri-ken—or a nod to Japanese-market commercials that featured characters named Ken and Mary.) Nissan built only 197 examples before killing production in 1973. The GT-R faded to black, the name dormant, unused on a Nissan for the next 16 years.

The everyday Skyline kept going, however, without the GT-R. Nissan continued building more Skyline sedans and coupes through the '70s and early '80s as consumers valued efficiency over power. In the late 1980s, the drought finally ended. Flush with cash from a strong domestic economy and increasing overseas profits, Nissan spared no expense in research and development. For the 1989 Skyline GT-R, the R32, four whole iterations of Skyline past the Kenmeri, the company designed a monster of an engine, a 2.6-liter straight six-cylinder known internally as the RB26. Then it gifted that engine with two turbochargers, for bursts of speed and power.

Computer technology had improved by leaps and bounds since the Kenmeri. To help take advantage of the new engine, Nissan developed two game-changing secrets: rear-wheel steering, called HICAS, that made the car both more agile and more stable; and a four-wheel drive system, ATTESA ET-S, that helped make the R32 shockingly easy to drive at high speed.

The legacy of the mighty Hakosuka had been thrust into the future. Over the coming years, the new R32 GT-R would dominate motorsport in Japan and Australia, winning a vast majority of the races it entered and returning the GT-R name to glory. On public streets, the R32 devoured mountain roads, and became a favorite of illegal street racers who gained underground fame for their risky highway antics. Outside Japan, the GT-R became the star of video games, comic books, television shows and motion pictures. It also helped fuel Japan's feverish tuning and aftermarket scene, inspiring ambitious mechanics to open up shop and become cult stars themselves. An Australian magazine put the R32 GT-R on its cover with a simple description: "Godzilla on Wheels."

This was a comfortable, fast, affordable, and fiendishly tunable sports car to rival the best in the world, as advanced as anything on the market. People began to discuss Nissan's achievement in the same breath as cars from companies like BMW, Porsche, and Ferrari.

The two GT-Rs that followed, R33 and R34, pushed the name to even higher plateaus. Along with the R32, those groundbreaking machines formed a kind of GT-R Holy Trinity. With time, they would become some of the most coveted vehicles on earth.

ONE AFTERNOON, a notification popped up on my phone. It was a text message from Morris:

"GT-R meetup at our shop Wednesday night. Hopefully not too many people."

I arrived early, pulling up to the Toprank office about an hour before the meet was scheduled to start. A few GT-Rs had already been parked outside, planning an easy departure for the evening cruise. I found Morris tidying the office waiting room, then followed him out front. It had rained earlier, so he used a push broom to sweep away puddles and debris, spitting out his latest frustrations with the government's inane importing policies as he worked.

Owners began showing up. First came Toprank sales chief Brian Jannusch, a towering six-foot-six sales director with a long mop of blond hair, in his black R32. Then a yellow R32 Skyline, not a GT-R, but still a favorite for its exaggerated aftermarket widebody kit. The building's small side lot was soon full—a grey R32, then a red one; a purple R33, then a silver one. As more cars arrived, they filled up the street parking spaces, too.

A few attendees were well-known in GT-R circles. The influencer Dustin Williams, with more than 750,000 subscribers on YouTube, arrived in yet another purple R33. Mickey Andrade, the head of content at parts company Throtl, with his trademark bushy beard, had brought the bright-yellow widebody. A professional racecar driver named Dai Yoshihara climbed from a silver R33 he had built and customized with the hallowed aftermarket supplier GReddy.

By that point, there were more than a dozen GT-Rs in all directions. Everyone milled around, saying hello and poking at cars, but the center of the action was unlikely, given the star power nearby: Everyone wanted to see Chris Payne's car.

MANY COME to the GT-R community bearing huge fanbases or large windfalls of cash. But your car always does more talking than your Internet status. Within the Skyline GT-R world there are dozens of different hard-to-get models, with special names like GT-R Nismo, or V-Spec or M-Spec. Nissan's performance arm, Nismo, made a dizzying number of rare upgrades, too—the S-Tune suspension, the Fine-Spec motor. With enough cash you could order the RB26 as a limited edition S1, R1 or N1. At one point, Nismo even made their own complete cars, the hallowed 400R for the R33, and the elusive Z-Tune for the R34.

They all mean different things, and can further be outfitted with hundreds of different hard-to-get parts from any number of workshops. Having the right car, and the right set of "How'd you get that?" parts, often comes down to who you know and how long you've been in the game. It also marks you as a true GT-R junkie. It's often the more secretive owners who pull up, without anyone knowing their names, in the most jaw-dropping cars at the meet.

Many owners dream of finding a traditional Japanese workshop to partner with, getting them to build a custom one-off machine. Japanese mechanics are famously detail-oriented, and often meticulous to a fault. But with patient clients, their slow pace can lead to extraordinary results. Some of the most famous are the high-octane specialists at Blitz, based in Tokyo, or the outlaw attitude of Top Secret from its base in Chiba City.

One shop, called Mine's, became a global sensation in the 1990s when its rebuilt R34 GT-R spanked a tuned Toyota Supra on a nationally-televised Japanese program called *Best Motoring*. The hosts, professional drivers famous in their own right, were visibly shocked and hailed the car's speed and precision. The Mine's R34 GT-R later brought its iconic look, white with ghostly silver graphics, to video games like *Gran Turismo*. This only made it more famous. GT-R owners around the world clamor for anything born out of its tiny shop on the Miura Peninsula, at the mouth of Tokyo Bay.

Payne, a tall and slender visual effects artist with a quick smile and disarming staccato laugh, flies under the radar compared with some high-profile folks at the Toprank meet. And his R32 GT-R looks like nothing else. He popped the hood and invited people to see.

The most notable addition is an enormous rear wing rising high above the trunk. The suspension has been lowered, and it features striking gold wheels. Up front, an aggressive bumper with large intakes feeds more air to the engine. The RB26 engine is fairly advanced but it's also straightforward and easy to understand. There's a large engine block in the middle, a metal intake tube to the left and twisting turbocharger pipes to the right. Payne's car, however, was painstakingly assembled by an elite custom house called Garage Saurus. It had a lot more going on.

Garage Saurus is known for its ability to fit seemingly impossible combinations of parts under the hood of a GT-R. On Payne's car, the center engine cover is gloss black and has the shop's dinosaur logo cut into it. Around the cover is a who's-who of the top names in Japanese speed parts. A Nismo strut brace stands over the engine bay, bridging one side of the suspension to the other. HKS turbo pipes tangle themselves to the right. An aluminum Evolve radiator is topped by a GReddy cap. White hoses weave their way around and through various components; bright purple fuel injectors stand atop the engine; a series of blue tubes punctuate the layout. The whole system is a serious upgrade from the advertised 276 horsepower in a stock RB26 engine.

Payne's car isn't insanely powerful—some GT-Rs easily top 1,000 horsepower—and its overall value is far from the upper echelon of the rarest cars priced like unicorn tears. But with the help of Garage Saurus, he has created a true one-of-one, lovingly tailored to his particular tastes. It's the culmination of a process begun when he was a teenager. Inspired by a next-door neighbor who had lived in Japan, Payne entered a student-exchange program in the late '90s, and at just 17 years old he lived in Tokyo with a host family for three months. One day, a man Payne knew only as Mr. Yana invited the host family to visit the U.S. military outpost for a fireworks show. When Mr. Yana pulled up to the house, Payne forgot about the fireworks. The man had arrived in a black R32 GT-R, the first Payne had seen in person. Climbing into the back seat, he told himself, "I gotta have one."

Payne would later buy a modern GT-R, a new one called the R35—Nissan's latest, launched in 2008 and sold in America from the start. He also has an R33 that he's converting to electric propulsion. But his true vision didn't really come together until he acquired the R32, and met a Japanese native by way of Canada.

NON FUJITA LIVES in Southern California, but he made his name in Vancouver, and he is sought after for his distinctly Japanese approach to his work.

Fujita-san, as he's known, is the GT-R specialist for Garage Saurus. (The "-san" suffix means "dear," or "honorable Mr. or Mrs.," in Japanese.) Over his entire 30-year career he has worked exclusively on the more affordable Nissan S-chassis, or "Silvia," and the Skyline GT-R. Back in Japan he owns an R34 GT-R he converted from two doors into a four-door by himself. His two grown children are a daughter named Silvia and a son named Skyline.

In 2007, Fujita's prowess under the hood of a GT-R caught the attention of Garage Saurus, a fixture on the Japanese drag racing scene in the late 1980s. Its founder asked Fujita to move to Vancouver and open a Garage Saurus offshoot there, servicing the growing Canadian market. So that's what he did, going on to build behemoths like a 900-hp R34 GT-R aimed at drag racing and a track-focused R34 in stunning Midnight Purple III paint. The latter was less powerful but, noticeably, more meticulously assembled.

That meticulousness became Fujita's calling card. As his work gained a reputation for abnormal attention to detail, the man himself became known for having absolutely zero fear of telling a customer that their personal vision isn't the best path.

"I always tell the customer, when I [start cutting on] the car in the garage, that's no longer the customer's car—that's my car," he told me. "I don't want to do some Mickey Mouse car. That's why I'm slow. I'm not fast. I need to double-check, triple-check. Because no one touches —only I touch. So if something happens, it's my fault. I need to do it right."

In Chris Payne, Fujita has found a kindred spirit. The two Skyline fanatics met in 2017, as Garage Saurus turned its attention to the United States. The R32 GT-R was slowly becoming legal at the time. Fujita opened a space in California, the hotbed of GT-R owners in the U.S.

At the same time, Payne was sitting on an R32 GT-R he'd purchased, sight unseen, in Japan. He paid $12,000, he told me, and though that's a paltry sum for a true Godzilla today, Payne fretted that he'd made a huge mistake. At the time, R32 GT-Rs were typically valued around $8,000. Add in the cost to ship and import the car, plus some needed refurbishments and upgrades, and the fact that parts were beginning to strain and crack, and Payne found himself in a deeper and deeper hole.

The last straw came when the GT-R started belching white smoke. Payne was in the middle of a lap on a racetrack in the SoCal desert when the oil pan cracked. Now he needed an expert. Meanwhile, Fujita was ready to start the first Garage Saurus build in the U.S. After linking up, they sourced a new engine and outlined the project's goals: Payne wanted a suitable amount of power, just not so much to produce component stress and major failures. That was fine with Fujita, who prefers sensible upgrades and high-quality parts that help ensure longevity. Most of all, Payne gave him the time he needed and stayed out of the way.

Today, the result is a 600-hp car, with a completely reworked engine bay, and fully customized suspension. Fujita-san calls 600 horses "the sweet spot." At that point, he said, the car is enough to turn heads and delight eardrums on the street, yet it retains the lightness and balance required to take down Porsches at the track.

That's what drew the crowd to Payne's car at the Toprank event—the functionality on display, the craftsmanship of Fujita's work, and the fact that every part had a role to play and hadn't simply been stuffed under the hood without rhyme or reason. It was designed to perform, not to attract likes and subscribers, and because Fujita had poured into it his decades of experience, the end result was genuinely useful for his client. It demonstrated that Garage Saurus had officially taken its place in the pantheon of hallowed GT-R tuners. I couldn't wait to hear it on the road.

PAYNE FIRST CAME across Sean Morris on Internet-forum chat rooms. Through the early 2000s GT-R culture thrived online, where fans could share stories and rumors, speculate over who would get busted next, and gawk over whatever scraps of old videos and magazines were scanned or uploaded through quasi-legal torrent sites. Before GT-R importation was legal, Payne called Morris to inquire about "creative" ways to bring a car into the country. Morris told him to forget it. Later, when the R35 hit dealers, he helped Payne secure a spot to buy one. And when Payne finally found his R32 in Japan, Morris organized the transport and importation.

Still, most everyone else on the cruise had a more recent relationship with Morris and Toprank. As the R32 and R33 GT-Rs turned 25 and became legal to own in the US, it's been easiest for customers to simply call up the Toprank office and roll all the associated costs for an import and purchase into one transaction. The trade-off is how, as each model from the Holy Trinity has hit 25, it's become more and more expensive.

No one has found a $12,000 R32 GT-R in a long time. The models gathered at the Toprank cruise are typically valued somewhere between $60,000-$70,000, with some topping $100,000. That may seem odd, a car somehow becoming more expensive as it grows more common on American streets. Plus, for all the pomp and circumstance, at the end of the day, these are still 30-year-old Nissans. But the demand is so high that the supply can't possibly keep up.

As the cruise got underway and the cars rolled away from the office, I hopped into the passenger seat of a maroon R32 GT-R with a Toprank associate at the wheel. Within minutes we were part of a 15-vehicle parade through Orange County surface streets, in cars that were famously not allowed here. For more than two decades they'd been practically nonexistent. Now they were ripping and roaring past Wienerschnitzels and In-N-Outs like they'd been here all along.

On the road, no longer static, Yoshihara's brilliant silver R33 with racing stickers looked far more menacing. Andrade's yellow Skyline hugged the ground unapologetically. The high wing on Payne's R32 could be seen slicing through traffic from blocks away, like a shark fin through the waves, the car seemingly stalking traffic in search of a snack. We were stuck in a GT-R feeding frenzy.

It's difficult to overstate the rarity of this experience. It simply does not happen.

At one point, the group came to a stop at a red light behind the R33 of Dustin Williams and Payne's R32. When it turned green, they each hit it. Nissan used the RB family of engines in a variety of models, but in GT-R trim, its sound is distinct. When modified, it can turn maniacal. The exhaust starts as a low rumble, and the vibration rises in your chest as the car pulls away. When the driver digs into the throttle, it becomes angrier and higher-pitched. Soon it is screaming. The note reaches a crescendo and turns to a song—the pistons pump up and down, 6,000 revolutions per minute, then higher still, if the owner is confident, brave, stupid, or all three. With each shifted gear, the brief pause in engine load causes the turbocharger to release pressure through an external valve. The resulting whooshing sound, and "turbo flutter" that follows, is unmistakable. It's addicting. Then it's back on the power, the growl accompanied by a stinging whine, perhaps leaner and meaner this time, until the driver decides the point has been made. They back off. And the whole process starts over.

Everyone took turns showing their stuff. Payne's car lurched forward in fury. Williams lunged to catch up, then let off the gas, the pressure blow-off causing his exhaust to briefly shoot flames. As they lined up to make a turn, we rolled by in the next lane, passing each car in quick succession. It was like walking the red carpet at the Oscars, one A-lister flashing by after another.

In culture-saturated Southern California, seeing a few Ferraris or Lamborghinis cruising along is no big deal. GT-Rs, however, are royalty. At one point a car full of teenagers leaned out the windows of their sedan, straining to see through the traffic, jaws agape and fists pumping.

THE SUN WAS GOING DOWN, turning the skies over Seal Beach into a watercolor of orange and purple. As the light dimmed, the outline of each Skyline grew more stark; their circular red taillights looked brighter, like a warning for anyone thinking of trying something at a stop light.

We pulled into the parking lot of a brewery, palm trees and the Pacific Coast Highway in the background. Everyone backed into their spots, trying to position just right, then hopped out to snap photos or talk into a camera and narrate what they saw. After a minute, the group began to gravitate toward one person, an older gentleman climbing out of the driver's seat of an R32 GT-R. As he stepped into the evening air, people approached with wide smiles and asked for photos.

This was Hiroshi Tamura, a slight and impeccably dressed 61-year-old visiting from Japan. His arrival was the reason the cruise was organized in the first place. It was Tamura who made everyone there drop what they were doing on a Wednesday night, some of them driving several hours, one-way, to accept the invitation.

Tamura-san, as he's known to most, isn't merely a GT-R expert. Nor is he simply a Nissan executive or some legendary driver with rare talent at the wheel. He is also the head of Nissan's GT-R development and engineering program, one of a select few individuals in the car's seven-decade history who can accurately be called a "father" of the GT-R. Tamura was in the United States to attend an annual drag-racing competition in Texas called TX2K—an event in which modified GT-Rs have become a mainstay, with some attendees cresting 2,000 hp. Tamura prides himself on keeping his ear close to the ground, and in this case, that meant spending time with Toprank before returning home.

Tamura smiled jovially, but he was being pulled in all directions. He climbed in and out of the GReddy car to inspect the work done while Yoshihara snapped pictures. He posed for photos near other cars, patiently answering a conveyor-belt of questions about the meaning behind certain GT-R names or Nissan decisions.

It was soon too dark for photos, so everyone headed into the restaurant for nachos and burgers. The cruise was a convenient and unique way for Toprank to bring together star clients, and to offer access to a GT-R icon in Tamura, helping cement the company's unique status. At one end of a 30-person table, I was meeting writers from YouTube giant Donut Media and getting to know Larry Chen, one of the world's most famous and respected motorsport photographers. At the other end of the table, Tamura sat holding court, telling stories from GT-R lore. It felt like the center of the GT-R universe. When the Father of the GT-R stood to deliver a toast and thank everyone for coming, it was with Morris taking patient sips from a beer at one side, and Toprank chief executive Yaska Kosuge at the other.

WHILE EVERYONE WAITED for their chance to meet the guest of honor, I tried to learn more about what brought them there. Every sports car has its devotees, whether they're BMW M3 diehards or Ford Mustang evangelists. After spending years in and around car culture for work, however, I can safely say that GT-R enthusiasts separate themselves from the pack—they're chasing something different. It might be the feeling they got from a story or a video first encountered in their youth, a feeling they're determined to recapture now that they have the time and means. Or maybe it's the obvious relief and freedom of simply being able to do something that was illegal for so long. Either way, simply possessing a GT-R is rarely enough to fulfill the dream.

For Dustin Williams, the YouTuber, the GT-R represents an authentic connection to Japanese culture. As a kid in Mississippi, the idea of owning a then-illegal sports car and one day visiting its homeland couldn't have seemed further from reality. The only GT-R Williams managed to see before as a kid wasn't one of the Holy Trinity models—it was the relatively common R35 version, available at Nissan dealers in all 50 states. Even so, he was starstruck.

Dustin grew up a huge fan of Godzilla. He absorbed the terrifying lizard's films, cartoons, and comic books, fascinated by the story, the art, and the portrait of daily life in Japan they depicted. It all felt like a different planet. As he grew older, he heard of a machine so monstrous in motorsport that, out of the thousands of cars ever developed in Japan, it was the only one given that nickname.

"After that," he told me, "it was kind of game over."

The R32 GT-R is the one Skyline people have in mind when they use the word "Godzilla." Now 28, Williams has one of his own. He also owns the aforementioned purple R33, and an R34 purchased through Toprank that is currently stored in Japan, waiting to turn 25. It was one of the cars I gawked at in that warehouse outside Tokyo.

This is all part of Williams's livelihood. Since starting his YouTube channel in 2013, he has posted more than 1,300 videos garnering 136 million views. Williams also owns Subaru and Mitsubishis, and he has a content partnership with Honda. But the majority of his videos are about GT-Rs: purchasing them, modifying them, driving them, and getting frustrated when they break. His content works best when viewers get a shotgun seat to his rare experiences. Williams travels to Japan between four to six times each year, documenting the places he goes and the people he meets. He'll pick up his R34 from Toprank and drive it around the country for a few days, showing viewers what it's like to own and drive a dream car on its home turf. Along the way, he films the food he eats, the landmarks he visits, and his gradually improving attempts to speak the language with locals.

It's easy to look at YouTubers like Williams, a musclebound Millennial comfortable sharing his private life on camera, and write them off as attention-seeking. But his channel shows the difference between craving the spotlight and inviting you along for the ride. There's a gentleness to his travel vlogs that suggests more than just a desire to show off a car collection—Williams cares about celebrating Japanese culture, and provides a window in for those who might never get the chance to experience it themselves.

"Back before it was legal," he told me, "you had to know what a GT-R was to understand why it's important, and that means understanding Japan. It goes so far beyond cars, even down to the food and how intricate it is, and it always boils down to the people."

For him, Toprank has been the connector. Williams has purchased five cars from the company, and the Toprank connection to Japan encouraged him to travel and learn more first-hand. "It's an entirely different experience to drive those cars where they're meant to be driven," he said. "It's the ultimate nostalgia. We have this idea of what Japan is and what they're like, we watch all the media and come to conclusions, and then you get there and you think, 'Holy shit, it's all real. It literally is what it's like in the anime.'

"And you already know, but it's this shock, almost like déjà vu. Japan car culture is so unlike anything else. It's different to see and feel and realize that it's all real."

Initially, riding along in that California cruise, I had assumed that being part of an event like this was akin to the ultimate GT-R owner's experience—Tamura-san in attendance, an Instagram-worthy moment that could establish someone as a person of importance in the Skyline world. As my journey through the scene progressed, however, I came to learn that, as much as the owners enjoy their cars, they are generally motivated by more than just four wheels and a motor. After all, given current values, most of them could have bought some showy Italian exotic, some flashy German status symbol, or some pavement-pounding piece of American muscle instead. Why a Nissan, and why this one in particular?

Many owners told me their ultimate GT-R dream is less about the car, and more about feeling a connection to Japan. Particularly, they mean the nostalgia-dripped 1990s era with its grainy film photos and illegally pirated Internet videos. To some extent they've all grown up on it, whether through reading Japanese graphic novels known as "manga," seeing imagery through films or experiencing it by playing video games. Several cited the Mine's GT-R in a hair-raising performance on *Best Motoring* as the clip that got them hooked. Now they can't shake it.

Whatever sparked their interest, GT-R fans are among the most passionate of any car nut. Some owners regularly use words like "obsessed," "addicted," or "junkie" to describe themselves. Many own multiples, or stay up deep into the night bidding on obscure parts to upgrade or personalize their ride. They had always been excited by GT-R ownership, they said. But combining the car with the scenes that inspired them as children—that was the holy grail.

"If anyone tells you they aren't obsessed," Mickey Andrade said to me, "they are lying."

CHAPTER 3

Twenty-five years is a long time to wait for a car. But that impediment, annoying as it may be to a Skyline superfan, is but a blip compared with the time it took to build the modern Nissan corporation. The story of Nissan is the story of Japanese automotive dominance, a dominance that grew from the ashes of defeat in World War II and was spurred on by the incessant meddling of a nation 6,000 miles away. It begins centuries ago and kicks into gear in 1853, when an American officer led a fleet of warships into Tokyo Bay.

LOOKOUTS STATIONED along the Japanese coast could not believe their eyes. For more than 200 years, their country had been closed off in near-total isolation. The ruling class, known as the Tokugawa, had imposed this period of *sakoku*, or "closed country," due to its distrust of the outside world. Long ago, Europeans had stormed ashore attempting to spread their religion. The Tokugawa sent them all away, particularly the Portuguese, which were derisively referred to as *nanban-jin*, or "southern barbarians." For more than two centuries, Japan had expelled all visitors, keeping pace with the outside world by reading books imported by a small faction of Dutch people who were permitted to live on a man-made island in the Bay of Nagasaki. That way the *Komo*, or "red-hair," were not technically touching Japanese soil.

But immediately, it was clear there was little to be done against these new foreigners. The lookouts stood aghast as a fleet of massive steam-powered ships, black as night and spewing thick clouds of smoke, churned through the ocean and advanced rapidly toward Japanese shores.

Each of the four ships was easily the largest vessel anyone on shore had ever seen. Japan had not yet advanced to engineering steam ships, and even the whaling boats that sometimes strayed too close to shore were dwarfed by comparison. In fact, next to the largest Japanese-made boats of the time, each of the steam ships, these "veritable castles," was roughly 20 times bigger. And not only that: each black ship towed a mighty sailboat behind it, plowing along against the raging current. This was nothing less than a show of power.

Aboard the lead ship, a 257-foot frigate called the Susquehanna, stood Commodore Matthew C. Perry. At 57, Commodore Perry had risen to become an experienced officer in the United States Navy. He directed the fleet, at the behest of President Millard Fillmore, directly into the heart of Edo Bay, or modern-day Tokyo Bay. The Japanese had affixed floating signs in the water, warning all comers—in French —that they were entering forbidden territory. But Perry took no notice and blew straight past them. He positioned the ships so that they blocked access to the bay, preventing others from entering or leaving. And he turned the ships sideways, so lookouts on the coast could stare straight down the massive cannons pointed in their direction.

Perry carried a letter from President Fillmore that would alter the course of Japanese history. It requested that the country open its borders to engage in trade with the United States, granting the U.S. an exclusive partnership, as well as provide safe passage to American ships and whaling vessels. Perry and Fillmore both knew this was a tall order. Japan had made it clear that all foreigners were unwelcome —there were rumors about harsh treatment of shipwrecked sailors that washed up on Japanese land, and soldiers following a Tokugawa decree had previously fired upon Americans attempting to return Japanese sailors to their home country.

Even in the face of this, Perry was determined to succeed. He promised his superiors, "We will demand as a right, not solicit as a favor, those acts of courtesy due from one civilized nation to another." He also believed whole-heartedly in American colonialism. Many were convinced Japan was sitting on vast reserves of untapped coal, a resource the young United States craved as a means to fuel its westward growth.

America had recently won possession of California in the Mexican-American War of 1846-48, and envisioned a new revenue source in building ports that could handle trans-Pacific trade. There was also the desire to introduce their God to the Japanese people, convinced that previous European colonizers had failed because the Japanese simply disliked Catholicism, not Christianity in general. (Unbeknownst to them, the Tokugawa had decreed the religion a capital offense in Japan.)

Perry came to shore and demanded to deliver the letter to the emperor. The Japanese were taken aback. His insistence that the message be viewed only by the emperor, or one of his princes, was simply not possible; Japan was ruled by the Tokugawa and its regional governors, the emperor little more than a figurehead. The *gaijin*, or foreigners, were instructed to leave immediately, or else.

That was a bluff, and Perry knew it. He refused to turn back. Surprisingly, the maneuver seemed to impress the Japanese. Locals dubbed the American's massive vessels the "black ships," not for their darkened hulls, but for the smoke that belched skyward from their stacks. This was not the oversized sailboat that others had swanned in on. Through a translator, Navy officers said the commodore was "committed to delivering the message or dying in the attempt."

In short, Perry was brash but formidable. He had arrived uninvited and unwelcome, aimed high-powered weapons at his hosts, and demanded they break centuries of tradition. Could it be possible, the

Japanese wondered, that this was a partner worthy of their great nation?

Nearly a week after Perry's ships steamed into Edo Bay, two of the emperor's imperial princes arrived at the shore. American sailors delivered to them a rosewood chest containing letters from both President Fillmore and Perry, and that chest was then taken directly to the emperor, just as Perry had insisted. The job was done and a dynamic had been established. In his thorough modern retelling of the encounter, American historian George Feifer wrote that, the moment the Japanese accommodated Perry, it kicked off a "big brother little brother relationship" that persists to this day.

Perry stayed in the bay for three more days, just to show that he could, then turned and sailed away. The Americans needed to restock supplies, and the reprieve also allowed the Japanese time to process what just happened. Perry had not accomplished all of his goals on the first go, but his visit marked the most significant meeting between Japan and a foreign country in some 250 years, and he left a promise to return in six months for further discussions. When he came back, in February of 1854, it was with twice as many ships. Formal negotiations began on March 8th. Whether the Japanese were resistant or reluctant at first is unclear. What we know for sure is that Perry considered the result a victory. The treaty that resulted, the Convention of Kanagawa, was signed by both sides on March 31 under an American flag, then with only 31 stars, flown almost inconceivably on Japanese soil.

In that agreement, Japan promised to protect American castaways, and to open two ports for ships to safely station and load. The Japanese did achieve some moral victories. Critically, the agreement did not open the two countries to trade, one of Perry's main objectives. Nor did the Japanese sign the treaty's English-language copy, owing to a Tokugawa edict forbidding the signing of a document written in another language.

These conditions were hard-fought, but short-lived. A formal trade agreement arrived four years later, making the United States the first foreign nation in centuries to convince Japan to open its borders, its resources, and its society to the outside world. No single event has shaped the course of modern Japan more than the arrival of Commodore Perry, and the effects still resonate. By some reports, Perry remains "perhaps the most widely known foreign historic figure in Japan," even today.

According to the New York Times, these days a typical junior high textbook in Japan devotes three lines of text to the attack on Pearl Harbor, and three full pages to Perry. This event that is scarcely mentioned in American, and practically never taught in schools, in many ways rules the collective psyche for Japanese people hundreds of years later. Feifer, the historian, wrote that the country still experiences deeply imbedded humiliation, an "unconscious hatred," over the event.

The name given for this national, internalized condition? Black ships trauma.

ONCE THE OUTSIDE world got into Japan, its spread could not be contained. Within a few short decades, by the late 1880s, the country had a new constitution, schools based on Western ideals, and a structured process for both immigration and emmigration. Compared with the 250 years prior, the period immediately following the arrival of Commodore Perry moved at breakneck speed. Perhaps no one embodied the rapid change occurring during this time more than Yoshisuke Aikawa.

Born in 1880, Aikawa was born into revolution—his great-uncle had helped topple and dismantle the Tokugawa regime. Acting on his advice, Aikawa attended the newly-opened Tokyo Imperial University, graduating from the college of engineering in 1903 with a thesis on the design and performance of water-turbine blades used at a nearby mine. The degree did not come easy; at one point in his studies, he fell so ill that he nearly died. His Western-style diploma in hand, a direct product of the new approach to life in Japan, Aikawa went off to face the world.

He found work as a mechanic at an early version of the company that would become Toshiba, where he earned the equivalent of a meager 45 cents per day. But the work aligned with his belief in the concept of "site first," the importance of knowing a system's inner workings. The only way Aikawa could understand the ins and outs of the company, he felt, was by learning from the ground up. And besides, the job meant something to him—after his college sickness, Aikawa had vowed to do work that made him feel alive, to not waste a second of his life.

When he wanted to learn more, there was only one place to go. Aikawa arrived in the United States probably in 1905, going to work on the factory floor of the Gould Coupler Company, near Buffalo, New York. Gould Coupler produced railyard machinery, and Aikawa learned how to work with cast iron in ways that hadn't yet crossed the Pacific. While there, he formed another of his core beliefs: "Dare to do what others don't." If he could produce iron in complex forms that remained affordable and strong, he thought, it would elevate Japanese industry to a level playing field with countries like America.

Aikawa returned to Japan for good in 1910. Once home, he started a foundry, Hyotan, that worked with malleable iron, a relatively flexible form of the metal that lends itself to being twisted and shaped. The business grew, yet Aikawa found himself gripped by something he had seen in the U.S. There, he witnessed the growth of the fledgling American car industry. Japan had few roads at the time, and privately owned vehicles were basically nonexistent. Still, Aikawa was convinced the automobile's ubiquity was inevitable. "If you have a strong belief," he would later say, "it penetrates even the sun."

Aikawa was patient. He spent more than a decade building Hyotan into a widely respected corporation, and himself into a sought-after executive. In 1928, he agreed to take over and lead two ailing mining and energy companies. (In a twist of fate, this meant Aikawa now ran the mining firm that had been the subject of his college thesis.) In an effort to move those brands past their previous financial troubles, he began a corporate reshuffling. Aikawa took an existing subsidiary, that produced automobiles, and broke it off into a new independent company. Then he named the operation by combining the words for Japan (*Nihon*) and Industry (*Sangyo*). The new venture, the Nihon Sangyo Corporation, was ambitious, and Aikawa would specifically pattern its business methods after those of titanic American corporations like Standard Oil, Du Pont, and U.S. Steel. At a 1934 shareholders' meeting, the company's board of directors approved a motion to shorten the name. To Nissan.

THE EARLY DAYS were slow going. In 1933, Nissan built just 202 cars, fewer than Sean Morris and Toprank now import to the United States each year. By 1940, that number had risen to 940. There were still few personal automobiles in Japan, and the country's roads, where they existed at all, were in rough shape. Aikawa had established Nissan as the nation's first mass-production automaker, and he had seen firsthand the growth of American industry, aiming to bring similar success to his home country as a public good. But reality had failed to keep pace. Though Nissan had begun to export cars outside Japan by the late 1930s, the volume was a fraction of what the competition was shipping around the world.

The 1940s were no better. Japan, once sequestered from the world by choice, now sought to expand its influence. In 1931, the Japanese military seized the nation of Indochina as part of its effort to establish a Southeast Asian empire. It officially entered World War II in 1940, and companies like Nissan, at the forefront of Japanese technology and mass production, pivoted to making trucks and airplanes for the military. After the devastating atomic attacks in Hiroshima and Nagasaki in the summer of 1945, that killed hundreds of thousands of Japanese civilians, the fighting ceased. Allies moved in. Nissan's factories were seized, and Yoshisuke Aikawa—the father of "Japanese Industry"—was labeled a war criminal and arrested.

The immediate postwar years saw Japan endure yet another transformation. This period, known as Reconstruction, took a severe toll. Starved of resources, stripped of economic autonomy, and left helpless as two of their major cities were flattened, the Japanese populace had lost more than two million people to the war effort. The proud country had also been embarrassed on a national stage and forced into a restrictive treaty orchestrated by Americans less than 100 years after Commodore Perry had barged in and done the same thing.

The country that once demanded Japan open its borders now took swift action to dictate its future. The Americans established military posts throughout the country, building new and prosperous "cities" of wealth and abundance. For Americans, at least. Servicemen and their families, as one historian wrote, "clogged the area with jeeps, military buses, and new automobiles brought over from the U.S." These areas, known collectively as Little America, were walled off and isolated from the reality of their host country. English was spoken almost exclusively. As one woman recalled, "We could walk from one end [of Little America to the other] without being out of sight of an American face or an American vehicle."

Outside Little America, nearby communities suffered. The few private vehicles around were mostly powered by charcoal, which was cheaper than gasoline—but far dirtier. They spewed thick black smoke and frequently broke down. (As a child, the great Toyota test driver Hiromu Naruse developed a knack for engineering because, during Reconstruction, he so often had to fix the charcoal-powered car that his family relied on for survival.) The Japanese were forced to live on government rations containing barely enough calories to keep a person alive, prompting the growth of an underground gray market for basic food and goods. This allowed wealthy families to flourish while skirting the law, as the poor and downtrodden suffered in squalor.

With time, this period would be remembered for its call to "endure the unendurable." The Japanese rallied around a collective grit and spirit to rebuild their country and themselves. But life under American occupation was hard. After a prominent 33-year-old judge in Tokyo wrote to his local newspaper announcing that he intended to consume exclusively government rations without resorting to gray-market supplies, he died of starvation.

THOUGH THE AMERICAN takeover had been swift and stark, many Japanese had taken a liking to the man in charge. General Douglas MacArthur had orchestrated and ultimately signed the Japanese surrender on behalf of the United States, and he was tapped to lead the ensuing occupation. MacArthur, a divisive figure then in his sixties, had served as a chief commander of the U.S. Army in World War II, overseeing combat actions in the region then labeled the Far East. At the surrender, he had particularly irked the Japanese government by forcing its representatives to sign papers under the exact flag, 31 stars and all, flown by Commodore Perry in Edo Bay almost a century prior. (MacArthur even insisted the flag be flown in from Annapolis specifically for the event.) But the General quickly won over many Japanese by promising that the coming occupation would rebuild the nation. While in Japan, he would frequently and fondly remark on his interactions, noting his respect for local culture and customs, and the Japanese viewed him favorably as a result.

It was with great surprise, then, when they learned how, in a 1951 Congressional hearing, MacArthur, apparently trying to save his job, had told politicians that Japanese culture was "like a boy of 12" compared to "the Anglo-Saxon, [which was] 45 years of age." He clearly did not anticipate the resulting backlash.

Not that his view was uncommon. Yoshisuka Aikawa, the Nissan founder, had seen both countries up close, sharing his concerns privately about "the immaturity of Japanese industry" on at least one occasion. But MacArthur's betrayal was seen as an insult too far, and reaction was swift. Japanese newspaper headlines insisted, "We are not 12-year-olds!" and MacArthur's remark was seen as an attempt to denigrate those he had been charged with helping in order to save his own hide.

If that was indeed the plan, it didn't work. The U.S. President,

Harry Truman, fired MacArthur anyway, then moved to accelerate the end of the American role in Japan's recovery. It was clearly time for the relationship to change, and Japan would need to reinvent itself yet again.

THE VERY FIRST car made under the Nissan banner was a small and rudimentary vehicle called the 1933 Datsun 12 Phaeton. It had two doors and four seats, and the driver sat in the right front seat. The body was similar to Ford and Chevrolet models of the time, with a flat roof and curving fenders. From the front, two massive headlamps stared out like bulging eyes. There wasn't much in the way of muscle, roughly 12 hp from a four-cylinder engine. But the Phaeton set a standard.

In the early days, Nissan focused on selling small cars to Japanese families. The few exciting products the company produced were an attempt to spur public interest in personal vehicles. There was the Datsun Sports of 1952, a stubby little bulldog of a convertible boasting a whopping 20 hp. Then the 1959 Datsun Bluebird, a sporty four-door sedan that proved hugely popular. Nissan sold more than 20,000 Bluebirds at home, the car enough of a star in the market that the company even experimented with exporting the model to the U.S.

Americans also took renewed interest in helping Japan become an economic power. By the late 1940s, China had established a stronghold in Korea, cheering on the communist revolution then ravaging that country. The United States intervened, sparking the Korean War. While that choice all but guaranteed years of vicious fighting and millions of lives lost, the Japanese cheered privately, calling the war a "gift from the gods."

America now had serious motivation to improve conditions in Japan, if only to prove the merits of capitalism. The United States introduced Japan to Western customs like bureaucracy—the most famous instance of which involved the 1949 formation of Japan's Ministry of International Trade and Industry, or MITI. The ministry would morph into an overwhelming influence that steered the country's growth into an economic powerhouse, often through secret or questionable means. And while the Allies had forced Japan's wartime companies to break up postwar, they did the Japanese a favor by not disbanding their society's elite class, as they had with other Axis nations.

In this way, Japan's most shrewd business minds were allowed to maintain their positions at the top. As the prime minister of Singapore would later write, the Japanese "realized this was their chance and kept a low, humble posture." They also set their industrial and cultural sights on catching up with, and eventually surpassing, the rest of the world.

As Nissan grew steadily, other car companies also built from the ashes. During the war, Japan had assembled an impressive roster of aircraft manufacturers and high-performance warplanes. One such plane was the Ki-43 Hayabusa, or "Peregrine Falcon," a machine that shocked Allied pilots who had underestimated Japanese engineering. Like a lot of war materiel, the Hayabusa was built by two corporations working together—its engine was made by the Nakajima Aircraft Company, and its fuselage was built by the Tachikawa Aircraft Company. In the occupation, with Japan prohibited from building aircraft, many aviation manufacturers were forced to divest into a series of smaller offshoots.

When Nakajima was dissolved, one of its offspring became a company called Fuji Precision Machinery, which made automobile engines. Tachikawa tried marketing an electric car, then switched to gas-powered models and changed its name to Prince Motor Company, after Japan's Crown Prince.

In 1954, Fuji and Prince merged, and in 1961, they adopted a single brand name, Prince. One of the first projects to come from the union was a powerful two-door sports car, the Skyline Sport Coupe. Just as with the Hayabusa, one side made engines while the other built the bodies.

The Skyline was a revelation. Like that first Datsun 12, and like so many Japanese cars of the period, it carried a strong American influence. The side profile was long and elegant, and the enclosed dual headlights bore a resemblance to popular U.S. models like the Lincoln Continental. In a distinctly Japanese touch, the front grille boasted a unique pear shape. Yet there was more to the Skyline than mere design mish-mash. To shape the car, Prince had tapped the stylist Giovanni Michelotti, an Italian who had drawn masterworks for Alfa Romeo, Maserati, and Ferrari. When production began in 1962, Prince flew in Italian craftsmen to build each body by hand, an unheard-of approach for a Japanese automaker and an extravagant move, then or now. The Skyline was intended for global appeal, a resident not just of Japan, but of the world.

Unfortunately, the car fell short of expectations. Thanks to its high cost of some 1,850,000 yen, about $70,000 USD today, only 60 Skyline Sport Coupes were sold. Still, the car won an important convert: Prince had captured Nissan's attention. The two sides began discussing a merger, and Nissan completed the purchase in 1966.

In the months that followed, the larger company made it a top priority to continue development of Prince's marquee products. In Nissan's hands, the large, Italian-drawn Skyline was shrunk to more traditionally Japanese dimensions and split into two- and four-door variants. Engineers strengthened the chassis, swapped the front drum brakes for discs, and exchanged the old four-cylinder engine for a larger, 125-hp six. That figure represented more than double the output of the old Skyline Sport Coupe, and it came in a stronger vehicle with greater stopping power. When the 1965 Prince Skyline 2000GT debuted—2000 for its 2.0-liter engine, GT for the Italian *gran turismo,* or grand touring—the car was called "a wolf in sheep's skin."

Nissan wasn't done. In 1969, it debuted the Skyline GT-R. The R was for racing, and the model had genuine competition roots . Under the hood was the six-cylinder S20 engine from the sleek Prince R380, a car that had famously won the 1966 Japanese Grand Prix against favored entries from Porsche. Producing 160 hp in GT-R trim, the S20 had been dialed back from its tune in the 200-hp R380, but it still made more than enough. On top of that, the GT-R got independent front and rear suspension to help it corner at high speed.

The first GT-R was a four-door, with a two-door version introduced in 1970. Officially, the model was called KPGC10. But like so many Japanese trademarks, it was soon known by a merging of two terms. The GT-R's nickname blended *hako*, the Japanese word for boxy, with *sukarain*, a type of mountain road the car was designed to tackle. Therefore, Hakosuka.

In the months that followed, Nissan began to adopt shorter production timelines, an attempt to keep up with the automotive industry's feverish pace. Just three years after the Hako was introduced, a successor began rolling off assembly lines. This was the Kenmeri GT-R, the model influenced by period American muscle cars, still powered by a 160-hp S20, but with dramatic new styling. It featured a long hood, giant side windows, and a sloping fastback roof. Even the front grille looked more Detroit than Yokohama. The only distinctly Japanese elements were the sideview mirrors mounted to the hood, up near the headlights, and the bulging overfenders that made the Kenmeri's American-inspired width seem even wider.

The gamble would not pay off. The global oil crisis of 1973-74 was in full swing, and skyrocketing fuel prices depleted the market. Nissan made the Kenmeri GT-R for only four months, selling less than 200 examples. After that, the company put its sports cars on ice, focusing on smaller and more efficient commuter cars. Nissan had tried applying Japanese technique to an American style, and it had gotten burned. It would not make that mistake again.

The economic conditions that killed the Kenmeri hit Nissan's competition much harder. With the know-how to produce small and efficient vehicles already in place, Japanese companies had clear advantages over American brands, and they intended to double down on them. Having attempted to build Skyline into a world-beater, the company retreated and withdrew inward.

THE OIL CRISIS caused several countries, including Japan and the United States, to rush into law strict regulations on vehicle emissions and fuel economy. American automakers, Ford and General Motors in particular, struggled to adapt. They produced uninspired cars with tired, bloated designs and dated engineering. But for the Japanese, who had learned, over the 20-plus years of Reconstruction, to build efficient, small cars for fair prices, the moment presented undeniable opportunity. As the placard in a Nissan museum would later describe, it was "the first technological race in which Japanese automakers did not have to play catch-up with their Western rivals." The entire industry was ready to pounce.

Honda first entered the U.S. market in 1970. Toyota, having brought its first model stateside in 1958, already had hundreds of American dealerships. Nissan, selling cars in America under the Datsun brand, made great strides in public perception of Japanese performance with two successful models, the Datsun 510 sedan and the Datsun 240Z coupe, each of which won multiple Sports Car Club of America racing championships. Japanese automakers were winning on the track and in quarterly financial statements. Next to the average American brand, a typical Japanese automaker spent about $1500 to $2000 less to produce each vehicle.

That gap was telling. Few Americans realized it at the time, but by the early 1970s, Japan had become the world leader in the export of both steel and automobiles. Pushed by its manufacturing industry, and encouraged by the MITI agency that America created, the country's economy grew to unforeseen heights. American industry was mostly caught flat-footed. In the occupation years and after, the United States government had aimed to build up Japan as a "strong anticommunist bastion," as one historian wrote. After becoming just that, the nation did more than simply embrace capitalism—it grew into the world's second largest economy, thanks largely to huge investment in the development of leading technologies, a policy of open global trade, and a large domestic market of affluent consumers. To Western astonishment, the country's market cap eventually exceeded that of the United States. Who was the 12-year-old now?

Nissan was flush with cash. It had successfully navigated a complex web of global regulations and trade issues, establishing footholds in markets across the world. Meanwhile, more experienced rivals lost their home-field advantage. Japanese automakers no longer needed to convince people of the value of car ownership: consumer attitudes had shifted from "one car for every home" to "one car for every person." The promise of Reconstruction had finally been realized. Perhaps, some at Nissan thought, it was time for the company to return to its roots, to show the world what Japanese engineering was truly capable of.

IN THE SKYLINE, Nissan had built and fostered a popular sedan that could double as a sports car. But the model wasn't immune to criticism. After the Kenmeri's eye-blink production run ended in 1977, Nissan followed up with the C210, the R30, and the R31, the third, fourth, and fifth Skylines, respectively. But these were not sleek sport sedans or performance boundary-pushers. Instead, they were boxy, underpowered, and slow.

That run of product planning reflected Nissan's deep understanding of the market, and it helped the company turn massive profits as consumers sought fuel efficiency over fun. But the Skyline had lost something. There were no GT-R versions during those years, and Nissan's racetrack results were a mess. People who knew the history began to doubt that the company still had greatness in it.

If nothing else, Nissan still had a stable of experienced project leads. An engineer named Shinichiro Sakurai had started with Prince in 1952, long before the merger, and he had worked on the original Skyline. He first gained acclaim after stuffing the six-cylinder engine from a Prince Gloria luxury car under the hood of the smaller Skyline for the 1964 Grand Prix of Japan. In that race, a Prince briefly took the lead from a Porsche, and Princes finished in second through fifth positions.

The performance shocked and delighted fans. Learning from Sakurai's success, Prince executives gave production Skylines a six-cylinder engine from then on. After the Nissan merger, Sakurai was named the model's development head, a job that saw him helm the launch of the Hakosuka. His legend was sealed. Sakurai became project lead for the next four of the model's revamps, the first to proudly wear the title, "Father of the Skyline."

By the early 1980s, though, things had become complicated. In the run-up to the launch of the R31, Sakurai fell ill. No longer able to lead the project, he handed the reins to his protégé, Naganori Ito, a technical designer who had worked under him for more than 20 years. By the time of the changeover, the R31 Skyline was nearly done; Ito became project lead in little more than name, mainly filing paperwork to complete the project and prep for its 1985 launch.

The R31 had grand ambitions, and many were successful. The car was the first Skyline to use the esteemed RB six-cylinder engine, and it marked the debut of Nissan's HICAS rear-wheel steering technology. But time had made the Skyline larger, more comfortable, and less inspired overall. While passenger cars flocked to front-wheel drive layouts for better fuel economy, Nissan had stuck with rear-wheel drive for performance and balance, then seemingly forgotten to include the performance part.

Enthusiasts and the media gave the car a lukewarm reception. When tepid reviews came in, Ito took them especially hard. He had only captained the R31 launch from the very end, yet he felt responsible for tarnishing his boss's legacy. He vowed to restore the Skyline name. Conveniently, the two men were already cooking up something radical.

SAKURAI HAD ALSO FELT the Skyline slipping further and further from its roots. Though it was too late to help the R31, he dedicated a team to a total reimagining of Nissan performance. No idea was deemed off the table, and his engineers looked to motorsport for inspiration.

In recent years, Nissan had been trounced by competitors as the company failed to adapt to two growing trends. On the racetrack, its front-engine cars had been punished by mid-engine machines with better balance and weight distribution. Meanwhile, dirt-road rally racing was booming in popularity, and deep-pocketed automakers had used the sport as a development lab for making great strides in turbocharging and all-wheel-drive. The most successful rally racers used both turbos and AWD at once, combining massive engine power with nimble handling in every weather imaginable. Nissan was behind there, too.

Sakurai and his team took notice. In the spring of 1984, their project began as an exploration of their brand's sports-car future. Led by Sakurai, who at this point was widely considered a walking embodiment of Nissan performance ("The Skyline is my alter ego," he once said), the team envisioned a machine that could win on the track first and foremost.

The prototype they designed and built, the MID-4, looked nothing like a Skyline. For one thing, the MID4 was an all-wheel-drive two-seater, its engine mounted "amidships," or behind the driver. For another, the car was wedge-shaped, with a pointy front end, a stubby wheelbase, and pop-up headlights. The MID4 looked like a budget Ferrari, all expertly crafted proportions, just without the Italian flair. When the car debuted at the 1985 Frankfurt Motor Show, Sakurai and his team had every intention of bringing it to market, even going so far as to produce four running prototypes to show they meant business.

The MID4 never made it to production, but they were on the right track. After Frankfurt, the team began work on an even sharper version, dubbed MID4-II. They further tuned the all-wheel drive system, added twin turbochargers, and refined the suspension for greater agility. By now, though, it had gotten out that Honda was hard at work on a mid-engine exotic of its own, the car that would become the Honda/Acura NSX. Toyota was frequently sending testing teams to Europe for marathon testing sessions at the wheel of its forthcoming Supra coupe. And Porsche had set the world on fire with a twin-turbocharged, all-wheel-drive cheetah called the 959—the fastest road-legal vehicle of its era, the first truly modern supercar, and the first true production car to eclipse 200 mph.

The 959 cost around $225,000 USD in 1987, or roughly $600,000 today, far past Skyline territory. But it was a line in the sand, and proof of how far you could go. Nissan quickly recognized that the playing field had shifted. It was one thing to unveil prototypes like the MID4 as proof of the company's imagination, but it was another thing entirely to bring a car like that to market. Porsche could afford to absorb the massive development costs associated with a world-beater like the 959, and Honda could afford to gamble on a low-volume prestige play like the NSX. Nissan's balance sheet looked different. The sunk cost to engineer and produce a complex vehicle like the MID4-II could leave the company vulnerable in a rapidly changing economic landscape. If the car failed in the market, the red ink could cripple the company.

Nissan engineers were bold, but its leaders made decisions based in reality. The MID4-II ended in defeat. Still, there was plenty of good to come.

WHILE SAKURAI WAS RUNNING the MID4 program, his pupil remained hard at work. The R31 Skyline had left Naganori Ito with a bad taste in his mouth. The car had failed to inspire the brand's devoted fans and further failed to win over new ones. The Hakosuka seemed like a distant memory. Ito became convinced that the next Skyline had to use track wins as a guiding principle. This would mean designing the R32 as a pure athlete from the ground up. It would mean calling all previously held notions into question and rethinking the GT-R name from scratch. More than that, it would mean a lot of money. For that last reason, Ito decided to keep his plans close to the vest. He shared his real ambitions only with select Nissan executives. And in March of 1986, he authorized a team to begin work on something called Project GT-X.

The GT-X team worked first on balance and chassis setup. In the interest of advanced road comfort and handling, it was decided that every R32 Skyline would receive a newly developed multi-link suspension front and rear. Next, they agreed that upgraded versions would also have an advanced version of Nissan's rear-wheel-steering system, Super HICAS, for stability. Every model would use a version of the RB engine that had debuted in the R31 Skyline—it was strong and dependable, and it could handle serious strain. Some of the new RBs were basic, while others had efficient and power-friendly upgrades, or an alluring turbocharger. Internally, those engines were designated RB20E, RB20DE, and RB20DET, respectively.

Then there were the GT-Rs. For this grand rebirth, the GT-X team took as much knowledge from the MID4 and MID4-II as possible. ATTESA E-TS, Nissan's intelligent all-wheel drive system, controlled by a then-powerful 16-bit onboard computer, came standard. The engine would have to remain front-mounted (the Skyline was still based on a family sedan and needed a traditional trunk) but there was still lots of MID4 tech left. There would be an RB engine, of course, and the team would slap on two turbochargers, as the MID4-II had. But even with two turbos, the "ordinary" Skyline six, the 2.0-liter RB20, would not do. The GT-R deserved more. They could have gone with a 2.4-liter design, or a 2.8-liter. In the end, racing was the deciding factor.

Ito and Project GT-X wanted to dominate the Japanese Touring Car Championship. Not do well, or simply win the title—but dominate. For homegrown Japanese brands, winning the JTCC was the most prestigious honor an automaker could achieve. And the most competitive division within the JTCC was Group A. For three straight years, from 1987 to 1989, the crown of Group A champion had not even gone to a Japanese company. Instead, it went to Ford, who had stormed the series, taking advantage of underpowered Skylines, Toyotas, and Mitsubishis. Once again, the Americans had sensed a weakness, brought the big guns, and left victorious.

The choice was critical. JTCC rules dictated that the racing version of Project GT-X would be mechanically tied to the street version. If the development team went with 2.4 liters for the street GT-R, the racecar would have to use that displacement, too. An engine of that size might not produce enough power to win on the track. If the team went with a 2.8, the rulemakers might deem the car too powerful and force it to take on weight, slowing it down. Toyota, for example, prioritized street performance for its upcoming Supra and chose a 3.0-liter engine, the legendary 2JZ six-cylinder. That car proved brutally fast on the road, but the decision essentially disqualified it from winning the JTCC—the weight was simply too much to balance effectively.

The Nissan engineers went with a 2.6-liter, guessing it would translate, first and foremost, to success on the track. With this size, plus powerful upgrades and twin turbochargers, the engine powering the R32 GT-R would adopt the name RB26DETT. They guessed right.

As the car inched toward final approval, a few select Nissan employees were tasked with pushing it beyond the limits. These were the test drivers. At automotive companies around the world, test drivers carry an almost mythical aura. Often as skilled as professional racecar drivers and facing the same risks, they are required to find the breaking points hidden within every car, on some of the world's most challenging roads and surfaces, then diagnose the issue and suggest potential solutions on the spot. The greatest difference between test drivers and racecar drivers has little to do with skill. It is how test drivers do their jobs with less capable equipment and less crash protection, and without fame or trophies. With Project GT-X, Naganori Ito instructed his engineers to "listen to the test drivers as to the voices of the gods."

Hiroyoshi Kato was one such driver. Born in 1957, Kato had grown up enthralled with books about cars. One of them had told the fictional story of two rival automakers gearing up to launch competing models, and how their respective test drivers attempted to sabotage each other to gain an advantage. To young Kato, he said later, "the words 'test car' sounded fresh and new," and so he dedicated his life to working on secret projects like those he'd read about.

In modern times, becoming a test driver requires lengthy qualifications and a long list of prerequisites. Things were different in the 1970s. Kato enrolled in the Nissan Automobile Technical College, a factory vocational school, and he earned a recommendation from his teacher to work in the Vehicle Test Department at only 17 years old. In Japan, then as now, the minimum age for a driver's license was 18. Kato had somehow become a test driver who was too young to drive.

Before getting his license, Kato was allowed to practice for the driving test at work, using an old company-owned Nissan Cedric P130 luxury sedan. He eyed it with anticipation—finally, a chance to get behind the wheel. But before Kato could climb into the driver's seat, his boss laid down a condition: If he wanted to use the car, he had to take the whole thing apart. Kato was forced to dismantle the entire Cedric piece by piece, and when he came to components with small moving parts inside, like the engine and transmission, he had to take those apart, too. When Kato was almost done, the boss announced one final task: He had to put the car back together.

Kato later said he took two lessons from the experience: first, that his boss "probably wanted to see how good a mechanic I was." And second, that he "needed to care of the car" he drove, that he "should maintain it in the best condition at all times."

Kato passed the exam and joined Nissan's test team in full, working first on an updated Cedric and then on the Fairlady Z sports car. As Project GT-X ramped up, Kato caught the eye of project lead Ito; before long, he was testing an R31 Skyline outfitted with an early version of ATTESA E-TS all-wheel drive. When Kato joined the R32 GT-R project, he was testing prototypes on frozen icy lakes, measuring traction; he later went to Japan's Fuji Speedway, checking high-speed stability; and finally, to measure overall performance and reliability, he traveled to the mighty Nürburgring, in Germany.

A team of test drivers accompanied early versions of the R32 GT-R to "the Ring," as it's known. More than 12 miles long and deep in the forests of Germany's Eifel mountains, the track is an unforgiving gauntlet, a nonstop barrage of blind corners, high-speed straights, and steep elevation changes wrapped in a blanket of dense trees. The Formula 1 driver Jackie Stewart famously called the track "the Green Hell," and manufacturers have long used the place as a prototype proving ground, each lap a battering ram of tests. By the time of Kato's first visit, Japanese automakers had become determined to prove themselves against European brands, and a lap time at the Ring was the end-all barometer. Nissan, Toyota, and Honda each spent millions every year to prepare, ship, and house massive teams of people and cars some 5,600 miles from home, all in hope of besting Porsche, BMW, and Mercedes on the greatest road in the world.

Kato was shell-shocked. He was an experienced test driver who had recently turned 30. Compared with others at Nissan, though, and especially with his German counterparts, his experience seemed hopelessly inadequate. The Ring, he later admitted, "was way too much for me," and so he was suddenly back to being an underaged dreamer, living out a fantasy from children's books, talking his way onto the world's biggest stage without a license.

Early on, a more experienced driver took Kato around the course in a GT-R prototype. When that man invited him to drive, Kato declined, sticking to riding in the shotgun seat. The car set off again, but this time, Kato kept his eye on the car's gauges, simply for lack of anything else to do. On the first lap, the engine's oil temperature shot past 130 degrees Celsius. Kato knew the engine would blow if they continued, so he alerted the driver, who limped the prototype back to its garage, where a crew of 20 engineers scrambled to fix the problem.

Kato felt better. His first trip to the Ring hadn't gone as expected, but he had found a way to contribute. And over the years, he returned with more and more confidence. During one trip, Kato suggested a fix aimed at improving the GT-R's cornering ability. Nissan had organized a test with the goal of beating a record set by the Porsche 944, a lap of 8 minutes and 45 seconds. With his suggested fix installed, Kato set out onto the course and lapped in 8 minutes and 20 seconds: record smashed, and the marketing magic that Nissan needed. Years later, while back at the Ring, he developed a three-fingered driving technique that, he said, allowed him to "make subtle adjustments, as if I were slightly pushing back the sidewall distortion of the tires." Today, he's known inside the company as Technical Master and Nürburgring *Meister*.

Meister is German for "master." If the R32 GT-R engineers knew what was good for them, as their boss Ito had suggested, they'd listen to the kid who was too scared to drive.

Ito put the finishing touches on Project GT-X, the vehicle the world would know as the R32 Skyline, and the car made its official public debut in May of 1989. It was quickly hailed as the modern successor to decades of history, one that could carry a storied name into the future. From the jump, Nissan intended to sell the car by the hundreds of thousands.

The true accomplishment, however, was the return of the high-performance model, the GT-R. Unveiled in August of 1989, three months after the Skyline, the GT-R made immediate waves. It looked sleek, it looked modern, and it looked aggressive, with no mistaking its intentions. The design carried hints of past Skyline models but ramped them up, with the wide-hip fenders and large front intakes offering sly hints at the ability hidden within. No sports car coming out of Japan at the time was anything like it, and yet, with all the technology under the skin, Nissan intended to keep it relatively affordable. Next to the stratospherically expensive Porsche 959 or even the Honda NSX, the R32 GT-R was a bargain and a half, nearly as potent as either but priced within reach of the penny-pinching Japanese professional. On top of that, it was a Japanese car for Japanese buyers, through and through: right-hand drive only; five-speed manual transmission only; no accommodation for sale in other markets.

Nissan limited sales of the R32 GT-R to the Japanese homeland, forecasting sales of around 5,000 units over a production run of several years. The company had no idea what was coming. The GT-R's launch set off a domino effect of victories in the press and on the racetrack, one that knocked sales into a dimension unforeseen by even the most optimistic GT-X engineer.

First, the R32 GT-R garnered worldwide media acclaim. One journalist called it "by far the most advanced touring car to come out of Japan." Another hailed the ATTESA E-TS all-wheel-drive system as the star of the show, writing, "the GT-R flatters your driving, making ham-fisted drivers smoother and giving extra traction and security where a normal car would bite." Nor did the car have an equal on the track. In Japan, the model won three consecutive JTCC Group A championships, finishing first in each of the 29 races it entered. In the lower JTCC N1 series, GT-Rs won 29 out of 30. Outside of Japan, GT-Rs raced to victory in the famed 24-hour races at Spa and the Nürburgring. In Australia, the GT-R landed three straight road-racing championships but also back-to-back wins in the Mount Everest of endurance races, the Bathurst 1000, in 1991 and 1992. Nissan had set out to vanquish the Americans from its home series and ended up expanding its empire by two whole continents.

By November of 1990, barely one year after the GT-R's launch, more than 12,000 road cars had been sold, eclipsing that 5,000-car estimate years ahead of schedule. Australia was a particular highlight: The company had always planned to sell a limited number of GT-Rs there in order to meet local racing regulations. When the time came, Nissan restricted the country's total volume to 100 cars and instituted a massive $110,000 base price, about $260,000 USD today. Even with that astounding markup, dealers received over 5,000 orders. All told, over a six-year production run, 1989 to 1994, nearly 44,000 R32 GT-Rs found homes, an increase of almost 900-percent over internal projections.

Sakurai had set out to revive the Skyline name. Ito had wanted to restore his mentor's legacy. Kato just wanted to drive. None of them could have imagined the firestorm their work created. The R32 Skyline and its GT-R alter ego had achieved superhero status the world over, a massive success for the company as a whole. How did they do it? By remaining true to Nissan's roots, and by marketing almost exclusively to the tastes of domestic consumers. They had put Japan on top by keeping the outside world out.

Nevertheless, for better or worse, Japan's place on the global stage was now deeply interwoven with its ties to America. And throughout the 1980s, an arcane and seemingly unrelated U.S. law had been inching its way through the legislative branch—a law that would change the course of Skyline history.

CHAPTER 4

Three days before my flight to Tokyo, I started staying up late. I would spend all night watching movies, playing video games, or diving into GT-R research, then go to bed around four or five in the morning. Pacific Standard Time and Japan Standard Time are 16 hours apart. I was going to leave California exhausted and arrive in Tokyo no matter what, and there wouldn't be time to waste. So if there was a chance to lessen the effects of jet lag, I had to give it a shot. I avoided alcohol, ate healthy, and drank plenty of water. And I knew it was possible that I might just be miserable, anyway.

I first went to Japan in 2017 on assignment for *Road & Track* magazine. It was a tremendous opportunity. After a couple of years spent toiling as the only editor of a small automotive news website, I had left automotive journalism completely and entered the public sector, working first for the Long Beach Airport, then in higher education. But the whole time I was out of cars, all I wanted was to get back into cars. I spent my lunch hours at the airport imagining my ideal automotive project, reading feature articles in *The New Yorker* or sports analysis on *Grantland* and wondering if I could take what made those outlets tick—intensely researched, professionally written journalism —and apply it to cars.

In 2016, I thought I might have found my *Grantland*-style subject.

Chapter 4 | 51

As a teenager in the early 2000s, at a car show at Pasadena's Art Center College of Design, I had caught a glimpse of a jewel, a stunning, hand-built Ferrari FX. The FX is no regular Ferrari; it began life as a standard Ferrari Testarossa but was then commissioned by the royal family of Brunei to be rebodied, upgraded, and outfitted with a Formula 1 transmission. The family had six of them built, but the example I saw was the only one not still parked in their massive storage warehouse deep in the jungle. It belonged to an Orange County museum, but no one seemed quite sure why or how it ended up there. The museum itself, when I visited, had conflicting information from one placard to another.

Telling the FX story became my white whale. I googled the car incessantly, looking for an in, a tidbit of information that might lead me in the right direction. I looked up experts on the Brunei car collection: no good. I emailed Ferrari expert after Ferrari expert: nothing. Then, one day, I found a video on Twitter of the museum car from the mechanic who maintained it. He could tell me what was hiding under the skin, I thought. I also located the former head of special projects for Pininfarina, the Italian design house that had restyled and rebuilt all six FXs.

The Pininfarina veteran lived in Italy. I would wake up at three in the morning to call him on WhatsApp, pounding frantically on my keyboard as he talked. He told me stories, not just of designing and testing the car, but of the many other projects he had overseen for the family. How he and his team had personally escorted custom Bentleys and Jaguars into Brunei, finishing their builds on the palace grounds (once while cronies held their passports hostage overnight because of a broken turn signal). How they had presented those cars to the Prince and the Sultan for personal sign-off. After each call, I would drag my drowsy butt out of the house and head to work at the airport, my wife more than once wondering aloud if anyone but me would care enough to justify the lost sleep. (The truth was, I had no idea.)

When the story hit the front page of *The Verge* later that year, under the headline "The Secret Six," the Internet lit up. It was the top post on the homepage of Reddit throughout the morning, and the comments section was on fire. My editors were ecstatic—the story was being aggregated by automotive websites and Twitter praise was pouring in. I took congratulatory calls and received a standing offer from *The Verge* to do more stories just like it. The problem is, stories like that are extremely rare.

I HAD JUST one other idea.

I wanted to tell the story of Hiromu Naruse. The test driver who learned to wrench on his family's charcoal car in the aftermath of World War II. At Toyota, he had worked his way up from floor-mopper to being the company's most trusted engineer. He took driving seriously. He had logged more laps of the Nürburgring than anyone else at the automaker, and he was known within Toyota as the *Nür* Meister. Once, when an incoming CEO arrived to take the company helm, he met privately with Naruse, who promptly informed his new boss that he would not take orders from "someone who doesn't even know how to drive." He became that CEO's personal driving coach.

In short, Naruse was formidable. Perhaps his greatest achievement came in his later years, when he convinced Toyota brass to invest billions in building a futuristic mega-supercar to rival the world's best. He stewarded that machine, the Lexus LFA, through nearly a decade of development and frequent setbacks that nearly killed the project. Finally, when the LFA was complete and ready to be delivered, Naruse seemed happy. He returned to the Nürburgring one last time, for final testing on a special-edition LFA, but on the short drive from the course to Toyota's corporate garage, he crossed the center line, slammed into an oncoming BMW, and was killed. He was 67.

The internet held even less information on Hiromu Naruse than on the Ferrari FX. Stuck after weeks of digging, I reached out to Toyota's American arm directly. We went back and forth for months, me sending questions and them checking with Japan for feedback. They sent me a copy of *Toyohido!*, a Naruse biography by the author Inaizumi Ren. Unfortunately, it was printed entirely in Japanese. Every night for two weeks, I would put my three-year-old daughter to bed, then stay up until midnight copying each page into Google Translate and transcribing the broken English into a Microsoft Word document.

Nearly a year after first pitching the story to Toyota, my contacts returned and said there might be a chance to go to Japan. The success of the FX piece had gotten *Road & Track* interested in a Naruse feature story, and the magazine offered to cover daily expenses. Toyota booked me a flight, and a hotel, then organized four days of back-to-back marathon interview sessions with Naruse's closest colleagues and assigned me a chaperone so I didn't get lost.

That trip resulted in "The Last Long Road," a stunningly designed, five-page print feature in *R&T* whose art depicted Naruse superimposed over traditional Japanese-style paintings of winding roads and floating lanterns. To me, it seemed like a story that could have run in all those non-car outlets I had been devouring. I thought it appealed to more than just car folks. And I wanted to do it again and again.

WRITING the Naruse piece opened my eyes to a part of the world that I knew I didn't understand. While in Japan, I had no idea what any of the street signs said or what we were ordering for dinner. I didn't even know what part of the country I was in. I was a total *gaijin*, and I found that fascinating. The vast majority of people who drive Japanese cars will never have any concept of what went into making those cars work—the people who made them, their daily habits, their hopes and dreams, their favorite foods and music. I wanted to know what inspired them. I wanted to know their favorite anime.

In Naruse's case, one of those inspirations was a principle called *genchi genbutsu*, or "go and see for yourself." It's a popular saying in

Japanese business culture, one the Toyota master embodied to the fullest extent. He learned it early in his career while spending long hours in the garage of Toyota's secret motorsport division, tightening lug nuts and fastening body panels. Later, as an executive, he refused to sit in his office, working exclusively from the service bays in a hot, musty warehouse, where he could direct young employees and climb underneath a car when they still weren't getting it right.

Japan held quiet revelations. Tourists regularly remark on the cleanliness of its large cities. I assumed there were aggressive policies or regulations to enforce this. One day, after leaving my hotel in Nagoya, I brought a soda with me on a walk. After finishing it, I looked everywhere for a trash can but found nothing. For blocks and blocks, I carried an empty bottle. What had started as a quick jaunt turned into a 30-minute mission, and I felt dumber with each passing second. At one point, I looked around and realized that no one else was carrying drinks, food, or anything disposable. Curious, I asked my handler why it was so difficult to find a trash can.

He turned to me with a puzzled scowl: "Why would anyone leave their house with trash?"

Silly as it was, this was my *genchi genbutsu* moment, in a way. It wasn't laws that kept Japan clean, it was a shared cultural practice. I left the country thrilled with what I'd learned about Naruse and Toyota, but also knowing that I hadn't begun to understand what the place could teach me.

ON MY SECOND trip flying across the Pacific, in March of 2023, I actually slept pretty well on the plane. Over the course of that 12-hour flight, I got five, maybe six hours of rest. We landed at Haneda Airport around 4:45 a.m. local time. After passing through customs, I exchanged the dollars I was carrying for Japanese yen, then tried, unsuccessfully, to book a reservation at a public shower station. Oh well, I thought, it might just be a smelly day. I had a change of clothes, a bar of deodorant, and a fresh jacket in my bag, and they would have to do. A few minutes later, a very nice guide at the visitor's center showed this ripe *gaijin* how to buy a train ticket from Tokyo to Yokohama. He also gave me a free map of the metropolitan area, which I would hang onto for dear life for the next three days.

Yes, three days. Two meetings per day, then home, in and out of the country in less than 72 hours. It was going to be a whirlwind.

When the train doors opened, perfectly on time, I stepped inside and took a seat. The car began to move and I snapped a video of the swinging *tsurikawa*, the suspended grab handles, for my daughter. Days earlier, we had gone to a women's car meet in L.A.'s Arts District. She had giggled at all the anime splashed across the cars, asking the owner of a Toyota FR-S about the heart-shaped ring hung above her passenger window, and gasping when she learned they're for passengers to squeeze when you're drifting sideways at highway speed. Watching the tsurikawa sway gently as the train sped off made me feel oddly at home and at peace.

NISSAN KNEW I WAS COMING. Deep in the bowels of its corporate headquarters in Yokohama, just a few miles outside Tokyo, I stood waiting with a member of the media-relations team. They had wanted to facilitate my trip, to help further my research, so they had provided a car.

When the Millennium Jade GT-R T-Spec pulled into sight in the parking garage, I nearly had a panic attack. A Nissan servicemember showed me where to sign my life away on a release form, then walked me around the vehicle, pointing out the slightest dents and imperfections. After that, he handed over the key and bid me farewell.

I tossed my bag inside and slid into the driver's seat on the right side. That, I thought, was going to take some getting used to. This was an R35 GT-R—no Skyline in the name, just the letters—the model that had debuted in 2008 as successor to the Holy Trinity of R32, R33, and R34 GT-Rs, the cars I was mainly writing about. The R35 would help me understand how the idea of the GT-R changed over the years, but also where that idea stands currently, and where Nissan plans to take it next.

Before I could do that, however, I had to fight traffic on the way to my first appointment. Punctuality is big throughout the country, and Masa at Toprank Japan, with the company's treasure-trove warehouse, was waiting for me. I notched the GT-R into drive and gingerly rolled out of the parking garage, only lightly nervous, waving kindly to the man with the release form, to show him everything was fine. Convincing myself of that fact was another matter entirely.

Driving in Japan, at first, takes a bit of mental gymnastics. The steering wheel is on the right side of the car; you drive on the left side of the street. I've driven in foreign countries before, but the combination of processing your new position on the road, your new surroundings, your jet lag, and unfamiliar street signs is always a doozy. And that's not even counting the 565 hp that was under my right foot.

Time to get on with it. I crept onto a public road, slowly growing more confident. Heading toward the highway, I entered the leftmost lane, then stopped for a stoplight and hit my left turn signal. Except, Japanese cars have their turn signals on the right side of the steering wheel, and what I thought was a blinker was actually the stalk for the windshield wipers. So in broad daylight, with a heavy workday crowd on the crosswalk ahead, the *gaijin* in the bright-green supercar advertised to everyone that he had no idea what he was doing.

That was my first big mistake of the trip. I would do it again at least five more times.

Oh well, I thought, again—like so many of the GT-R owners I had interviewed over the last few months, I had been thoroughly humbled by a JDM car. Nothing like being in good company. I forced a chuckle. A turn or two later, climbing onto a narrow two-lane highway, anticipating freedom, I came face to face with lunchtime Tokyo traffic. The car slowed to a crawl.

I had nearly 600 horses under the hood of an icon, I had traveled thousands of miles to drive Japanese roads, I was in one of the greatest cities in the world, and I couldn't go faster than 5 mph.

I laughed once more, this time for real. The *gaijin* had been humbled yet again.

GETTING out of Tokyo was a struggle. But after around 90 minutes of lurching and stopping, lurching and stopping, the road's lanes split off, the trucks headed in another direction, and the mass began to flow. The GT-R growled over the Arakawa River, cherry blossoms, the *sakura*, in first bloom along the waterline. People were posing for selfies with the trees or resting in the sun nearby. The countryside appeared, green and vast, the highway stretching out ahead. The car began to feel smaller and more alive, far less cumbersome than it had in the tight roads of Tokyo, where you're always within centimeters of other cars, pedestrians, and sometimes even brick walls and concrete buildings.

I took a deep breath and settled into the leather. More than any GT-R before it, the R35 was designed to be an all-in-one solution, a comfortable luxury car and world-beating performance tool at the same time. It is bigger and heavier than its predecessors, stuffed to the gills with technology and features. Which is not to say it coddles. Even with the chassis in Comfort mode, you have to be awake. Turning the wheel works your shoulders and elbows. The huge brakes squeal with displeasure in a gradual stop. Two banana-sized shift paddles behind the steering wheel never stop calling to you, beckoning you to drop sense and sensibility and slam the accelerator.

You are aware, they seem to be saying, *that this car can find 60 mph in three seconds flat? You are aware, yes, that it makes enough grip to stay glued to the road as you zip through corners and leave traffic behind? Grab the paddles and feel alive for once in your life, for chrissakes!*

But I didn't. I dutifully followed my phone's navigation, heading deeper into unfamiliar country. Finally, after passing a seemingly endless line of golf pro shops—the Japanese spend more than $2 billion on golf gear every year—and crossing several of the rivers that helped make the region famous for its edamame farms, I made a left and pulled into a 30-car parking lot just off the main road. I had a date with forbidden fruit.

Masaki Sawada is, he admits, a bit jaded. Every day, he walks past rows and rows of cars that some see as buried treasure. Sawada is a car fanatic himself, and he seemed to understand that simply walking into his facility was a little overwhelming. I knew what to expect, but it still took me by surprise.

This was Toprank PDI, the company's Pre-Delivery Inspection center, one of eight Toprank facilities in Japan. In addition to the California location in Cerritos, there is also one office each in Sri Lanka, Thailand, and Myanmar. Where some people have a cubicle, Sawada has a building full of sleeping R34s. An enthusiast through and through, he recently "over-extended," as he put it, to buy a Toyota GR Yaris, a performance hatchback not sold in America, for about $50,000 USD.

Over-extended, he told me, "Especially for a toy. But it is definitely fun."

Sawada films his drives for his YouTube channel, and he often accompanies foreign buyers when they come to visit their cars, showing them local roads and restaurants. His Instagram handle is @masalovescars. His exuberance tends to go a long way with clients, many of whom want to know that he understands their reasons for spending so much money with Toprank, instead of less with someone else.

Besides the GR Yaris, Sawada also has an R34. His father bought it more than a decade ago, a Bayside Blue GT-R, totally stock, with 19,000 kilometers on the clock. It was a stretch back then at 3.5 million yen, or about $25,000 USD. Today, even with 96,000 km on the odometer, it has likely quintupled in value. "The sheer amount of demand for the car is absurd," Sawada said. But the R34 means too much to the family, Sawada said. They will never sell.

He took us on a walk through the parking lot wrapped around the warehouse. JDM cars of all kinds were just sitting out in the open, a laundry list of makes, from sold to available, pristine or in need of repair. At the moment, the most in-demand GT-R is anything with official Nismo factory performance upgrade parts, because Nissan produces originals so infrequently. Those parts are so desirable new that ordering one usually means putting yourself on a waiting list that is months or years long.

Some of the cars we stroll past, hidden under tarps, undoubtedly wear Nismo bits. Others, like the M-Spec Nür or Midnight Purple III models I see, are incredibly valuable even without those parts, but as the warehouse is currently full, they wait outside. In January of 2024, Sawada said, when the oldest R34 GT-Rs turn 25 and become legal for export, their departure will make room, and other cars can move in.

We walked into the facility's garage bays and office. After Toprank purchases a car in Japan, either at auction or through private transaction, the vehicle is listed for sale on the company website. Once a buyer is found, that car is brought to the garage, which Sawada calls "the Pit." There, master technicians conduct initial inspections and perform routine maintenance, as well as any larger jobs needed, like engine tuning or paintwork. Only then will they begin the exporting process, "once the car is up to our standard."

On the day of my visit, the Pit held a cherry-red Honda Accord Euro R on a lift. That's another car not sold in America, a sporty, Japan-only version of a bland four-door sedan, with an aggressive body kit. As I stood there, a technician with a flashlight stuck his head deep into a rear wheel well.

That car, Sawada said, was destined for an American service-member stationed at the naval base on Okinawa Island. American military comprise a large portion of Toprank customers, and the company can help them navigate Japan's tricky vehicle-registration procedures for non-residents. The Honda, for instance, will be required to use a special license plate whose number begins with a glaring Y, denoting U.S. military affiliation. That plate is a mixed bag —it allows foreigners to drive in Japan, but it also lumps trouble-makers in with those on good behavior. Servicemembers have a reputation for causing accidents in Okinawa, and the statute of limitations for victims to claim benefits is only two years, as opposed to the regular Japanese standard of three. Locals thus whisper among themselves to "beware of Y-plates," a phrase that suggests long history, or maybe a subtle nod to Japan-U.S. relations historically.

Another fascinating service separates Toprank from other importers: the visiting process. It is for foreign residents who buy a car, usually a Skyline, and keep it in Japan. Earlier, in the outdoor lot, Sawada had pointed to a Bayside Blue R34 with another unique license plate, one that denoted the car as a rental.

"A rental?" I asked, confused. The car belonged to an American, he said, but as the owner was not a resident of Japan, they were not legally allowed to own and register a vehicle there. In that case, Toprank will register the car itself, as a rental, and the owner will "rent" it for the duration of their stay. (I would later discover that Mickey Andrade, from Toprank's California brewery cruise, and many other owners I spoke with had all toured the countryside this way.)

"It's only us doing this in this market, because we have a specific license to run a rental service," Sawada said. "People say Toprank prices are high, and in the end, sure, we're higher. But that doesn't mean we jack it up without services."

From another area of the Pit, Sawada led me deeper into the building, past an assortment of spare parts and files and into a corner with a special resident. Seconds later, I was blinking in disbelief at the rich silver paint of a two-door Hakosuka, one of around 1,200 originally built and one of the few hundred known to remain. The car still had its original engine—when Sawada opened the hood to show me, we were met with a combination of rare vintage hardware and the jumbled disarray of a dusty work in progress.

This, it turned out, was a long turnaround. Toprank's chief mechanic, referred to only as Sato-san, has led the Hako's restoration, on and off, for 20 years. "It's kind of a Toprank project car now," Sawada said, adding that the team is in no rush to finish simply because they enjoy working on it. (When I asked if the engine ran, he said, "Pretty sure.") If they were to get the car in complete working order, Sawada noted, it would then be so valuable that they'd have almost no choice but to offer it to wealthy customers. So they're in no rush.

That topic, Sawada told me, has come up a lot in recent years. It is difficult to overstate the impact that the Hakosuka had on Japanese enthusiasts in the early 1970s, he said, particularly on people his father's age, who were kids when the model debuted and began winning races. Along with cars like the Toyota 2000GT, the Hakosuka was one of the first Japanese models that proved the country was progressing into a new era. Then, in the late 1980s, when those kids were in their twenties, the R32 GT-R, the modern Hako, hit the JTCC and had the same effect. "It was so sensational," Sawada said. "It was just so strong that all the teams started buying them, even though it wasn't supposed to be a GT-R series." In this way, then, the GT-R built a legacy in the hearts of the Japanese, one that could be shared between generations and that continued into the early 2000s.

Much like the Hakosuka, the R32 was overbuilt, proven in motor-sport, and relatively attainable. The latter model's performance alone would have been enough to cement its legend, but external factors fanned the flames. The GT-R's inclusion in games like *Gran Turismo* and movies like *The Fast and the Furious* (amazingly, for Japanese audiences, the film was retitled *Wild Speed*) only added to the mystique. Cult car-culture manga—Japanese graphic novels—have featured the R32 heroically for years, as has the 24-hour hype fire hose of social media.

The result, as Sawada echoed, has become something of a GT-R super-market. A tornado of pent-up demand, released just as a generation aged into disposable income, and, in the case of American enthusiasts, wrapped within 25 years of waiting. The fever, Sawada told me, is out of control: "As a Japanese car guy and enthusiast, the cars are just too expensive." It's also beginning to affect more affordable JDM sports cars. In one period, he added, values of the cheaper and slower R34 GT-T rocketed up some 300,000 yen in a single month.

At those prices, Toprank is more likely to receive inquiries from foreign buyers who discovered the cars on YouTube than from Japanese locals who were passed down stories. The GT-R accounts for 70-percent of Toprank's business, Sawada said, but it was never supposed to be a 35-million-yen car. Imagine watching an iconic piece of America, a Mustang or a Camaro, price itself out of the U.S. market.

"It's mixed feelings," he said. "But those customers will treat it as a 35-million-yen car. As long as people enjoy it, that's how it should be."

AFTER GETTING accustomed to Toprank's overstuffed California facility, in that nondescript business park, seeing the operation's scale in Japan put things in perspective. Toprank isn't just America's premier GT-R importer; it's a 360-degree service operation, handling storage, registration, regulation, inspection, and service. As I waved goodbye to Sawada and headed toward my next meeting, a picture of the GT-R world began to form in my head. Not the backroom garages and tiny mom-pop shops I had envisioned, but the interconnected network of amenities and supply chains that it really is.

Toprank has competitors, but it has no direct equal. In fact, in many ways, no company is the polar opposite of Toprank more than the one I visited next: a humble parts reseller that grew from scrappy beginnings to become an Internet giant.

About an hour further out from central Tokyo, in the middle of a field of overgrown grass and weeds, sits Trust Kikaku. The firm is located on a massive plot that was once farmland, which is good, because Trust Kikaku specializes in bulk. The grounds of its headquarters are blanketed with an abundance of 1990s sports cars. There is an abundance of decay in those cars, missing wheels or missing bumpers, or fenders with rusty holes the size of cantaloupes. One

R34 Skyline is missing its left front fender and its left set of taillights. Another has fenders but no hood or engine. Most important, Trust Kikaku has an abundance of parts on hand, either ripped from the cars outside or purchased new from Nissan or Japan's vast ecosystem of aftermarket shops.

That bulk of components is Trust Kikaku's greatest strength, the ability to sell virtually any part or accessory a Skyline owner could want. But those parts are also the company's greatest stain. Trust Kikaku will buy almost anything, as much of it as they can get, from five or 10 examples of a rare part in a single batch to multiple identical vehicles at once. The sheer quantity of product controlled by the company, some believe, allows it to control market prices. Depending on your perspective, Trust Kikaku is either a savior, with the one obscure piece you so desperately need; or an opportunistic vulture that generated that desperation intentionally, and built a GT-R pricing phenomenon by artificially creating scarcity and preventing the competition from stocking inventory of their own.

That last perspective is awfully sinister, and for someone who's read about Trust Kikaku for years, the grounds can be foreboding and eerie to enter. So I crept through the automatic front gate with caution, rolling slowly past the rotting chassis hulks to a parking spot near the front door. At which point my sleep-deprived brain was shaken awake by the appearance of a wiry, six-foot-four Russian bounding toward me. He gave a giant smile and a dramatic, cheery wave.

"Hello! Wow! Look at this car! This is fantastic. We are so happy you have come to visit us. Please, let me show you around."

This was Pawel Kmiec-Shibuya, head of Trust Kikaku's overseas sales. An instant later, he was bounding around the property, giving an overview of his employer's history while I attempted to process the never-ending stream of gutted cars we rolled past.

Trust Kikaku's CEO, Minoru Terada, founded the company in 1993 while still working full-time in his previous career. A sports-car enthusiast, he wanted to buy cars and work on them, then flip them for profit. In the process, he figured, he could make small improvements to each, like switching out dented bumpers or faulty parts. So he started collecting replacements.

If it sounds like Trust Kikaku rose to prominence by accident, that's because it mostly did. Terada's flipping process saw him accumulate a mountain of spares, but he didn't think to sell them until a friend visited his crowded shop in the late 1990s and suggested advertising some of it on eBay. The three warehouses of cars and parts that now exist under the Trust Kikaku umbrella came about not through some grand plan for expansion, but because Terada can't help himself. When he needs more space, he simply buys a new building. In the beginning, the man was a Supra fan, and he didn't particularly like Skylines or GT-Rs. Now, his company has staked its entire future on them.

As Pawel talked, I followed him around the corner of the main office building, and we stopped to look over an expansive open field. Below, at the end of our dirt path, was a massive gravel parking lot—though you could also call it a graveyard—with each of the lot's sides the length of a football field. The space held all manner of neatly parked JDM cars, row after row after row, lined up like eggs in a crate. There were hundreds. It looked like an optical illusion, the result of mirrors or trickery, a quantity and lineup that couldn't have been real.

From our elevated position, I tried to count, pointing down at each car with a finger, one at a time, like a kindergartner. I stopped when I noticed that the cars disappeared over the horizon, their end impossible to see. Maybe 250 in total? Three hundred? Even Pawel didn't know.

In one sweeping vista, that was the root of Terada's success: volume. By keeping an almost absurd amount of product on hand—other Trust Kikaku facilities are sprinkled around Japan—his company can sell what it wants, export what it wants, and rip what it wants from any car it wants. The world holds enough buyers to make any of those choices financially viable.

Predictably, growth seems inseparable from Trust Kikaku's business model. And the stranglehold that the company now wields over the GT-R market allows them to charge almost anything they want.

While it could be a coincidence that the GT-R market has exploded as Trust Kikaku has grown, it's more likely that the two curves are at least tangentially linked.

Standing on that hill, I couldn't decide if the lot below was feeding an appetite or sucking it dry. I only knew the answer was complicated. Earlier in the tour, Pawel told me about how, seven years back, he had tried to buy an R34 GT-T in good condition. The car had the desirable two-door body and a manual transmission, but its $10,000 USD price was just out of reach. Now, he lamented, that money will barely get you a slower Skyline, with the smaller engine, an automatic, and way more miles. Looking out at the mass of GT-T and other Skyline models taken off the market to be raided for parts, I wondered if he saw the irony.

NATURALLY, Trust Kikaku is taking aggressive steps into the American market. In late 2021, it established TKGT, its first U.S. branch, and in mid-2022, that offshoot set up shop in a small business park in California's Huntington Beach. Weeks before flying to Japan, I visited the location to learn about its plans for expansion, and to meet its 24-year-old supervisor.

Octavio Sato was working at Target when he heard about a Japanese auto-parts company looking to expand. A SoCal native, Sato had grown up watching YouTube car videos on channels like The Smoking Tire, and GT-R-specific content from big-time creators like "Adam LZ" and "Tommy F Yeah." He had always wanted to work in cars but didn't see a practical path to get there, so he earned an undergraduate degree in computer science and cybersecurity and got ready to start a more traditional career.

Sato followed Trust Kikaku on Instagram because Tommy F Yeah did. One day, the company account posted a job listing for a new position in California. At the very least, Sato thought, it would be good résumé fodder. "Even if it's something temporary," he told me, "hey, cool, at least I got to work in cars." He got the job and said goodbye to Target.

Early on, Trust Kikaku had hired a consultant to help establish U.S. operations. But after a few months on the job, the home office had built such a good relationship with Sato, they decided to get rid of the consultant and work through him directly. He now manages a team of TKGT reps, his office logging and packing sales made through the company's website. Twice a month, massive inventory containers arrive from Japan, carrying everything from fenders and turbos to stickers and T-shirts, and every day, the team loads an 18-wheeler to the brim with shipments for stateside customers.

Parts are one thing, but Trust Kikaku wants U.S.-based TKGT to fulfill another critical aspect of its planned growth: vehicle imports. In close proximity to the legendary Japanese auctions where many of these cars come up for sale, Trust Kikaku has enviable access to cars that have lived their whole lives in their home country, a quality that can bring a premium on the market regardless of mileage or condition. As the R34 GT-R approaches its twenty-fifth birthday, Terada's organization wants someone on the ground in the States—Sato—to manage the complex web of laws and regulations.

"I don't know how successful we're going to be," Sato admitted. "But we're going to try." Then he acknowledged, as his superiors in Japan would weeks later, that vehicle importing can be extremely difficult, whether the cars are legal or not. Sato has already grown frustrated with both the process of registering a GT-R in California and the state's glacial DMV processing times, but, he said, he has been encouraged by the clear requirements and open communication lines from his contacts at places like the Environmental Protection Agency (EPA) and the National Highway Traffic Safety Administration (NHTSA).

That last part was nice to hear, though I couldn't help thinking about how Sato's counterpart at his largest competitor, Toprank's Sean Morris, had been professionally importing cars longer than Sato had been alive. Still, there were encouraging signs. TKGT's Huntington Beach lobby had two R33 GT-Rs on its floor, which suggested the company had successfully imported two R33s—no small feat. The outpost had also managed to quickly connect with a hungry base. Word spread fast when the Huntington location popped up, with customers thrilled to pay domestic shipping on a wide array of parts that had previously required international rates. Tommy F Yeah even came to visit in 2022, and both he and fellow YouTuber T.J. Hunt had filmed videos at TKGT, driving up awareness even more.

Before I left, Sato walked me through his inventory warehouse. Shelves there were stacked to the edges, product piled high and close to the ceiling. There were fenders, axles, fuel pumps, and more—used components sat in protective bubble plastic, with new ones still in their boxes from Nissan. The building held smaller items, too, like iconic heritage badges costing more than $400 apiece (down from a high of more than $600, in 2022, when the yen was stronger). The big sellers when I visited were original R32 and R33 transmissions and rear quarter panels. The latter were hot, Sato suspected, because R32 owners want to make their cars look like R34s.

Naturally, the Golden State is by far TKGT's biggest market—"The amount of Skylines in California is insane," Sato said—but shipments to Florida, Texas, and the northeast are increasing. Several GT-R owners I spoke with said they had happily shopped with TKGT and would probably do it again, though they might not admit that fact publicly. In other words, Trust Kikaku is well and truly here now, an established part of the community.

"People are looking for one place to get it all done," Sato told me. Then, laughing: "It's crazy that, because of this car, I get to take a paycheck home."

THE DIFFERENCES between Toprank and Trust Kikaku are telling. The latter appears to make its decisions by reading the tea leaves, and it has much catching up to do in terms of importing know-how. The Japanese company doesn't host homeland tours, organize "rental" registrations, or offer after-sale support, either. Referring to an R33

GT-R they had recently brought to America, Sato called the car basically an experiment, "just to see if it would get taken," or seized by the feds. It's hard to imagine those words leaving the mouth of the minutiae-focused Morris.

The similarities are meaningful, too. Toprank and Trust Kikaku are each a major gateway to American GT-R ownership, and each is a lightning rod for controversy. Like Trust Kikaku, Toprank's operation shows evidence of being caught off guard by its own success. That magical warehouse I visited, the one with the fifty-plus R34 GT-Rs, was far from modern, with bare walls, a lack of climate or moisture control, cars dirty from sitting, and a mostly dirt floor.

Still, vibe counts for much in enthusiast communities, and if Toprank is proof of anything, it's that customer service can go a long way. I spoke with multiple owners who store their cars in that dirt-floored facility, and none of them seemed bothered by the grime. They did mention, however, that other customers have complained about their appreciating assets sitting in an old building without a fire-suppression system. Toprank has reportedly offered to install such a system, but the clientele balked when told the cost would be rolled into their monthly fees. (For what it's worth, most of the Toprank customers who described themselves as "obsessed" said they found such bickering funny, and that they didn't care either way.)

It's perhaps most accurate to describe Toprank and Trust Kikaku as two separate but vital parts of an ecosystem. To some extent, both companies need each other. Every year, Toprank brings in 20- and 30-year-old cars that will always need parts to stay running, and Trust Kikaku has more of those parts than anyone else. By the same token, when Trust Kikaku brings cars to America that they won't service or support, Toprank will be there to pick up the slack. A rising GT-R market lifts both boats.

BACK IN JAPAN, Pawel, the six-foot, four-inch Russian, explained his company's philosophy: buy everything they can get their hands on.

Partly, it's because they can't predict which parts will be needed the most down the line.

"It won't be good for business," he said, "if we sell the cars and then, after two years, they break down and that's it. In the future, there probably will be more focus on running parts"—simple service items required to keep a machine healthy—"instead of performance parts. As time passes the focus will switch."

"You can make the engine bigger," he added, "but if you don't have the gasket, then it won't work properly."

Leaving the graveyard lot behind, Pawel led me inside Trust Kikaku's sprawling storage facility where I saw that strategy on full display. Picture a JDM Costco. The shelves were lined with stock engines, original gearboxes, authentic Nismo front seats, items that were rare 20 years ago and even more uncommon today. As time goes on, they'll be increasingly difficult to find.

That purchase strategy, Pawel conceded, borders on hoarding and raises pricing. But he claimed that Nissan's reluctance to increase GT-R parts production in the face of demand pushes prices higher still. Nismo, for example, makes and sells a coveted strut-tower brace. Buy it from the factory and the part costs a few hundred dollars, assuming you can wait months to get it. Trust Kikaku keeps the same item in stock, Nismo branding and everything, priced at around $1,000. The markup is roughly 300-percent, but you're paying for how the brace can be on a truck to your driveway by the end of the day.

"In the case of the GT-R especially, if something's cheap, it probably means it's not in really good shape," Pawel said. "You have to provide as many parts as possible. Those won't be cheap, sorry. We just keep anything we can, to make sure we have enough."

For their part, the people at Trust Kikaku strongly believe the hype around GT-Rs will only continue to build. Like many others, they're watching as the R34 GT-R nears American legalization, knowing that change will impact their business, if not knowing exactly how. After all, once those cars are old enough to be here, they will need service, they will need replacement parts, and they will need performance upgrades.

The R34 may have had its original launch in 1999, but 25 years later, it faces an impending rebirth in January of 2024. And an entire industry waits to support it.

"It's our main focus right now," Pawel said. "Business in Japan is good. But it probably won't be comparable to what happens in the U.S."

As the sun crept toward the horizon, Trust Kikaku began to close up for the night. I waved goodbye to Pawel and walked back to the parking lot. As I squeezed the R35 through another round of narrow streets and headed for my hotel, I grew convinced that these companies had smartly positioned themselves to capitalize on an incoming wave. Even if it was mostly accidental.

Americans had demanded, over and over again, that Japan abandon its old-fashioned ways and adopt more modern business practices. And one more time, the Japanese were going to use their exports to sell those lessons right back to us.

CHAPTER 5

GT-R owners can get a bad rap. As the cars have become more valuable and more expensive to maintain, they've attracted more people with money to spare. In some cases, that means a wealthy collector for whom funds are no object, a person chasing a rare item that holds value. In others, it's a social-media influencer looking to gain followers by exploiting the latest trend. Either way, enthusiasm isn't automatic. It might sound obvious, but holding the keys to a GT-R or posting photos or videos of one doesn't always equate to a deep appreciation for the model or Japanese culture.

It helps to remember that the car isn't universally beloved. Loads of auto enthusiasts are badge snobs—it's "only" a Nissan. Others hold a simple cultural bias—historically, few Japanese automobiles have been hyped as "blue-chip" automotive collectibles. Whatever the reason, mainstream car culture has long dismissed the GT-R as the stuff of cult fandom. Even now, with certain models becoming six-figure investments, industry experts who readily accept high prices for rare Porsches and Mustangs are often flummoxed that anyone would pay $50,000 for an old Nissan, let alone twice that or more.

Several of my colleagues, automotive journalists paid to understand historical significance and cultural subtlety, told me they view the GT-R as just another Nissan. "It's not bad, for a Japanese car," one said. Another described the R32 driving experience as "kind of like an '80s Buick." When I explained to one dyed-in-the-wool veteran the process of buying an R34 GT-R in Japan, how buyers will pay rent to have their car stored there for occasional visits, he snarked, "So you're telling me they've got more money than brains, then."

Just as being a GT-R owner doesn't require enthusiasm, it doesn't mean you're rich, either. Plenty of folks of limited means have fought and scratched their way to a GT-R title. These people come from modest backgrounds, work regular jobs, and save for years to bring home a piece of their personal dream. They might store their pride and joy in the open car park of an apartment complex. They might fix it with their own tools, and whatever parts they can find or kludge into working. Their GT-R might be the only vehicle they own, driven to and from work in all four seasons. Several owners insisted to me that a friend of theirs, down on his luck, slept in his GT-R rather than sell it.

Whether it's financially responsible to pour most of your net worth into a 30-year-old Japanese coupe is another matter entirely. But that doesn't mean it doesn't happen. Unsurprisingly, those "budget" owners are often the ones who become influencers and connectors in the GT-R world, not for the pristine condition of their cars, but for their depth of knowledge and willingness to share their passion with others.

All of which is to say that the GT-R, more than so many machines like it, inspires people to pour in everything they have. According to one former Nissan insider, when the company conducted a consumer-research study with its target demographic, it discovered that, in extreme cases, Porsche and BMW buyers might spend a sizeable chunk of their available funds on a car. GT-R owners, the study found, regularly spend 100-percent on their cars.

You could say that's a poor financial decision. You could also argue that the return on investment with a GT-R, the excitement you get from actually driving it, is likely to be greater for a budget enthusiast than for one of high net worth. Many of the budget folks I spoke with told ownership stories, the experience of owning your dream car and feeling like a rockstar, that mirrored the ones from those with deeper pockets. This makes sense: Driving a GT-R with a few lumps and scratches will still get you looks on the street. Flawed and damaged paint won't keep someone from approaching you at a gas station with a smile and genuine interest. You may not get to take a vacation to drive your car in Japan, but you'll still get a thumbs-up from kids on the sidewalk.

One person who was an extraordinary help in connecting me with other GT-R owners was Steve Ellis. Ellis, a native Texan and Millennial, runs an automotive event space for the collector-car insurance company Hagerty. He owns a silver R33 GT-R that he paid for in part through several years of buying and selling cars at Toprank alongside Sean Morris and Brian Jannusch. Ellis drives his R33 to work every day, taking it to meets and rallies across Southern California in his spare time. His schedule regularly includes beachside morning car shows and evening canyon runs in the same day. He saves for weeks or months to buy parts, he does most of the work himself or with the help of friends, and he doesn't seem to stress over wear and tear.

In many ways, these GT-R owners have even more fun than their high-end counterparts. Ellis's favorite story to tell involves meeting a Ferrari driver and his young son at an L.A. car show. The father, Ellis said, watched in exasperation as the boy sprinted over to his R33, asking question after question about it.

"When he was done," Ellis said, "his dad came over and said, 'Okay, I can't get him to give a shit about my car. What's the deal with these things?' I thought that was so freaking cool."

If anything, people like Ellis are relatable ambassadors for the lifestyle. They're using the means they have to get where they've always wanted to go. A cracked oil pan or a blown RB26 won't be easy to replace, but people like Ellis will hammer a mountain road or hit the track anyway.

Before Skyline ownership became mostly legal in America, getting caught with one on the street could lead to your dream car getting impounded or crushed. And yet people in the budget group were often the ones spending their life savings, anyway, crossing their fingers to avoid chance meetings with a traffic cop. By taking such risks willingly and happily, that group carried on a rich tradition of working with what you've got. It's a tradition that goes back as far as the invention of the automobile itself, blossoming particularly in that very first GT-R of the 1960s and the tuning culture of late 20th-century Japan.

FIFTY YEARS AGO, when a tiny engineering shop unveiled the world's first turbocharger kit, few realized the impact it would have on the automotive industry. That kit, sold as the FET, was the first mainstream product from HKS, a newly formed company operating from an old dairy-farm shed at the base of Mount Fuji. In just a few short hours, the parts in the box could make a non-turbo car turbocharged, and thus far more powerful. Because the package was designed to work without costly or time-consuming changes to an engine's insides, it was a revelation, easy to install and set up. It was the world's first "bolt-on" turbo kit.

HKS began when a young Yamaha motorcycle engineer named Hiroyuki Hasegawa decided to venture out on his own. Hasegawa secured funding from two partners, setting up shop in the shadow of a mountain. He branded his company by combining his backers' initials with the first letter of his last name. Brought to market in 1974, the FET was designed to fit—what else?—the Nissan Skyline.

Like many of his generation, Hasegawa had been transfixed by how the Hakosuka felled the competition at Fuji Speedway. Now he wanted to help Kenmeri GT-R owners land their own Fuji dreams. The simple addition of an FET could take a stock Kenmeri engine from 115 hp to 160 hp, an increase of more than 40-percent. It was the beginning of the aftermarket industry that would help define the GT-R.

The FET was an attempt to establish HKS as a producer of quality parts, one that could not just equal the work of big automakers, but improve upon it. Hasegawa wanted to make his own racing engines, his own exhaust systems, and his own turbo kits, all of which anyone could purchase and fit to any car. In time, HKS would grow to become one of the most powerful and influential aftermarket firms in the world, closer to a major global manufacturer than the tenant of a farm shed.

A few years after the FET, HKS released a package containing both a rebuilt engine and a turbocharger kit. It was designed to fit both the Skyline and the Toyota Celica coupe, inching the company closer to Hasegawa's goal of being a one-stop shop. Not satisfied to stick with driveline components, HKS would later become one of the first firms to explore digital engine accessories. The idea of an aftermarket speed part is almost as old as the wheel, but the advent of affordable and relatively compact computers, and the software to manipulate an engine's power and torque, helped kick off the modern era of vehicle "tuning."

HKS went on to produce popular fuel-control units, ignition systems, and intake parts, all of which helped make it a leader in a new age of performance. Competitors like Trust/GReddy, Blitz, Spoon, Mugen, and JUN Auto soon came on the scene, cashing in on a growing flood of customers. All were flush with cash from Japan's newly ascendant 1980s economy. And that economy showed no signs of slowing down.

A FEW YEARS after Commodore Perry's arrival in Edo Bay, Japan began to relax its strict isolation policies, allowing residents to freely leave the country. Taking off for America became popular immediately, first to Hawaii for new job opportunities, then to the mainland during the railroad boom in the late 1800s. Immigration to California grew wildly shortly thereafter. But with the onset of World War II and the establishment of government internment camps for Japanese Americans—camps that displaced thousands of families and marked one dark period among many for their adopted country—scores of

Nikkei, the descendants of Japanese immigrants, searched for a safe place to settle.

L.A.'s South Bay gave an opportunity. South of Los Angeles, tucked up against the Pacific Ocean, the area holds a collection of several mid-size cities and communities. There, the Japanese once scattered across Southern California found refuge from much of the discrimination they had experienced during and after the war. The available properties, largely unsettled farmland, provided ready access to jobs at the ports of Los Angeles and Long Beach. They also represented one of the few places that Japanese were not expressly prohibited from owning land.

Crucially, the area would become home to Japanese automakers and industry leaders. In 1963, Honda moved its U.S. headquarters from a tiny facility in Los Angeles to a far larger building in the South Bay city of Gardena. In 1985, seeking more space again, it moved five miles south, to the coastal community of Torrance, where Toyota also kept its stateside campus. Among medium-size American cities, or those with populations between 100,000 and 250,000, Torrance still has the largest percentage of Japanese residents in the country, at 10.1-percent. Today, the area is known for its many Japanese markets and restaurants, where you may find udon or yakitori more easily than a cheeseburger and fries.

Nissan, for its part, established its American office in Gardena, just up the road. Gardena also boasts, for its size, the highest concentration of Japanese residents in the country, at 11.6-percent. The Japanese Cultural Institute established an office there in 1988.

For all these reasons and more, the South Bay would become the epicenter of Japanese car culture in the United States.

IN THE EARLY 1990S, without social media or widely available Internet access, anyone in America interested in Japanese cars had two choices: Read mainstream car magazines like *Road & Track*, where Asian vehicles shared space with European and American ones and tuner coverage was rare, or locate something like *Option* magazine, which focused on Japanese performance exclusively. And the best place to find *Option* was in the South Bay's many groceries and bookshops. You could head to markets like Yaohan or Kinokuniya to pick up the latest editions while also grabbing copies of similar publications like *Carboy*, *Carisma*, *RevSpeed*, and *Autoworks*. All were published only in Japanese, but each provided a small window into advancements and culture half a world away. The stories they told seemed like the stuff of movies.

HKS had sparked a movement: Japan had a thriving tuning scene for Japanese cars, and America simply didn't. They had cars that Americans couldn't buy, roads that Americans couldn't drive, and shops that Americans couldn't visit. There was no better example of the intersection of those qualities than the Skyline GT-R. In the JDM pantheon, it had the strongest culture, with deep ties to motorsport and street racing, plus a close association with dozens of tuning shops. And if magazines like *Option* were to be believed, enthusiasts in Japan were obsessed.

In the bookstores and supermarkets of Torrance and Gardena, kids ran straight to the magazine sections. They would inhale issues regardless of whether they could read Japanese, learning who had built the latest monster GT-R, or who had dared to tempt fate and the law with the fastest high-speed run. The most famous example is the story of Smokey Nagata.

A gentle-looking man with moppy hair, famous for his shyness, Kazuhiko "Smokey" Nagata began his career as a mechanic at Trust, but he left to start his own company when he was repeatedly caught working on his own projects at work. He called the new shop Top Secret, and opened its doors in the early 1990s. Immediately he set about building some of the craziest creations Japan had ever seen, often highlighted by his signature gold paint. Nagata's legend exploded in 1998, when he took a heavily tuned GT-R engine and installed it under the hood of a Toyota Supra—painted, of course, bright gold—and shipped the car to the United Kingdom. In England, armed with a camera crew from *Video Option*, Nagata tore down public highways in the dead of night, attempting to hit 200 mph.

He made it to 197 before the police pulled him over. Hidden cameras caught the entire interaction as officers searched the RB-powered Supra, seeking to confiscate his video tape, and Nagata repeatedly protested that he didn't speak English. "Do you think this is a bloody playground?" an officer yelled. "What?" Nagata said. Then the cuffs came out. The video that resulted, and the accompanying spread in *Option's* print edition, made Nagata an icon. After a night in jail and a small fine, he returned to Japan a hero. It was the street-racing version of Michael Jackson's "Thriller."

STORIES like that fueled the Southern California street scene. Yearning to live as in the myths and legends of Japan's giants, aspiring modifiers turned to their own machines. But they lacked access to the JDM Toyotas and Nissans they had read about. So they turned mostly to Hondas. Cars like the Civic and Accord were affordable, reliable, and common, and Honda's VTEC engines, like Nissan's RB26, had plenty of tuning potential. These cars were mostly front-wheel drive, which is normally reserved for slow and boring commuter machines. But dedicated customizers could still make big power.

Hondas were everywhere in the scene. Once each year, a giant celebration and drag-race competition called Battle of the Imports was organized outside Los Angeles. All makes were invited, but the "imports" tag usually translated into a field roughly 90-percent Honda. When the president of GReddy traveled from Japan to visit the 1995 Battle of the Imports, he was perplexed by the lack of Toyotas and Nissans, reportedly saying, "What the hell are all these Hondas doing here?"

Being accessible, mostly. With a little saving from a weekend or summer job, even a high-school student could afford a used Civic. They'd head to at a friend's tuning shop to devour the latest aftermarket catalog from across the Pacific, pen in hand, scanning a dizzying array of upgrades and drawing circles around their favorites.

Lots of young drivers were dreaming big. Unfortunately, the streets of Los Angeles bore little resemblance to those of Tokyo. Freeways like the 405 and 105 did not lend themselves to extended high-speed runs, and heavy traffic even late at night meant drivers would often slice and weave their way around other vehicles at a dangerous pace.

Why didn't they take it to the track? Money. Street racing costs pennies compared to running on a closed course. What's more, in Southern California, local tracks had grown fewer and fewer. Lions Drag Strip in Long Beach had shut down in the 1970s after two decades of operation, and the intermittently operating Brotherhood Raceway Park—run by a larger-than-life former bodybuilder named Big Willie Robinson, who had fashioned the place into a safe haven for wayward youth—met too much local resistance and was finally forced to close in 1995. "We used to baby-sit all the kids from San Pedro and Wilmington who had nothing to do," Robinson told the *San Pedro News Pilot* in 1993. "We actually made this area safer because we were watching out for everybody."

With nowhere to go, they raced on darkened streets. Cars would gather in largely industrial areas, the few places in Los Angeles with long, straight roads and no stoplights or intersections. Traffic would be illegally blocked off at each end of a half-mile stretch of pavement. This was the beginning of the street-racing era that police would later characterize as something of a warzone, citing the danger and telling reporters tales about the "sheer audacity of their operations." It wasn't uncommon for teenagers from a dozen different cities to be arrested at a single meet.

Authorities acknowledged that street racing had been around for decades. Still, the import events of the 1990s were usually described in a more sinister sneer. One thing that had changed was the type of vehicles in use. As the *News Pilot* said in 1997, there had been a transition away from "old American iron, the Chevrolet Novas and Malibus with massive V-8 engines." Instead, the paper added, "there are mostly Japanese vehicles, lowered, turbocharged, and injected with nitrous oxide for a short but neck-wrenching burst of speed."

The people on the ground also represented a change. Though rooted in Japanese communities, the scene drew drivers, cars, and spectators from the nearby cities of Inglewood, Hawthorne, Carson, and Compton. Those areas included populations that were heavily Black and Latino, making the scene largely people of color. In a 1996 *News Pilot* profile of the manager of a local car dealer, the white subject of the article described her younger years of drag racing Americans cars on those same streets as "just having good, clean fun."

Few saw the import racing scene that way.

BY KEEPING their well-loved cars on the road, low-budget GT-R owners chase their dreams in their own way. But when hard times come, they get hit harder.

"You've definitely got to have a love for them," Jesse Iwuji said. Iwuji, a NASCAR driver and team owner who owns an R32 GT-R and keeps an R34 GT-R stored in Japan, echoed advice others had shared with me before. Prospective buyers, he suggested, should make sure to have a large savings account, access to a vast array of replacement parts, or both.

Non Fujita, the chief technician at Garage Saurus, told me that he constantly sees GT-Rs with evidence of shoddy work from previous shops. He shudders at the thought of working on older models, especially the R32, because those cars have had more time to be exposed to hands that don't know what they're doing. Remember Chris Payne, his customer with the cracked oil pan? The pan cracked, Fujita said, because someone used an incorrect bolt and overtightened it—a common mistake, but a costly one. The only way to have known there was an issue in the first place would have been to remove the entire pan and inspect it inside and out.

There was an R34 GT-R at Garage Saurus, Fujita said, with an issue with its multi-function display screen. That feature was seen as extremely advanced at the model's 1999 debut, but at some point in the last 20-plus years, another mechanic had swapped wires on the wiring harness. To find the problem, Fujita explained, every wire would have to be double-checked, one at a time, from its pin-out. An R34's harness has 114 wiring pins.

Why would a person work for years to acquire an object needing more attention than they're prepared to handle? Anyone who gets into the GT-R world simply to look cool on the Internet may soon realize they are in over their head. "Imagine someone who decides to have a kid," Iwuji told me, "just to post baby pictures."

It helps to look at how humans are themselves wired. In early 2020, researchers at the universities of Munich and Vienna published a study on the effects of marketing unhealthy foods to children. Young people, they found, were more likely to pay attention to advertisements that depicted bright, unhealthy foods. And especially so, if those foods were expressly prohibited at home.

In fact it was already well understood that telling children they aren't allowed to have something only makes them want it more. These researchers, however, wanted to know why. First, they showed junk food ads to a group of children who were allowed to eat candy at home. Those kids showed mild interest in media that showed other kids eating candy, which made sense: If you can shovel cookies and sweets into your mouth at home, then sure, the prospect of shoveling more will sound good.

Next, the researchers showed ads to children who weren't allowed to have candy. Those kids showed much, much more interest. When the prohibited foods came on-screen, the children became fixated. The chemicals in their brains shifted. Their pupils dilated. The researchers paired their findings with previous studies, and determined that the subjects were experiencing something called "emotional arousal." The response, they said, was an example of the forbidden-fruit effect, where being denied something only makes you want it more.

There was more. For one thing, the subjects were only somewhat interested when the candy was shown in still pictures. Yet when the same food was shown in television commercials, they went berserk. This, the study theorized, might be from something called incentive sensitization—a term typically used to describe drug addicts. Photographs kept a certain distance between the viewer and the candy. But seeing the ads in video form "leads to the impression of the availability of this specific food group," the researchers wrote.

It turns out, seeing another person enjoy something you can't have can make that object—that candy bar, that puppy, that JDM Nissan—seem more attainable in real life. Whether it was the Mine's R34 dominating a Supra on the track, or Smokey Nagata ripping toward 200 mph on a British roadway, these and other glimpses of the GT-R culture in faraway lands became irresistible to many.

The key was the impression, whether real or imagined, of attainability. Even though you can't have it now, you could have it one day. And look at how sweet that would be.

In the junk food example, the researchers wondered how this attachment, this dream-like fantasy world existing in their minds, would make the children act out in the world. "How this emotional arousal then translates into behavioral preference," the study said, "has to be investigated further."

But I can tell you something about emotional arousal. How it translated into the behavioral preferences of GT-R enthusiasts. How almost to a person, they explained that they grew up admiring the driving heroes they saw in videos, or read about in magazines. They idolized the people in Japan wrangling cutting-edge racecars to victory, sliding around mountain edges, or using high-speed antics to evade the law. It was all proof that the GT-R and its culture did, in fact, exist in the real world.

From there, playing video games and flipping through anime allowed these budding super-fans to put themselves in the story. Even though they couldn't be part of the culture directly, they could absorb it from afar. They imagined a future with them in it, one where they could be welcomed and included. They thought about it incessantly. They created an ideal scenario in their minds—the perfect car, the perfect road, the perfect crew—until it all felt real. And nothing would stop them from making it real.

Even as they moved through the world around them, they were working toward a different world—one that their peers couldn't see. One way or another, their story was always going to end with the outcome they envisioned. They prepared themselves for the day when they would have the chance to put down a deposit, figure out the shipping process, and park a Skyline GT-R in their garage. Almost by any means necessary. "You have to understand," one anonymous importer told me, "that to them, this is normal."

All they needed was an in.

ANDRES DIAZ and Nicole Chiong sold cars. Their Florida business, Soho Imports, opened near Miami in 2010, specializing in the importation of rare JDM models, especially Nissans. Diaz was named president, and Chiong, an authorized notary public, was made secretary. The business stayed in good standing for a decade, selling people the Japanese-market vehicles they had always wanted. Miami's car scene is one of the most vibrant in the country, and Chiong and Diaz were well-known within it, the couple frequenting meets and road rallies. Diaz in particular was a noted Honda enthusiast, with long-standing ties to the passionate South Florida JDM culture. They seemed like some of the good guys.

Soon after its founding, Soho was moving loads of cars every month. Those vehicles ran the gamut, with all the cult-hero models represented. Most of them were unavailable in America when they were new. Between 2015 and 2020 alone, Diaz and Chiong imported 11 Mitsubishi Lancer Evolutions, 14 Honda Civic Type Rs, and 27 Toyota Supras—numbers of that size indicated this company was working above-board. And yet. Importing insiders chatting on Internet forums began to raise eyebrows as early as 2012. If you knew what you were looking at, certain details of Soho's offerings didn't always add up. Those insiders obtained documents showing that Diaz and Chiong had imported R33 GT-Rs and Japanese-market Nissan Silvia S15s, cars not easy to bring in or convert for legality. When those papers were scrutinized in online discussions and blog posts, there were hints of fraud.

But what if you weren't on one of those forums? It's easy to imagine how a relatively uneducated customer, new to the market, could have assumed things were on the up-and-up. Soho had been doing business publicly for years. Diaz and Chiong were tied to the community. And really, if none of this was okay, wouldn't some government regulator notice? And of course, people wanted to trust them. They could make dreams come true, right?

The thing is, regulators had noticed. In 2022, the Florida Department of Highway Safety and Motor Vehicles released a list of 348 cars that Soho had imported. Each, the agency said, was evidence that the business constituted "an immediate serious danger to the public welfare." They suspended its dealer license, arrested Diaz and Chiong in their home, and demanded that every vehicle on the list be immediately surrendered to authorities.

GT-Rs accounted for nearly 90 of the vehicles Soho brought in, more than 25-percent. And as the feds were closing in, and the end of that 12-year run approached, the very last car Diaz and Chiong brought into the country was—you guessed it—a Skyline GT-R.

KALVIN MALLI IS a mechanic who moonlights as a YouTuber, and gained a steady following for filming well-executed engine swaps, other automotive work, and the occasional funny skit. He longed to own and build an R32 GT-R, and in March of 2021, he posted a video about the one he had found and purchased, sight-unseen. He titled it, enthusiastically, "I Bought The Cheapest R32 GTR From Japan And I'm Going To Rebuild It!" The seller had promised Malli that the car was in good condition. "Rust is to a minimal," the seller said. Malli believed him.

Four days later, Malli posted a second video. This one was titled,

"My 'New' R32 GTR Has MAJOR INTERNAL DAMAGE." By August, Malli was calling every new entry in his video series "R32 GT-R SCAM." He had decided to conduct a full chassis teardown to remove rust, which had been found everywhere. He began selling T-shirts with the phrase, "Rust is to a minimal." His efforts to restore his R32 became an ongoing series, one still going strong at press time.

While Malli was discovering the depths of his troubles, a self-proclaimed "Nissan Skyline Specialist" was setting up shop in an unlikely GT-R hotbed: South Dakota. Public records show that Derek Allen Banks opened his shop, SimplyRB, named after the RB26 engine and its variations, in February of 2021. By the end of that summer, multiple clients of his had filed lawsuits against Banks and his business. Those suits alleged he had accepted more than $100,000 in deposits without completing work. They also claimed he performed poor or questionable repairs, and tampered with VIN plates in an apparent attempt to make off with their cars.

In March of 2022, Banks was handed a two-year extended prison sentence and ordered to pay more than $116,000 in restitution. One year later, barely two years after his now-dissolved company was incorporated, Banks admitted to violating the terms of his probation.

Stuff like this happens in the GT-R world all the time. In 2021, a company called Hive Auto Garage formed as a used-car marketplace. A host of rare GT-Rs were quickly amassed, including an R32 with an costly rebody in dry carbon-fiber, an R34 owned by the movie star Paul Walker, and multiple vehicles customized by Top Secret icon Smokey Nagata. By early 2023, the company was listed as "Permanently Closed" on Google. Although multiple people I spoke with said they knew the parties involved, no one knew what led to the closure, and my efforts to track down former employees went cold. Millions of dollars in cars vanished into thin air.

After a while you stop being surprised by the stories. But I have wondered, many times over the course of reporting this book, what exactly is the dream all these people are chasing?

Owning the car doesn't seem to be enough. The car itself is just a starting point. Nearly every GT-R owner has a mission that's driving them: Step one is acquiring the car; step two is building a dream machine, or taking a particular trip, or recreating a certain experience.

One owner, who spends his spare time perusing Internet clips of old Japanese television shows, told me that one day, he noticed an unmistakable car on the screen. It was... his car. A gold-painted R32 GT-R with particular marks and rare parts identical to the one in his garage. He recognized it immediately. In the video, it was lined up to race against another GT-R tuned by Garage Saurus. His car didn't stand a chance.

"It just got destroyed," he told me, joyfully. The fact that his car had a moment of its own in the spotlight, however fleeting, was enough to send him over the moon.

A common theme is feeling a connection to Japan, the source of so much '90s inspiration and nostalgia, whether it was anime or manga or video games from the period. The U.S. consumed all of it – but to many people, the GT-R was always the missing piece. Now, some of them are seeking a bond with the alluring foreign nation. They think it will make them feel like a kid again, like it will return them to some sense of childhood joy.

Jesse Iwuji told me stories about his friend, an attorney who would only call himself Jay C., who grew up alongside Iwuji and first introduced him to the JDM world as a kid. It was Jay who convinced Iwuji they should both buy Skyline GT-Rs, and it was Jay who convinced him they should book a trip to Japan to drive their cars on the hallowed roads they'd grown up admiring.

To Jay, recreating the sensations of joy and excitement he saw others enjoying in anime and videos, back when he was a kid, was the whole point of buying a GT-R. There was a time when he thought all that was behind him. Like many in the GT-R community, Jay spent his early adulthood buying, tuning, and racing all kinds of Japanese imports. When he buckled down and focused on law school, eventually opening his own private practice, he figured he'd matured out of the scene. He considered buying a Mercedes S-Class, like other prominent attorneys, and settling into a life of refinement and status.

It was his wife who pulled him out of it. "She said, 'That's not you. Go get something else. Something fun.' So in 2018 I decided to buy an R35 GT-R." That car, the newer model that was available in the U.S. all along, reignited Jay's love for the car scene. But it wasn't his holy grail.

That came when Jay and his wife bought an R34 GT-R through Toprank, stored in Japan while it waited to turn 25. A few weeks later, unprompted, Iwuji called him to say that he had bought one too—through a different dealership, called Space Auto, but an R34 GT-R in Japan nonetheless. The two childhood friends had made good on their promise to buy Skyline GT-Rs together. There was only one more thing to do. Go to Japan.

"When I was planning the trip, I thought that since I'd already driven an R32, R33 and R35 here in the U.S., how much more cool could it be?" he said. "But the truth is, for a Japanese car lover, there's nothing that can top it. It's one of the best experiences money can buy."

When they arrived in Tokyo, Jay headed to Toprank to pick up his R34. Then the duo made a beeline for Space Auto to grab Iwuji's R34 from the showroom. Armed with their dream cars, the tandem took off in search of famous roads they'd played in *Gran Turismo* and *Need For Speed*, or seen during the chase scenes in *Fast & Furious* movies.

At one point, when the sun had fallen and Tokyo's lights took over the streets, the two friends merged onto highway roads and started cruising side by side. And all in a rush, a flood of nostalgia came rushing into Jay's brain. He looked around and realized he knew every streetlight, every lane marking, every exit sign. He'd played them before in video games, while driving simulated R34 GT-Rs and dreaming of experiencing the real thing.

Now that he was there, in real life, he felt "a high of some sort," he told me. "It feels like you're driving in the video game. I kept saying how it's so crazy driving an R34 in Tokyo, looking inside the cabin, seeing all this scenery that's just like the movies. I looked at Jesse's car and felt like I was playing in two-player vision at the same time. All of a sudden, you realize how real it is."

By the end of the trip, the duo checked more items off their bucket lists. They visited Top Secret headquarters and Jay called dibs on some floor carpets. They visited Mine's and Iwuji had stared, slackjawed, as the shop that built his all-time favorite GT-R hoisted his own personal car onto their lift bay and installed custom parts.

I told Jay that some people I spoke with considered it unfathomable to have to "visit" a car they owned across an ocean.

"I kept getting into this debate and I stopped," he told me, "because it wastes a lot of time. People try to view the world in a very objective way. You know, 'For that price you can buy this car or that car, which is faster from 0-60 mph or the quarter-mile."

He paused. And then with added emphasis:

"Do you really think I'm buying a 30-year old car because of a 0-60 time?" he said. "No. Absolutely not. It's the heritage, the motorsports, the cool, unique things about them. It's the culture!"

Jay said that not a single day passed without him thinking about that trip. He can't wait to do it again, and when his R34 GT-R at Toprank finally becomes legal to import to the U.S., he plans to bring it in and immediately buy another one in Japan that he can visit.

"It's a vibe, it's a lifestyle, and if you let it be part of your life, it's irreplaceable," he said.

"Unless you're obsessed, who in their right mind would do that?"

CHAPTER 6

Augusta, Kansas, doesn't have a lot going on. The small suburb of Wichita is primarily farmland. It has a small municipal airport, an on-again-off-again relationship with oil discovery, and a population of slightly more than 9,000 people. So it was big news when, in 1979, a local optometrist named Robert Whittaker was elected to represent the state in Congress. A 40-year-old Republican with a flashbulb smile, Whittaker would go on to spend 12 years in office. During his tenure, he focused mainly on issues related to the railroad industry, likely due to the BNSF tracks running through his hometown.

Over that dozen years in Congress, Whittaker introduced 43 bills and resolutions. Only nine made it to committee for further consideration, and just three were approved into law. One of those three served to officially designate National Blood Pressure Awareness Week. Another changed the name of Marion Lake, an hour north of Augusta, to Marion Reservoir.

The third was the Imported Vehicle Safety Compliance Act of 1988.

By the early 1980s, U.S. automakers had reluctantly acknowledged they were outflanked by their Asian rivals. Over the decade prior, Japan's crowded cities and expensive fuel prompted the Nissan, Toyota, Honda and others to perfect the process of building fuel-sipping small cars. They learned that efficiency and profit were not mutually exclusive. Those companies had also invested heavily in the development of advanced manufacturing methods, including a pioneering use of robotics.

As American fuel prices rose in the 1970s and early 1980s, the honing and investment began to pay off. Japanese automakers saw their U.S. sales increase as Detroit fell back. Panicked U.S. executives began a stumbling attempt to catch up, feverishly trying to copy anything Japanese that seemed relevant, but the sales shift continued. From 1978 to 1980, Nissan's share of the American market doubled, from 3-percent to 6-percent. Toyota and Honda saw similar growth.

Americans wanted new cars from across the Pacific, but they also had a growing desire for other specialty vehicles. Like Japan, Europe held appealing new models not sold in the United States. What's more, during the early 1980s, the U.S. dollar grew stronger and stronger. That meant American currency could purchase European machines at what amounted to steep discount.

Americans were sitting on an incredible opportunity. At the time, almost anyone could call a broker and get a quote for the purchase of a brand-new car located in Europe—buying a new BMW in Germany, for instance—and end up paying thousands less than if they had bought a virtually identical car at the local BMW dealer down the street. Those brokers, known as gray-market importers, advertised savings of between 15-percent and 40-percent after shipping. It was the deal of a lifetime, and prospective customers flooded gray-market outfits with calls. Demand grew, as a National Automobile Dealers Association newsletter said in 1985, "from a trickle to a tidal wave."

In a way, the government had created this headache. The dollar's strength led to demand, but lopsided exchange rates drew people to the gray market for fast or flashy foreign vehicles never intended for sale in America. In 1980, driven by rising public concerns for air pollution and road safety, the government enacted strict new rules for both. Many foreign brands faced a choice: conduct expensive modifications specifically for U.S. market; or simply not sell here at all.

A door was left open. The modifications that manufacturers justify making at scale made far more financial sense for individual buyers. Many cars could often be made U.S.-legal through relatively inexpensive conversion work, the modification or addition of things like seatbelts, bumpers, door reinforcement, and emissions components. So people began to bring those cars in and do just that.

Naturally, there were loopholes. In California, privately importing a brand-new vehicle was against the law. If the vehicle was "used," however, a condition the state's government defined as 5 years old or at least 7500 miles, that importation was fine. Before long, sports cars and luxury sedans began rolling out of shipping containers with 7501 miles on the odometer. The state's requirement had, as the Los Angeles Times wrote, "failed to faze the shady," and in the years before a federal mandate officially halted the process, a full third of all gray-market cars that came to America did so through California.

The most notorious gray-market character was Albert Mardikian, the "millionaire president," as the Times said, of an Orange County firm called Trend Import Sales. Mardikian was among the first to capitalize on the gray-market loophole, and he built T.I.S. into an import-and-conversion shop in one, sourcing rare and exotic vehicles and modifying—"federalizing"— them to government standards. A Syrian-born engineer, Mardikian was cunning and ambitious. T.I.S. eventually saw such demand that Mardikian came to employ a staff of 50 technicians and gross roughly $100,000 per week in conversions alone. He was said to have inspired the Tom Cruise character in the 1988 film "Rain Man," and local newspapers touted him as a rags-to-riches poster child, a portrayal he reportedly enjoyed.

European manufacturers were initially amused by this cottage industry. By the end of 1982, though, they couldn't afford to look the other way. More than 9000 vehicles were gray-imported to America that year, enough to impact the bottom line at the hundreds of authorized dealerships that companies like BMW, Mercedes-Benz, and Porsche had spent millions to establish.

In 1984, gray-market volume rose to 30,000 vehicles. BMWs alone accounted for 11-percent of that figure, with Porsches representing an identical percentage. But things were the worst for Mercedes, whose cars accounted for more than 60-percent of the total. Thanks to the gray market, one of every five new Mercedes-Benzes sold in the U.S. in 1984 had bypassed the company's dealer channels entirely. A year later, gray-market importing had become a billion-dollar industry.

Mercedes is generally viewed as the driving force behind what happened next, but BMW and Porsche were major players too. Ferrari and Volkswagen dealers were also beginning to fret about siphoned sales. By assuming U.S. restrictions would deter people from the hassle of importing, they had all underestimated the public and gotten in too deep, and the system was costing them money. Led by Mercedes, a group of European manufacturers launched an offensive, aggressively lobbying Congress to do something.

Little happened at first. In Germany, large corporations were accustomed to flexing their political muscles and seeing results. The U.S. had a more complicated and arduous system for passing laws, and the Europeans had a hard time getting get the government to act. (It probably didn't help that more than a few representatives kept gray-market luxury cars parked in the garage beneath the Capitol building.)

Rebuffed, the manufacturers began to write letters. They reached out to the banks first, persuading them to not issue loans for gray-market vehicles, arguing that the titles of those cars were too questionable to use as collateral. Next, they worked to convince insurance companies that issuing policies for gray-market vehicles—many of which were being converted by small and shady shops—represented greater than average risk. ("We're just saying make your own decision," a Mercedes spokesperson said, "but be aware.") And finally, to instill fear in buyers, the European automakers told their dealerships to refuse to service gray-market cars. Porsche even sent a 13-page informational packet to national media. The mailing, which the company called a "rational overview," included phrases like "potential pollution time-bombs."

Still, the effort was not yet fully organized. It involved too many agencies with overlapping jurisdiction, and there were plenty of blind spots and sensitive issues. Mercedes in particular struggled with accusations that its true objection lay in how the gray market made its cars appear abundant instead of rare and unique. And while the storied German manufacturer was complaining that private imports were hurting business, its dealerships were simultaneously raving about rising sales. (In a nice stroke of irony, that success was likely tied to how independent Mercedes dealers often bought cheap vehicles from the very conversion shops the company was publicly fighting.)

Eventually, however, the conversation began to shift. The California Department of Motor Vehicles began to stamp "Non-USA" on the titles of gray-market cars, and NHTSA, the agency that processed gray imports, complained loudly about the six-month backlog it had accumulated. The EPA also came for Al Mardikian, claiming he had used photos of one properly converted vehicle to gain certification for dozens of different VIN numbers, i.e., dozens of different cars.

The agency would later submit evidence that 34 cars converted by Trend Import Sales had received certification despite having none of the federally mandated modifications whatsoever. Facing charges of perjury, mail fraud, and making false statements to federal agents, Mardikian pleaded out, serving six months in federal prison. The poster child had become the gray-market head mounted to the wall.

Not that the fight was over. European automakers wanted to kill the gray market once and for all. They turned their attention to one idea in particular: convince the general public that converted vehicles were unsafe.

THE ACCIDENT that changed the debate forever happened in June of 1984, when a Mercedes 500 SEC suddenly careened off the road in

Napa County, California. The two-door luxury car became airborne, then slammed into not one, but two oak trees. A fire started. The Mercedes smashed through a chain-link fence and finally came to rest in a grassy field. The blaze grew in intensity. A witness would later say the car "lighted up inside," and then exploded. Sadly, a young woman named Suzanne Zelonis was still in her seat. She died at just 26 years old.

Zelonis' boyfriend, however, was miraculously saved. The accident had thrown him, unbelted in the driver's seat, into the car's back row. That allowed an anonymous bystander to reach through the rear window glass, grab his hand, and yank him out of the car moments before the explosion. Disoriented, his hair singed and clothes tattered, he staggered away from the burning husk of the Mercedes. He collapsed in the grass next to a shocked woman who'd pulled over to help. As he waited for the ambulance, he asked if anyone else had made it out of the car. No, she told him. A few moments later, he asked her again.

As they sat, the woman learned that the man was John "Sandy" Walker, a prominent San Francisco architect. At 56, he was thrice-divorced and a regular in the posh Pacific Heights party scene. He was Zelonis' fiancée, as well as her boss—after graduating from UC Berkeley, she had been hired at Walker & Moody, which Walker had helped build into a high-profile firm for homes, restaurants and other signature buildings throughout California.

The woman also noticed that Walker had an odor on his breath. Like alcohol. Investigators would later learn that he and Zelonis had attended a wedding earlier in the day, drinking champagne. They then stopped by an afterparty, drinking wine. At the hospital, Walker's blood alcohol level was 0.14, over the legal limit of 0.10.

Prosecutors threw the book at him. They issued charges of felony manslaughter and felony drunk driving. Walker drew little sympathy: a highway patrolman estimated the wealthy socialite was traveling between 114 and 133 mph on the country back road. Walker's fiancée, 30 years his junior, was burned beyond recognition. Her identity could only be confirmed through dental records.

In trial, prosecutors painted Walker as the pampered son of a prominent, privileged family. An old friend described him as "One of the Golden Boys," and Walker's third wife said he was the kind of person who "always has someone to come along behind and clean up [his] messes." His own actions seemed to confirm this in the minds of many. The woman who waited with Walker in the grass, while Zelonis' body burned inside the Mercedes, remembered that "he seemed pretty sad about his car."

The only person in Walker's corner, it seemed, was his attorney. John Keker, a Princeton and Yale graduate who would later prosecute Oliver North in the Iran-Contra scandal, searched for any possible angle to gain sympathy. He had the trial moved from Napa County, where locals were angered by drunk out-of-towners treating the roads like their personal playground, to Sonoma County. He tried to have the results of the sobriety test thrown out. He even cast doubt on whether Walker had been the one driving. None of it worked.

But Keker wasn't done. In a moment that would echo far beyond that Sonoma courtroom, he made a new claim: The crash had nothing to do with speed or inebriation, he said. It happened because Walker's Mercedes, a gray-market import, had been improperly modified by a conversion shop. In fact, Keker alleged, the work was the product of the one and only Al Mardikian, whose shop's labor had caused the Mercedes-Benz's computerized brake system to malfunction and catch fire, throwing it into a skid and off the road.

Drunk or sober was irrelevant, Keker said. The crash was the result of shoddy workmanship by a convicted felon. No one could have prevented it.

The prosecution vehemently argued this narrative. To bolster his case, Keker called on Paul O'Shea, an "accident reconstruction specialist" and three-time national racing champion. Years earlier, O'Shea's testing of the Chevrolet Corvair had informed Ralph Nader's landmark 1965 book on vehicle safety, "Unsafe at Any Speed." Keker paid O'Shea $1,000 per day for his testimony. Unlike the authorities, O'Shea had gained underhood access to Walker's

Mercedes after the crash. The car, he testified, "went out of control" due to "a malfunction of the braking system."

Armed with that, and with a client who conveniently couldn't recall much of the event in question, Keker laid into the jury. In his closing argument, he looked at each juror in turn, and lambasted the gray-market conversion industry. "It could have happened to anyone," he said. "It could have happened to you."

On February 7th, 1986, John Clinton "Sandy" Walker was found not guilty of vehicular manslaughter. The defendant, journalists noted, "sighed and smiled" at the verdict. At the time, anyone found innocent of manslaughter in California could not be tried for felony drunk driving in the same incident, so Walker had beaten both charges. On his way out of the courthouse, he showed a flash of empathy. "I appreciate this," he told the assembled media, "but it doesn't change the tragedy of Suzanne's death."

Public opinion was little swayed. A spokesperson for Mothers Against Drunk Driving said "justice was not done," and a letter to the editor of the *Napa Valley Register* scorned, "Once again we are witness to what money can do... no justice, indeed." As for Keker, some of his friends reportedly stopped speaking to him, but his client was free. And regardless of what anyone thought, the legal record would forever hold that the car was to blame.

IMMEDIATELY, opponents of the gray market industry spread the story of the private import that had burst into flames and killed a young woman. Press coverage, a Mercedes-Benz spokesperson said, made it look as if "a Mercedes is self-combusting, and that doesn't make us feel very comfortable." It underscored their position that gray market cars were unpredictable.

"The testimony to the cause of the accident was that [the 500 SEC's anti-lock braking system] failed," the spokesperson said. "Not that he was drunk. Not that he was speeding."

Scrutiny on the gray market industry reached a fever pitch. A dealership owner shared the story of Zelonis' death in heartbreaking detail during a House of Representatives hearing in 1985, months before Walker was acquitted. A survey conducted by the National Automobile Dealers Association showed that, out of 400 gray-market vehicles serviced at members' dealerships, only four of those vehicles "appeared to be in full [regulatory] compliance."

Thirty-three percent of those cars had no catalytic converter installed, the survey found. Fifty-seven percent had no oxygen sensor installed. Both components were mandated on new vehicles for the purpose of controlling emissions—if you walk into your driveway and remove them today, it's a federal crime. It appeared as if conversion shops were simply ignoring federal mandates.

Even political scandals seemed to work in the dealers' favor. While preparing for a diplomatic event in Germany, President Ronald Reagan's deputy chief of staff, Michael Deaver, traveled to Europe on a scouting visit. He brought with him three White House staffers, two Secret Service agents, and three U.S. Embassy personnel. While they were abroad, each of those nine people visited BMW dealerships and purchased a new car to ship home. In doing so, they not only benefited from the lopsided exchange rate Reagan was traveling to Germany partly to address—a rate that had helped create the gray market in the first place—they took advantage of a BMW policy that allowed discounts for customers with diplomatic passports. Even after paying for shipping and conversion work, they had effectively bought new foreign luxury cars for half-off.

Newspapers caught wind of the arbitrage and the group returned home to public controversy, but an investigation by White House counsel turned up no foul play. Their conduct may have been inadvisable, but it wasn't illegal. Still, counsel banned the practice going forward.

This could have given the impression that the government didn't see anything wrong or particularly dangerous about the very practice they were trying to ban. Instead, lobbyists turned the issue on its head. The whole situation was a perfect example, they said, of people with power and access bending the law to their will. Meanwhile, normal Americans were relegated to paying full price. And, they added, it needed to be stopped.

Ironically, as public opinion turned against the gray market, the market began to show signs of dying on its own. More than 60,000 vehicles had been gray-imported in 1985, but volume didn't increase in 1986 as many had expected. Instead—as the dollar weakened, as oversight of conversion shops tightened, as fatal wrecks collected headlines—volume dropped to around 30,000, slowing to a trickle a year later. The practice simply wasn't worth the trouble any more. Moreover, some of the more desirable models of the past, like the 500 SEC and the Porsche 911 Turbo, were by this time officially sold in the U.S. The problem had taken care of itself.

Naturally, of course, European automakers like Mercedes didn't agree, and neither did the massive American dealer associations. Each had already poured millions into an aggressive lobbying campaign, and they wanted new vehicle imports gone. So they kept hammering away.

Rep. Whittaker, the Kansas congressman, proposed H.R. 2628 in June of 1987. The resolution received seven bipartisan co-sponsors, four Democrats and three Republicans, and moved on to debate in the House of Representatives. During that debate, Whittaker launched into a passionate defense of the bill. "This rapid change in the market," he said, "resulted in significant problems in enforcement of the law relating to market vehicles. Many vehicles slipped through the cracks and were not properly brought into compliance with our safety laws."

Here, Whittaker met resistance, in the form of Rep. Robert Walker, a Republican from Pennsylvania. Walker called the proposal "suspiciously similar to a bill that is billed in the automobile enthusiasts' magazines as 'the Mercedes-Benz dealers bill.'" He also noted that the current language, if enacted into law, would prevent customers from buying unique foreign models not available in the U.S., a practice that by definition could not steal business from American dealers. "They will not be able to bring that car in," he said, even if "they are willing to modify it to meet the standards."

The argument didn't exactly advocate for the average Joe, but it at least considered the proposed bill from a different angle, and in a way that would prove strangely prophetic. Further on in the discussion, Walker pointed out that some cars were effectively "never going to be allowed to come into the United States."

At that point, Rep. John Dingel, Jr., a Michigan Democrat who would go on to become the longest-serving House member in U.S. history, stepped in. The bill wasn't really about making people wait 25 years to bring in a noncompliant vehicle, he explained. Rather, he said, it was about stopping disingenuous importers who brought foreign cars into the country under the guise of modifying them to meet federal standards, "when, in fact, they do not do so."

The point of the bill, Dingel explained, was to create an orderly process that prevented people from gaming the system, and to protect legitimate importers and converters from unfair competition. "A lot of these vehicles will be modified by fly-by-nights and people of that character," he said. "This is an attempt to rationalize that kind of situation."

Both houses passed the bill as proposed in October, and President Reagan signed the Imported Vehicle Safety Compliance Act of 1988, or IVSCA, into law on October 31st, 1988. It was exactly one week before Election Day.

IVSCA DIDN'T FUNDAMENTALLY CHANGE the standards that imported cars must adhere to. What it did was direct NHTSA to rewrite an existing law, the National Traffic and Motor Vehicle Safety Act of 1966, with additional restrictions. In a nutshell, those additions limited who could import a vehicle and how they were allowed to do it.

Imported cars still needed to be brought into compliance with contemporary safety and environmental standards, but there were two key differences. First, the import process needed to be done by a government-registered company, or Registered Importer, from start to finish. And second, once it reached 25 years old, any vehicle not sold new in America could bypass those standards completely. Any sooner and the car would require extensive, and expensive, conversions. (There was also a not-so-secret third priority, championed by federal agencies like NHTSA, the EPA, and Customs and Border Patrol: reduce bureaucratic workload.)

Mercedes, BMW, and Porsche had gotten their wish. And Whittaker, Dingel Jr., and other legislators had streamlined the process. But there were still loopholes. And exemptions. And unforeseen consequences. The new law would discourage untrustworthy importers but not stop them. Automakers had underestimated the car-buying public before, and now it was Congress's turn.

Ten months after the IVSCA was signed into law, Nissan unveiled the R32 Skyline GT-R.

CHAPTER 7

My second day in Japan began early. To my extreme surprise, I actually woke up on time and felt pretty good. There was no dreariness, no full-body exhaustion from an overseas flight followed by a 16-hour day.

Was it possible? Had my preflight sleep regiment actually... worked? I leapt out of bed and grabbed another shower, practically flying out the door. After a quick breakfast in the hotel lobby, I sprinted across the street to a convenience store, where I grabbed a few snacks and a bottled green tea for later. This was going to be a big day.

Downstairs in the garage, I pushed through the doors and eyed the green GT-R, still sitting in the corner of the lot where I had left it. That big brute grumbled and clanked into gear, still cold, its wide tires screeching across the concrete as I inched out of the spot. Together we squeezed through the narrow gate leading up to the street, where I reminded myself to turn left, into the left-most lane, and stay there. Then I pointed toward the mountains.

To escape the city of Atsugi, I headed west. First onto the E1 expressway, also known as the Tōmei. It was a Thursday morning, and traffic was heavy in the opposite direction. I passed thousands of workers, truckers, and salarymen heading off to begin their workday.

My side of the Tōmei was clear, though, and for the first time in the trip, I could keep a constant speed.

With a clear mind and some open road, I took the opportunity to get comfortable with car and environment. As cumbersome and exhausting as the GT-R can be on city streets, it's a totally different car with a bit of room. You simply pick a speed, let your foot merely breathe onto the gas pedal, and keep a light touch on the wheel. Then you move as if locked into a groove.

For a two-door, the R35 is not a small car. The bluff and bricklike body that can be such a terror near high curbs—the car's corners are out there, somewhere, you just can't see them—seems to suck itself into the wind. The point is stability. After a while, you begin to feel as if you could take your hands from the steering and watch the GT-R hold a straight line for miles.

I could have gone much faster. But it felt good to keep a leisurely pace and enjoy the serenity of the ride. Things were starting to fall into place: I had the car, I had my appointment for the day, I had clear directions from my phone projected onto Apple CarPlay, on the GT-R's center screen. All that was left to do was keep a lookout for cool JDM cars passing by. My favorites tended to be the most mundane: a tiny hardtop convertible called the Daihatsu Copen, far too weird-looking to sell in the U.S.; and a no-frills, too-tall refrigerator of a work van on tiny wheels called the Suzuki Every. They were both just so... Japanese.

Heading west, the Tōmei whisks between the Pacific on the left and the Tanzawa Mountains to the right. Japan's Forestry Agency describes the Tanzawas as having a "gentle natural beauty," which felt right. Rolling, gradual, calming land.

The Tanzawas are home to several species of Japan's famous cherry blossom trees. They flourish naturally in the range's forests. I arrived in Japan expecting explosions of pink and purple lighting up Tokyo, but that wasn't quite what I met. The principal tint of a blooming cherry blossom is actually the color of the tree's petals, a surprisingly dull white with hints of pink and purple underneath. As they bloom over the course of a few days, some of the trees may shift to a more dramatic pink, but I only saw white. Paired with Japan's naturally blue-gray skies, it made the land look gauzy and delicate. It was as if someone had taken a giant strainer and given the mountains a dusting of powdered sugar—a tap here, a swoop there.

Thirty-five miles later, I exited the Tōmei and began to wind through small country towns. It was a dose of the kind of Japanese life you don't see in Tokyo crime dramas and cyberpunk anime battles. The streets had more space to breathe. I rolled down the windows as the GT-R cruised past beautifully crafted vertical houses, countless parks, dozens of walking paths.

Cherry blossoms would occasionally peek around corners or over rooftops. They seemed to vanish, meekly, back into the land whenever I looked too long. Once, I tried to park alongside a batch of the trees, only to be met with narrow, one-way roads and some foreboding signs. None were in English, and I didn't want to ruffle feathers. By now I was a long way from the city centers where people are accustomed to *gaijin*. Maybe the trees were just done with being fawned over on social media, had banded together, and lobbied to be left alone.

I passed out into more open land, heading into a properly dense forest. The GT-R and I were now on Route 23, which the map said promised an upward climb and lots of curves. But it was a cloudy day, and each corner was followed by another corner, and then another. Something kept me going slowly, never leaning into the R35's tires and brakes. The road was walled by skinny and spooky trees, their grayish-brown bark stretching high into the gloomy skies. They seemed to know something I didn't. I couldn't tell that Mount Fuji was looking down on me from directly overhead.

THE LEGEND HOLDS that the sport of drifting originated on Japanese mountain roads like this one. In the dead of night, drivers who couldn't afford true sports cars would take their cheaper and slower cars to the tops of mountains. Then they'd plummet down the twists and turns of local S-bends, or *touge*. Japanese for "pass" and pronounced "toe-gay," the touge were favored by teenagers who wrung their cars for everything they were worth.

Often, that worth wasn't much. But with the right suspension setup, the right roads, and a deft touch, you could control a low-powered car by kicking its back end out, and sliding nearly sideways around downhill corners. Link a turn after turn together in that fashion, and you might spend an entire mountain's worth of a road sliding around. Rather than following the correct racing line, where you aim to maximize speed at all times, you were dancing, from side to side, for maximum fun.

Touge passes are not traditional GT-R territory. The car is more synonymous with 100-mph speeds over miles of "Wangan," or long and straight Tokyo highways. Touge is for the light and nimble. A certain generation of the rear-drive Toyota Corolla has long been popular there; so have the Nissan S-chassis cars and nimble thoroughbreds like the Honda S2000 and the Mazda RX-7. Basically, anything tossable, preferably with an engine that enjoys having the absolute crap revved out of it. The practice is less about speed and more about control, the ability to skate the car around a winding road without vaulting off the mountain.

Of course, GT-R were spotted on the touge from time to time. One of the most famous GT-R photos in history shows an R32 that got a little too ambitious: The car is wedged between the guardrails of a curving road, nose on the ground, those four classic round taillights pointed straight up. The owner poses with his right foot on a back tire and an ear-to-ear grin. Early touge runners lacked the structure and the deep pockets of Japan's high-speed, highway-based street-racing organizations, but they were no less outrageous. And eventually, they inspired and fostered the talent that would go on to star in the professionally sanctioned Japanese drifting series D1 GP.

In the U.S., a similar spirit has existed since at least the midcentury, since the early days of hot-rodding. California especially has a seemingly endless network of roads carved into the sides of its canyons and coastal ranges, pavement that has long served as a playground for those who drive outside the law. The closest such road to L.A proper is the Angeles Crest Highway, a twisting stretch through the Angeles National Forest that automotive journalists favor for testing new vehicles. There's also Mulholland Drive, which snakes closer to the cliffs of Malibu and was immortalized in a 1978 article in the short-lived magazine *New West*. It told of Minis, Volkswagens and Ford Capris outgunning Porsches and their wealthy owners in the 1960s.

"Besides being dangerous," author Chris Banning wrote, "Mulholland racing is totally illegal and blatantly unfair to the unsuspecting driver who happens into a race on the way home from a party and gets several years scared off the far end of his life." His story focused on teenagers and college dropouts, shredding across the road in the dead of night simply because they could.

"The turns hurtle at you like screaming nightmares," he continued, "and G-forces pin you to the rail as the car drifts close to a sheer drop over the edge while the driver saws more lock on the wheel... The tires slip, then bite, the engine rages and slams you back in the seat before the next hairpin rockets at you at 40 mph faster than you know anything can get through it. It's like riding a roller coaster in the right-angle turn at the bottom of a ski jump going 50 mph over the limit."

Melodramatic, maybe—but if you've ever ridden with someone driving a little too fast on a back road, not entirely inaccurate.

Glendora Mountain Road is another popular Southern California spot. GMR, as it's known, gives a much shorter run than either Angeles Crest or Mulholland, only about 10 miles until you run into road closures. But there are challenging curves and wild changes in elevation that make it a blast to drive. And crucially, it's in the San Gabriel Mountains, which means it's easily accessed by the largely immigrant populations of East L.A. and the San Gabriel Valley.

My search for GT-R enthusiasts in the L.A. area brought me to Sean Lee, a Taiwanese immigrant who has lived in the U.S. for decades and become a prominent influence in SoCal automotive culture. Kicked out of the house by his mother as a teenager, Lee spent the rest of his youth without a stable home, often sleeping in his car and running from the law. But he had a knack for figuring out problems and didn't give up easily. Encouraged by a mentor to enter the world of business, Lee decided to turn legit. He purchased a shipping-and-logistics company that he built into a wildly successful operation.

Lee has owned dozens of sports cars, and he became a fixture at local racetracks in the 1990s and early 2000s, pushing those cars and honing his skills. He bought an R35 GT-R when the car hit the market in 2008, and he imported an R32 GT-R shortly after the model's 25-year eligibility. He typically favors Nissans or Porsches, enjoying both ends of those brands' bitter rivalry, waffling between his love for each depending on the car in discussion, the type of driving at hand, or simply his mood on that particular day.

Lee is a connector. Around 2010, he formed an enthusiast network known as Purist, which began hosting rallies and car shows to raise money for local charities. More than a decade later, Purist has hosted nearly 50 fundraisers, its events drawing huge assemblies of sports cars and supercars to benefit toy drives and back-to-school events. The easily recognized Purist logo, two stripes leaned heavily to one side as if whipped there by speed, is a fixture on windshields on L.A. freeways.

When I met with Lee at his garage in the heart of the San Gabriel Valley, he explained how his affinity for GT-Rs grew and matured. How he kept meeting fellow Skyline enthusiasts at meets and track events over the years. How those people became friends who rushed to help with the founding of Purist and its growth over time. And how many of these friendships began over unorganized, late-night drives through the mountains—gatherings of people who took to the hills to wring their cars for everything they were worth.

"These are people that can really drive," Lee said. At one point, he estimated, the group held more than 200 members. That number included prominent journalists at some of the most recognizable names in automotive media, employees at car companies looking to let off steam, and budding aftermarket executives testing the most recent custom parts before they hit the market. It also included talented but unproven kids—teenagers either bored or looking for an outlet away from the crackdowns on street racing, some of whom would later become the biggest stars in Formula D. They ran hard, fixed each other's cars when they broke, and formed a bond over those midnight runs. They called it GMR Touge.

"We were the bad boys on touge," Lee told me. He had a Toyota 86 at the time, one of the many members who would swap cars to learn the strengths and weakness of each. Sometimes, journalists would show up with the latest shiny model and allow unauthorized test drives. "Nobody could talk about the club. They could all drive pretty darn good—they've proven that since. It also included a lot of magazine people that actually drive and love cars. They weren't just journalists that copied the spec sheet for an article. They really drove the cars with us, and we would sit down privately and ask each other questions and get real deep input.

"Eventually, we began to understand, 'Holy shit, this is what it's all about.' And why one part of the car is good or another is not good."

When I pointed out similarities to the stories of Japan's street-racing organizations, the teams that famously ran the Wangan highways around Tokyo at triple-digit speed, testing parts and cars, Lee nodded in agreement.

"They did high-speed. We did canyons."

I WAS NOT DOING any traditional touge-running around Mount Fuji. With 565 hp at my disposal, it would have been overkill on those slow, sweeping roads. Instead, I took things leisurely, trying to process the sights and sounds, observing the gradual slope of the pavement, glancing from time to time at the thick clouds above the forest canopy, feeling present in the moment. I kept my eyes on the break in the trees ahead.

Once, as I swung wide into a looping, right-handed horseshoe turn, the clouds gave way. Blue sky suddenly stretched out above the trees, and the branches created a frame around a giant mass of rock with an ice-cream scoop of snow on top. The mass kept going and going, my eyes following it higher and higher until my neck was craned and I was staring, nearly vertically, at its peak.

Mount Fuji stared back down at me. The scale was stunning. The mountain sat atop Japan, majestic and close and distant all at once, like a king surveying his land. Probably wondering what new and strange visitor had entered its purview.

I felt my breath stick in my throat. An instant later, the road curved left, and Fuji was gone. The clouds were back, the opening in the trees closed up again.

I pulled into a rest-stop area with a visitor's center and no trash cans. Only when I walked to the opposite end of the lot, where a few long-term van-lifers had stopped for a break, did I find a place to dispose of my empty green-tea container. No longer burdened with trash—why would anyone carry it, right?—I wandered over to the visitor's center. "World Heritage Fujisan," a plaque said, in both Japanese and English. "Fujisan, sacred place and source of artistic inspiration."

Added to the UNESCO list of World Heritage sites in 2013, Mount Fuji is actually an active volcano. For millennia it's served as a symbol of national pride. Located almost smack in the center of Honshu, the largest and most populous island in the archipelago that makes up Japan, it stands more than 12,000 feet above sea level, which makes it far taller than the country's next largest peak. It dwarfs even the range that surrounds it. The effect of that disparity on weather is partly why the mountain is nearly always shrouded by clouds, why it has a reputation for "hiding."

"People have feared and revered Fujisan, which has erupted repeatedly, as the mountain in which the gods resided," the UNESCO plaque read.

Back at the GT-R, I tore into a bag of pistachios. As I ate in the driver's seat, careful to corral any crumbs, I could see most of Fujisan's base through a break in the clouds. But the break kept moving and changing, a fast wind constantly bringing in new condensation. I still had a bit of time before I had to leave, so I decided to walk the grounds, locking the R35 again and following a small dirt trail up the hill. The trail led to a set of wooden planks that formed a staircase and I followed. The steps were uneven, lopsided and held to the ground by large nails. I briefly worried about turning an ankle or muddying up my dress shoes, then said screw it and kept going. Even when the steps seemed to have no end in sight, I kept trudging my suede Dingman wingtips into the rudimentary path. First trip to Fujisan, and all.

Finally, the trees parted into a clearing. I stared up at a two-story wooden viewing tower. Walking up the tower stairs, I rose above the tree line, the view growing clearer with each step. By the time I reached the tower's top, I was nearly eye-level with the mountain's chest. Only a few miles of thin air stood between Fujisan and me. It towered above the horizon, perched above forest for miles in every direction, the trees gradually coming together at its base as if bowing in reverence. I stood there for a minute, silent, awed by the scale.

The geological record shows that Fujisan's gradual shape and immense size is due to the mountain erupting continuously for more than 100,000 years. It seem implausible that something so striking could have risen organically, aligning almost poetically with an entire nation's perspective on notions of modesty and continuous improvement. Or maybe it was the other way around.

In 2022, evidence from a series of earthquakes indicated the volcano was still active. Scientists declared it to be in "standby phase" for the first time in 300 years. One day, the mountain will awaken, and that snowy peak will not be white for a time, and the mountain will grow larger still. Odds are, none of us will be around to see it, but then, it's probably not wise to underestimate anywhere the gods have chosen to keep a house.

I CLIMBED down from the lookout post and hopped back into the car, heading onto the road. From there it was all downhill, coasting down through the forest on the momentum of the GT-R's mass, hurtling toward the ground, though I barely had to touch the car's brakes because its enormous carbon-ceramic discs were so adept at burning speed. The pedal needed only one light tap every minute or so.

After a few miles of gentle curves and spots of cherry blossom clusters, I reached level ground again in Fujinomiya, a city of about 130,000 known for its natural beauty and chewy soba noodles. Sadly, I didn't have time for lunch. I followed the nav system's directions through another dense forest, slowed when I came to a sign reading "HKS" in bright white letters.

Japan has plenty of famous aftermarket companies scattered up and down its borders. GT-R owners I spoke with told me of pilgrimages they took to visit the legendary shops of Mine's, Top Secret and Garage Yoshida. They mentioned these names as if they were temples. But HKS is less a shop and more a tuning behemoth. It is the Fujisan of Japan's aftermarket.

Fittingly, the company headquarters sits directly at the mountain's base. On a clear day, you can lock eyes with the volcano from nearly anywhere on the premises. This was not a clear day, but you could still feel the mountain's presence, and besides, the HKS grounds were laid out on a slope, most buildings uphill from another. When you're walking to lunch, or to a meeting with the boss, you have no choice but to stare deep into that piece of great national pride and possibly consider your place in the universe.

I parked the GT-R in the gravel employee lot, the lowest point on the property, where I met my hosts, Akira Yoshinaga, a young rep in the overseas sales department, and Nobuhijo Uchiumi. We exchanged greetings—"Wow, you brought an R35!" Yoshinaga-san said—and then I followed their climb toward Fuji, heading to the first building on our tour. On the walk up, you follow a paved road, past warehouse-looking structures staggered up the hill on either side, each the size of a football field. HKS is famous for its wild paint schemes, green, orange, and purple splashed across a black base. The offices were meditative by comparison: a dull white topped with a dull blue trim running the length of the building. Some had "HKS" in blue letters at their top, and if you let your eyes follow those logos up the hill, a natural progression, they would eventually land on the mountain. The poetry wrote itself.

My hosts led me into a quiet warehouse. Faded and dull green support beams framed plain white walls and a spotless white ceramic floor. The room was where HKS keeps many of its old racecars—a black-and green 1980s dragster, an all-black Seat rally car, various Toyota drift projects with wild spoilers and stickers and metallic candy-red paint. In the center of the group was an R32 racecar, number 87, in the classic green-purple-orange splash graphics, with the same thick white wheels it had it used when it raced to victory over factory teams in the 1993 JGTC. Next to that is an R35 GT-R, much like the one I had been driving minutes earlier, but draped in the same paint scheme. It sported dive planes the size of boogie boards around its chin, add-ons that helped it set lap records at Fuji Speedway back in 2015.

Over the past five decades, dozens of worthy cars have clamored for a spot on the GT-R Mount Rushmore. Those two certainly make a strong case, but they represent the past. Today, HKS is looking toward the future. My hosts motioned me over to the bare steel shell of a car —an R32 GT-R skeleton—sitting by itself in the corner. Without a roof, doors, or hood, the stark silver frame looked as if it were from any old boxy sedan. Inside the engine bay, however, lay a secret project HKS has been working on nonstop for several years, one the company hopes will endear its brand to a new generation of fans.

The lump of metal parked in the engine bay was clearly an RB26. But it was unlike any I had seen. Nearly every piece of it was jet black, bright and demanding of attention. The intake manifold on the left, on stock GT-Rs a large cast-aluminum piece that quickly flakes and corrodes, had morphed into a sleek housing made entirely from woven carbon fiber. The turbocharger plumbing to the right was a network of thick and twisting vinelike tubes, in graceful matte black, fastened with fuchsia metal rings. Plaques and logos adorned the entire system, reading "Complete by HKS | Advanced Heritage," a hint that this was HKS reaching above and beyond its typical work. This was an RB26 in an HKS acid dream.

"The purpose is to keep GT-Rs on the road," said Yoshinaga-san, or Akira for short. He gave a faint smile. "And to make them more fun." The sleek intake was shaped to more effectively feed the right amount of air to each cylinder individually, improving engine responsiveness, he said. The turbo system was 3D printed, a technique that allows company engineers to build and test new shapes with remarkable speed.

As a package, it was visually striking. But that engine won't hit public roads like this. Each of those parts were prototypes, first shown publicly by HKS weeks earlier at the Tokyo Auto Salon. At the time of my visit, they were still under development for production. (By the time they're ready for purchase, the 3D-printed black turbo pipes will be switched to hand-formed carbon.) HKS is investing heavily in developing those parts the right way; as Akira said, the stated intention is to make them more reliable while improving power and efficiency. "We're an aftermarket company, so performance must be increased, but the point is improvement," he said.

In HKS's Advanced Heritage department, three employees have been working full-time on new RB26 parts for the past two years. Take a step back from the flashy parts and the alluring power they promise, and the idea of something called Advanced Heritage can be baffling: Why would an aftermarket company pour so many resources into all-new parts for a 30-year-old engine? An engine that the original manufacturer, Nissan, doesn't even produce any more? Devoting three full-time employees that could be working on HKS's profitable powersports or government projects, instead of squeezing a few extra horsepower or miles per gallon from a low-volume engine that ended production two decades ago?

Akira told me to save my question for later, he had more he wanted to show me. We turned and head out of that warehouse, away from the historic racecars, heading up the road toward Fujisan before ducking into another bland-looking building off to the left. It was a mechanic's garage, spotless as well, but with large windows that allowed natural light to shine onto the floors, which were painted a shade most people simply call "Japanese workshop green."

The building, Akira said, was formerly used to develop engines for commercial vehicles like taxis, vans, and buses. Now it was empty, every loading bay unused and lonely save the one directly ahead of us, which held a pristine black R32 GT-R V-Spec II on a lift for work. Or display. Or both.

It was the boss's car, Akira told me. It belonged to HKS President Daisuke Mizuguchi, whom I would soon meet. For the moment, though, I learned about the man through his machine, a black V-Spec II that looked as if it had been Ziplocked and tucked away for three decades, not a scratch or dent in sight. Under the hood, I recognized the Advanced Heritage parts immediately. The intake manifold and engine itself were the stock, bulky Nissan components. But the right-side parts, the turbo pipes, the airbox, the windshield-washer reservoir, they were all sleek carbon.

Mizuguchi volunteered his personal car to test the parts, Akira said. His car will return to stock once completed. I wasn't buying it—it looked to me as if the boss commissioned an entire department of the company just to build brand new parts for his pride and joy.

"I don't know," I teased. "Maybe he's just saying that so he can keep it." My hosts laughed politely and quickly changed the subject. These particular parts, the right-side parts, they said, will come to market first. HKS originally wanted to bring out the entire Advanced Heritage line of products at once, but the timing didn't work out. They began to detail the exact construction techniques used for each part. I should have been listening, but I could only focus on the way the carbon weave made the twisting pipes appear to be in motion, perpetually slithering through the engine bay.

I snapped to moments later, right as they were saying something about how the full AH collection will produce 600 hp and help efficiency by about 15-percent. Just the right-side parts alone will retail for around $10,000, they told me. HKS was counting on the appetite of high-end customers looking for exclusive, high-quality parts from an established name re-entering the Skyline GT-R world with its first new parts in over a decade.

Yes, that made sense, I offered, but it's still a pretty penny. Is the demand really there to justify this kind of investment?

Akira changed the subject, leading me out of the building. We'll discuss it more with Mizuguchi-san, he said. We left the workshop and started walking toward yet another dull-looking building.

Akira owns a GT-R himself, he explained, an R33, which he prefers over the others for its longer wheelbase and high-speed stability. "You know *Wangan*?" he asked, referring to a form of high-speed highway racing. I nodded. "I like doing Wangan things," he said.

I asked Akira's associate, Uchiumi-san, what he drove. He had an R34 Skyline GT-T, he told me, the less-powerful, less-aggressive, non-GT-R model, power sent only to the rear wheels. I offered what were intended to be words of encouragement: that I was sure, one day, he'd be able to afford the GT-R he really wanted.

As it turned out, he didn't want one. Uchiumi-san lives here, in Fujinomiya, he said, and he likes taking his GT-T to the local roads and racetracks where lighter weight and rear-wheel-drive can be an advantage, especially at lower speeds and in tighter turns. I hadn't really thought of that, but it makes sense. I could certainly think of one application where it works perfectly.

"So," I said, "Wangan for you? And touge for you?"

They lit up, both answering at once: *"Yes!"*

HKS IS a big deal in its homeland. In Japan, the company is not just a manufacturer of turbos or an occasional racing team. It became a paragon of homegrown auto ingenuity in the 1970s when the company produced its own Formula 1 engine, and when it subsequently popularized the turbocharger as an aftermarket part. Revenue exploded during the tuning boom of the 1980s and 1990s, with a six-year run of nearly $70 million in annual sales through the height of the Japanese recession.

Today, HKS is publicly traded on the Tokyo Stock Exchange. In 2023, after another three-year run of explosive sales growth, the company celebrated its 50th anniversary. This is the tuning industry all grown up, a version of what Daijiro Inada, the Option magazine founder, had wanted, the aftermarket modification industry legitimized. This is turning turbochargers into ticker symbols.

"Since the beginning of the '80s," Inada said, in a glossy interview for the brand's 50th anniversary, "HKS has been on an uptrend and has become so powerful that no one can stop it."

Hiroyuki Hasegawa, the founder and "H" in HKS, ran the company from 1973 until his death in 2016. Weeks later, Daisuke Mizuguchi took over as the second president in HKS history. Mizuguchi began working at HKS in the 1990s, directing some of the aftermarket's most famous racing and record-setting programs, and he never left.

I was led into Mizuguchi's office and introduced to the chief boss, who greeted me with a warm smile. We traded handshakes and bows and business cards. His office is a long corner room adorned with plaques and trophies. Two potted orchids sat to the side, their long and blossoming vines in full bloom and stretching to the ground. Their leaves overflowed onto the carpet.

Mizuguchi was quiet and reserved initially, but when it came up that I was working on a book, he brightened. It turned out he was familiar with the importing process. In the 1990s, Mizuguchi had become possessed by the idea of importing that most American of vehicles, the Chevrolet Suburban. His Chevy took two years to finally arrive in Japan, and though I personally can't imagine driving something so bulky on the country's slim roads, Mizuguchi has owned it since and still drives it. "I always liked the Suburban, even as a kid," he said. "It's huge!"

Today, Mizuguchi is focused on "making customers' lifestyles more unique," a philosophy, he once wrote, that he thinks will help carry HKS and tuning culture in general through its next 50 years. His own relationship with cars is certainly unique. As a young engineer, one of Mizuguchi's first projects was the development of an R33 GT-R called the HKS T-002. Containing every advanced part then in the HKS catalog, T-002 was a potent record-smasher, the rare GT-R—the rare tuner car, period—that could be tuned to win in different environments. Among its achievements were an engine that could be tuned to more than 1,000 hp, a time-attack lap record at Tsukuba, and a 0-to-300-kph record in an Option magazine test, that last one with Inada at the wheel. Mizuguchi also worked on one of the most legendary and mystery-shrouded vehicles in Skyline history, a ground-up rework of an R32 GT-R that HKS dubbed the Zero-R. Just 10 examples were built, each priced at 16 million yen, roughly $260,000 today. If any were to hit the market now they'd likely be worth millions.

Years after Mizuguchi watched the GT-R help build his company into a powerhouse, he is determined to ride the wave again. The Advanced Heritage program in particular is one of his most important projects. He described it to me as everything he had wished he could do to the RB26 engine back in the 1990s. Decades of research and technology advancement, he said, have gone into the project.

Advanced Heritage has had so much time and investment dedicated to it because HKS views it as crucial going forward. Because of its close association with Nissan over the years, the firm is still known to many as a GT-R-customization company. Even today, R32-35 GT-R models account for roughly 10-percent of its annual global revenue. Only the Toyota 86, a small affordable two-seater, accounts for a similar amount of HKS business. As the R34 Skyline GT-R nears U.S. legalization, the tuner wants to still be seen as a leader, on the cutting edge of the model's potential and development. Up-and-coming rivals have threatened that position, and millions of dollars are at stake.

"The U.S. is our biggest overseas market," Mizuguchi said. "The population is three times more than Japan's. It's a big opportunity for us." He knows that American buyers who find the R34 market too rich or too crowded will look to import R32 or R33 models, with that same engine, and they'll all need parts. HKS products are currently sold in America by companies like Trust Kikaku. (At press time, the main Trust Kikaku shopping website held 18 pages of HKS products.) The market is much more competitive today than it was in the 1990s, however, in terms of both product and capturing attention. HKS is banking on its name and reputation, plus the promise of quality, to earn business.

"Twenty years ago, there was big demand for modifications in the U.S. We're not just putting out old things, we're putting [out] new things with 20 years of development [behind them,] to make more performance or [make our products] more environmentally friendly."

This is all well and good, but the process will hold speed bumps. Some of the same qualities that made HKS an aftermarket giant may also become a hindrance. The company has a long history and broad influence, but for some, it's become overly conservative. HKS is often late to follow sales trends, releasing key products several years after the competition. Its publicly available street parts typically don't produce enormous horsepower, focusing instead on efficient power delivery and improved fuel economy. In spite of all this, the brand charges premium prices, marketing an "OEM-plus" attitude that exudes refinement yet falls short of the horsepower-per-dollar ratio many GT-R fans in the States have come to expect. (OEM is automotive-industry jargon for Original Equipment Manufacturer, which has become shorthand for "high-quality.")

For many, the HKS name also represents the past. Though a titan in the 1990s, the brand hasn't done as much to remain relevant in the American market since. After the global economy tanked in 2008, HKS only stuck around the United States for a few years, pulling out of our market completely in 2011. (GReddy, by contrast, resorted to a declaration of bankruptcy in order to maintain a U.S. headquarters.) The company is now in an uphill battle to regain that footing. HKS reestablished itself here in 2017, with a new national headquarters in Chandler, Arizona, but hasn't been overly vocal since that return. (Search online for information about HKS in the United States, and one of the most popular queries that pops up is, "Does HKS still exist?")

Big ships turn slowly, and publicly traded aftermarket companies take time adjusting to change. But when I visited those famous headquarters at the base of Mount Fuji, there was a clear sense in the air of time running out. HKS had already pushed back the release of much of its Advanced Heritage line once, offering only the turbocharger and air box for sale, not the complete system as originally intended.

And when I ask for a summary of the HKS advantage and philosophy, it's met with answers that focus on efficiency and modest power gains. It's no great stretch to suggest those topics won't automatically resonate with buyers in a country where fuel is still relatively cheap and Skylines are generally owned by those who can afford it. (In fact, I'd go out on a limb and say those topics likely won't resonate at all.) The philosophy, I'm told, is to "enrich customer lifestyle through the production of unique high-quality products that appeal to customers on an emotional level."

Sitting at the CEO desk across from Mizuguchi, I don't have the heart to tell him this, but it all feels a bit... off-base. His company seems ill-prepared for the depth and breadth of competition it will face, much of it from brands firmly entrenched in our market. Outfits such as Australia's Platinum Racing Products, or PRP, push big-horsepower parts and have fostered a feverish fanbase; PRP's site in particular offers 89 PRP-branded products for the RB26 engine alone, many of them coated in the company's signature eye-catching purple paint, which looks great on Instagram. Crucially, those parts are already out for sale.

"They're such a traditional Japanese company," Larry Chen, the motorsport photographer who attended Toprank's L.A. brewery cruise, said. Over the years, he's partnered with HKS on multiple projects. "They do what they know and I love that so much. It's so much about reliability, [and] OEM fit and finish, and that Japanese philosophy of it being an overall good product."

But even Chen has concerns.

"One of the things I've told them directly is, I don't even know if they're ready for this resurgence. Once the floodgates open for the

R34, and people bring more R33s and R32s to the U.S., they might not be ready for how many people want HKS parts. Because if the motor goes, you may as well replace it with non-OEM parts. That's what I did. A rebuild would cost pretty much the same price, so you might as well go with more power and more reliability."

In that event, do Skyline GT-R owners turn to hot new upstart companies, with their in-your-face builds and designs? Or to a 50-year-old corporation across the ocean that's finally getting back in the game?

Mizuguchi and HKS certainly want to believe it's the latter. They welcome the fight. "It's exciting because we like a challenge," Mizuguchi said. He reminisces fondly over the days when aftermarket rivals would meet at the Yatabe test track for days of pitting their latest and greatest products against each other and duking it out to earn the cover of *Option*. Now they fight in the court of social media. Back then, Mizuguchi told me, the competitions made everyone better, steel sharpened steel, and HKS worried only about its own performance, not concerned with what others were doing. The industry he said, wanted to inspire young readers, to help them achieve their goals as a unified front.

I can't help it. "But you wanted to win, right?"

Mizuguchi-san smiles. "Of course."

IF THE COMING R34 GT-R invasion is a short-term focus, and the Advanced Heritage program is medium-term one, then HKS is also looking for long-term ways to stay at the top of the GT-R ladder.

When I asked Mizuguchi for his thoughts on developing parts for the next generation of Nissan GT-Rs, he noted how the GT-R has long been a vital part of HKS's business. We joked about how the peaks and valleys of the company's revenue chart aligned almost perfectly with the timeline of when the GT-R went in and out of production. (HKS revenues rose most sharply from 1989-2002 and 2010-2023, for instance.) He remained coy about what comes next, anything he knew regarding a possible R36, the R35's as-yet-unannounced successor. He had no inside information, he said. I recalled, but didn't mention aloud, that the only reason I was sitting in his office, surrounded by the beautiful orchids, was because the head of the GT-R program had called him on Facetime, wanting to help with the very book you're reading, and Mizuguchi had answered on the first ring.

Mizuguchi did make one prediction: The next GT-R, he said, could be a hybrid, pairing a traditional gasoline engine with one or more electric motors. Maybe that was true. Maybe it was deliberate misdirection. Whatever the case, he said, the R35 isn't the end of the line.

"The GT-R will not die," Mizuguchi said. "It will continue to evolve."

I thanked the boss for his time and was led out of the building, back to my car. On the way out, we passed through a hallway holding a bronze bust of Hasegawa, the HKS founder. In a suit and tie, his hair combed neatly to the side, he greets new entrants to the building with a face that suggests he's itching to tell you something. Perhaps some secret of the trade. Maybe he's just happy to see the company still around. Either way, I'm grateful for the visit.

Bounding through the doors, I was greeted by bright midday sun. The clouds had burned off, only blue sky overhead. After a second, I realized what that meant, and turned toward the mountain. There, staring back at me, was Fujisan in full glory. The snowy peak sat atop the roofs of the HKS buildings like a hat.

The mountain seemed less ominous now, having been revealed in full. Less like a disapproving teacher and more like a friendly grandfather. I pressed the GT-R's Start button and listened to the car rumble to life. As I drove back out through the HKS gates, I remembered something a Nissan insider had once told me, when I asked if an R36 GT-R was in the works. As the mountain dwindled in the rearview, I realized it applied to more than just a car—it could have been said about HKS's attempts at rebirth or Fujisan's peaceful slumber.

"Just wait," they told me. "Godzilla sleeps too."

CHAPTER 8

The first person to test the new rules was a billionaire.

By the mid-1980s, Microsoft founder Bill Gates was already a household name and one of the wealthiest people in the world. And like so many tech founders before and since, when Gates came into money, he started collecting Porsches.

The most iconic and recognizable Porsche is a sports car called the 911. Rear-wheel-drive and rear-engined, with trademark round headlights, the model set new standards of performance in the 1960s and 1970s, then went on to become an enduring symbol of excess and "Yuppie" nouveau riche glamour in the 1980s. Gates had owned several 911s. The Porsche 959, though, was something different. The same car that inspired Nissan executives to go back to the drawing board with the R32 Skyline also caught the eye of the world's richest man.

There was a lot to find appealing. Like the 911, the 959 was rear-engined, its six-cylinder powerplant mounted behind the rear wheels. Beyond that, similarities were few. The car was twin-turbocharged and all-wheel-drive, with a formidable 444 hp. At a time when the average road car sported one computer at most, the $225,000 959 had seven, its silicon brains managing everything from torque distribution to the electronically adjustable suspension. Even the body panels were advanced, hand-laid in a fiendishly light composite. The whole package looked and performed like a race car but was as comfortable and reliable as your Bellini sofa. Just 292 examples were made. This wasn't just a Porsche. It was a billionaire's Porsche.

Predictably, there was a catch. Developing the 959 had cost an astronomical sum, with Porsche basically inventing much of the car's cutting-edge technology from scratch. By the time the first examples rolled off the line, the project had gotten so far over its skis financially that the construction of each 959 was said to cost the company almost half a million dollars.

Porsche, then, was not about to outfit the model with garish bumpers, ruining the sumptuous lines. Nor was it going to spend additional funds on restrictive emissions equipment. And it definitely wasn't going to sacrifice multiple examples to federally mandated crash testing. The U.S. was going to miss out.

Gates wanted one anyway. He placed an order for a 959 in the late 1980s and had the car shipped to America. When you bring a vehicle, any vehicle, into the country, you must first declare it to U.S. Customs. If that exact model, from that exact model year, isn't on a federally approved list of legally compliant cars, you're stuck. The car can't come in.

We don't know exactly what happened when Gates's 959 rolled into the Port of Oakland. What we do know is that the Porsche was seized by Customs and impounded. A second 959 was with it: Paul Allen, a Microsoft co-founder, had a matching example brought in at the same time.

Then what? Long story short, the Porsches sat at the port. For years.

WHILE GATES and other well-heeled U.S. buyers looked for a way around federal regulations, car enthusiasts in Japan were living through a golden age.

Honda launched its compact and stylish two-door Integra, then the moonshot NSX. Mazda debuted a radically styled update of its RX-7 sports car, then radically updated the car again. Mitsubishi and Subaru had competing four-door sedans patterned after mud-splashing, all-weather rally racecars. Toyota sold a wide range of fun machines, from the tiny mid-engine MR2 sports car to the high-performance Supra coupe. At Nissan, fans looking for thrills could turn to the brand's sleek Silvia coupes, or to cushier and faster models like the twin-turbocharged 300ZX. There were the Skylines, of course, in both two- and four-door form, from the R30 of 1981 to the R31 of '85 and the R32 of '89. And of course, the R32 GT-R crowned it all.

All of this could be seen on the roads around Tokyo, plus the usual exotics from Europe. Porsches were popular. Every once in a while, you might spot a Lamborghini Countach.

There was a lot to choose from, and Japanese enthusiasts took advantage. They also enjoyed importing foreign vehicles into the scene, even American ones. It was not uncommon to see a Pontiac Trans Am, with its iconic fire-breathing graphic emblazoned on the hood, rolling through mountain curves or attacking highways at high speeds. Right behind it you might find a De Tomaso Pantera, the wedge-shaped, Italian-designed sports car with a raucous Ford V8 mounted behind the cockpit.

Groups of car nuts formed to tell stories, share secrets, admire each other's rides, and most of all, to drive. For honing their skills at speed, there were multiple options—the Tsukuba and Suzuka circuits lived just outside Tokyo, while the storied Fuji Speedway, fast and wide, sat at the base of the mighty Mount Fuji, two hours southwest of downtown. In the late 1980s, the Ebisu Circuit opened three hours north, a virtual playground featuring several short tracks and even a private mountain-pass road.

Naturally, young adults sampling their first taste of freedom didn't always take the legitimate route. They would mostly meet at night, to stay under the radar, then caravan into mountainous countryside. There, they would test skills and prove their bravery on winding roads with dramatic elevation change and sheer cliff drops hundreds of feet tall. It was dangerous and often reckless. The threat of crashing was ever-present. In fall and winter, when temperatures in the mountains dropped so low that the roads grew icy and impossible to drive, they would take to city streets. These drivers were known as *hashiriya*.

AT FIRST, the hashiriya were not well-liked by the public. Many Japanese citizens, including the police, associated the drivers with criminals or street gangs. Worse, the hashiriya were often lumped in with Japan's most notorious vehicle subculture, a group known for causing trouble and disturbing the peace: the *bosozoku*.

The word bosozoku means "violent running tribe," and the group's members did little to distance themselves from the concept. Born immediately following World War II, many early members were young men who had served in the military, former fighter pilots who expected to die in the war, and were struggling to adapt to civilian life. Bored and seeking thrills, they formed motorcycle gangs styled after American ones like the Hell's Angels, borrowing the leather-jacket aesthetic of 1950s films like "Rebel Without a Cause."

Motorcycles gave bosozoku the adrenaline rush they had experienced in war. But there was a layer of darkness to their motivation. Many bosozuku desired a return to "traditional" Japanese values like isolationism and the samurai code. They were disgusted by the direction their country had taken, and they espoused nationalist imagery like rising-sun flags and the graphics of the Japanese Imperial Army. They expressed their refusal to conform through deafening exhaust pipes, ripping down residential streets long after midnight in packs as large as a hundred machines.

When the bikers turned their attention to cars, the results were equally outrageous: modified versions of pedestrian four-door sedans, slammed to the ground, with scarcely an inch separating bodywork from pavement. Form trumped function to the extreme.

Massive front and rear spoilers extended four or five feet fore and aft, and the cars were painted dramatic colors, with stripes, zig-zags, and patterns inspired by Southern California lowriders in Latino culture. Finally, there was the exhaust—typically a long, thin pair of pipes shooting skyward at a 45-degree angle or more, extending 10 or 15 feet into the air. It was all designed to communicate that the driver wanted to be seen and didn't care what you thought. Most viewed them as a menace, and though its activity has since died down since the 1970s heyday, in 2013 the National Police Agency moved to classify the group as "pseudo-yakuza."

The hashiriya struggled to distance themselves from the bosozoku. By the early 1980s, it was difficult to customize your car's appearance or performance without painting a target on your back for authorities. But the hashiriya were all about driving enjoyment—it demanded modifications. Hashiriya cars were toned down compared to bosozoku style, but still, they often featured eye-catching touches like lowered suspension or pointy chin spoilers. One signature mod was finned oil coolers mounted to the outside of a front fender, fully exposed, rather than under the hood. But driving was the focus. And as interest in the movement grew, the hashiriya needed an advocate. Someone who could win over the public.

HASHIRIYA TOOK to mountain roads and public streets but also to racetracks. They would meet and compete to see who could tame a mountain faster, lap a course first, or hit the highest top speed. From almost the beginning, they looked for any edge they could find.

Every car had another level of performance hidden inside it. The secret lay in finding your model's particular strength, then upgrading that strong point until it couldn't be beat. Tuning shops dedicated to this work sprung up all over Japan, particularly in and around Tokyo and Yokohama. They developed and manufactured parts focused solely on making cars faster, sharper, or lighter.

There was no shortage of tuned machinery. But there was also no objective way to know how they stacked up. Manufacturers had the budget to go track testing or racing, then buy ads in major media to trumpet the results. A tuner's bragging rights traveled mostly through word of-mouth, spread by hashiriya in darkened parking lots or at highway rest stops. Rumors and outright lies often persisted, and the drivers themselves, of course, were biased.

Daijiro Inada offered an alternative. A car nut and self-trained journalist, Inada started *Option* magazine in June of 1981. He wanted to cover the industry from a street culture perspective, which meant including and legitimizing tuning companies in the same way that other car magazines covered major manufacturers. At the time, modifying your car in Japan was still largely criminalized, to the point that even having custom parts could warrant a friendly chat with local police. Inada wanted to end that.

Option immediately set itself apart by openly advocating for the hashiriya. The magazine didn't just run articles on the hottest cars or star tuners. It published step-by-step guides for upgrading your car, and it penned opinion pieces, aimed directly at the authorities, that espoused the legitimacy of the culture. Driving culture was given a voice in Japan and allowed to blossom, moving it from the days of being associated with illegal activity and convincing the public that car people were actually contributing to society. This wasn't a way for kids to commit crimes and get in trouble; it was a way to stay out of trouble, develop positive relationships, and maybe even build a career.

In October 1981, *Option* rented out Yatabe Test Track, a high-speed oval course in Tsukuba originally built by the Japanese Automobile Research Institute. Throughout the 1960s, both Nissan and Toyota had used Yatabe to set speed and endurance records that had become part of industry lore. Now Yatabe was needed again. As tuning had exploded in popularity and the cars had grown faster, the hashiriya had moved away from using quarter-mile drag racing as the measurement of a car's performance. Now they hunted top speed, a practice that required far more asphalt. This often meant taking to long public roads like the Tōmei Highway, endangering other motorists. It was time, Inada felt, to move to the track.

For *Option's* test to mean anything, it would need the right companies to participate and the right people behind the wheel. Tuner cars of that time could be unreliable and often reacted unpredictably when run at high speed for extended periods. With that in mind, the magazine enlisted the help of two experts: former Formula 1 (and Hakosuka GT-R) racer Kumimitsu Takahashi, and Mitsubishi test driver Osamu Mochizuki.

Together, the two men piloted the first batch of test cars to impressive heights. The fastest Japanese car ended up being a Nissan Fairlady S30 tuned by SS Kubo, a tiny tuner operating out of a cramped garage in a dense industrial neighborhood just outside Tokyo. The owner, as the car-culture site Speedhunters wrote, was "the guy everyone wants their engine set up by." At Yatabe, his S30 hit an astonishing 160 mph, beating Inada's own S30 by a full 6 mph even though Inada's car was turbocharged and the Kubo car was not. ("In that era," Inada would later write, "turbocharger tuning had just started.")

The fastest car overall, however, was a Pontiac "screaming chicken" Trans Am. Owned by Koichi Okawa, the founder of HKS competitor Trust, the Trans Am wore four exotic Italian Weber carburetors and had been painted a friendly flat blue. Tuned to a punishing 500 horsepower, it hit a top speed of 164.5 mph, claiming the inaugural Option championship.

Only four months later, *Option* returned to Yatabe for another set of tests. For all that had been accomplished in the first round, it paled in comparison to what came next: A De Tomaso Pantera, its Ford V8 built by a former NASCAR mechanic and tuned by ABR Hosoki, hit the magic 300-kph barrier: 186.4 mph.

The next hurdle was for a Japanese car to break that barrier. It took until 1983, but when HKS turned up with a Toyota Celica it called "M300," the firm's intentions were clear. The car's engine had been tuned to the moon, with two turbos and a host of internal modifications taking it from a stock 173 hp to a rumored 500. With Inada behind the wheel, the Celica rocketed around Yatabe, posting a final top speed of 301.25 kph.

The tuners had made it clear they weren't playing around, and the competition was getting serious. There was no going back now.

FROM THE MOMENT the early hashiriya began to scour maps for worthy roads and highways, they formed into cliques. In an effort to distance themselves from general automotive troublemakers, they began to fashion their informal crews after professional racing organizations.

Teams would form around a group of people who owned the same model of car or who liked to drive the same kind of road. They adopted names like TOPS, Ariya, and Tokyo Group Shadow, monikers that often had little or nothing to do with the people or cars involved but were chosen simply to sound cool.

One team, the American Car Club, was headed by Trust founder Koichi Okawa, and it boasted a particularly impressive roster. One of its members, a young racer named Eiichi Yoshida, owned a 1979 Porsche 911 Turbo and loved to drive, even by hashiriya standards. In 1982, however, he left the American Car Club, looking to strike out on his own. He wanted to found his own outfit, one rooted in principles he believed were important—honor, driver training, and secrecy.

That final value he felt, was critical. In the early 1980s, Japanese authorities did not take kindly to low-level lawbreakers, even those who committed nonviolent crimes. Street racers were considered some of the worst of the bunch, and the punishment for their offenses could be severe.

Ironically, Yoshida's 911 would eventually become one of the most recognizable outlaw cars in the country, and his club would grow into the most notorious illegal street-racing organization in the world.

Yoshida named his group Racing Team Mid Night, a phrase designed to double duty. The first two words were to emphasize how seriously the group took its mission to develop driving skill and improve the performance of its cars. The second two words hinted at the club's undercover nature: It met only under cover of darkness, after midnight and into the early morning, while the rest of the country slept. This was primarily to avoid law enforcement, but it was also because the roads would be mostly empty.

In the early days, races took place on the Tōmei Expressway, a long stretch of open highway beginning in Nagoya and running northeast, to Tokyo, tracing the coast for more than 200 miles. Racers would meet up, issue challenges, then blast down the road. You were expected to approach or meet your car's maximum speed and hold it for as long as possible, which often meant pinning the throttle to the floor for several minutes at a time. The race ended, the story goes, when the trailing car lost sight of the leader.

This practice obviously put enormous stress on man and machine. The driver had to grapple with the mental hurdle of traveling well over 100 mph for long periods, without losing control, on a surface in no way designed for that speed. The car was pushed to its limit, every component straining from load and heat, engine bellowing at top pitch while consuming gasoline as if from a fire hose. Some cars needed to be refueled once or even twice per night. Others would burn through a set of tires in the same period.

As time passed, the scene grew large and vibrant. Too vibrant; the situation was getting out of hand. Crowds of spectators would gather along highway edges to watch loud and dramatic cars rip past while their drivers literally risked death at the wheel. Police attention was inevitable.

Two things took the subculture to new heights. The first is that teams stopped using Tōmei as their racetrack of choice. Conveniently, a new highway opened up in 1985. The Wangan Expressway ran from Tokyo to nearby Yokohama, with its most race-ready portion running some 18 miles, from the small suburbs of Tatsumi to the city of Narashino. That section of road carved through a largely industrial area utterly devoid of traffic at night, elevated above warehouses, stockyards, and Tokyo Bay. It was well-lit and curved gently at most, key qualities that would allow cars to stretch their legs and stay stretched. Lacking on-ramps and exits, this part of the Wangan offered police nowhere to hide, and no spots where they could quickly enter the highway in pursuit. It was a playground tailor-made for Mid Night; just as important, it was right in their backyard.

The other critical escalating factor was the introduction of a new generation of high-powered sports cars. Mid Night had initially raced mostly Porsches, with the exception of the occasional Celica Supra or R31 Skyline. But as the 1990s arrived, so did the Honda NSX supercar and new versions of the Toyota Supra and the Mazda RX-7. And, of course, the R32 GT-R. Duly equipped, Mid Night's members hit the Wangan with more horsepower, less speed-sapping aerodynamic drag, and more tuning potential.

Cars like the GT-R made an immediate impact on the team and the attention it received. In this period, several myths emerged that are difficult to corroborate. It was rumored, for example, that the secretive club announced the times and locations of its meetings through coded advertisements in the newspaper—offering things like women's coats or shoes at wholesale prices at a particular parking lot in the middle of the night. (More likely, the team met at Yoshida's Tokyo garage not far from the Wangan.) It was also whispered that the team consisted only of wealthy titans of industry, each of whom could afford to spend hundreds of thousands, even millions of yen, buying and upgrading their cars. (Even into the 1990s, the members were probably in their late 20s or early 30s.)

What separated Mid Night from other clubs of the time was its hierarchal structure and difficult application process. The team kept its members in check by establishing a clear chain of command and handing out strict reprimands, including expulsion, if certain standards weren't met. New members had to first prove they could handle their car at over 120 mph for extended periods of time. During races, they were required to keep a one-lane separation from other cars at all times, to lessen the danger to civilians.

Having proven their skills, applicants had to attend every meeting for at least one year. They were given a pink Mid Night sticker to apply to their rear bumper, above the muffler, for that period. Upon graduating to full membership, they would earn a silver sticker or, even better, an adhesive club windshield banner that stretched from one end of the glass to the other. The sticker was unmistakeable —it often read "Mid Night Car Speciall," with two Ls. As members, they were expected to never lose to rival teams.

The prestige came from the structure and practices, but also from associations with the best shops in Japan. Each Mid Night meet-up was a virtual who's-who of tuner components and whole-car builds, from small A-list brands to titans still in existence today: HKS, Trust, Blitz, Veilside, JUN, Move, ABFlug, Espirit, Revolfe SA, RE Amemiya, Pent Roof, Auto Garage TBK. Famous creations included the ABR Hosoki Engineering Datsun Fairlady, with its wild and bright-red custom bodywork, and a white Porsche 911 Turbo with "Traction Master" graphics splashed across its hood, a reference to the nickname of the car's driver, who had averaged a blistering 88 mph over a particularly torturous 8.5-mile mountain course. Mid Night's runs helped validate and test the tuners' engineering, and tuners' involvement elevated the team above other drivers of similar makes and models. There are even rumors that not only tuners, but major automakers, used Team Mid Night as proxy prototypes for testing future product.

Within the team, the biggest rivalry was between Porsche and Nissan. Many members owned Porsche 911s, especially the Turbo, a model valued for its 160-mph top speed. But it's likely that even more owned Skylines—at one point, the ranks held at least nine R32 GT-Rs. The mighty RB26 engine needed only minimal tuning to produce 600 hp, and in the hands of the masters connected to Mid Night, it could see 1,000 hp and beyond.

Mid Night members famously will not acknowledge the club's existence, or their participation, to Western media. But they have worked with Japanese outlets in the past. In one instance, a conversation with multiple club members for *Option* magazine, owners of both the Skyline GT-R and the 911 Turbo compared and contrasted the cars. They agreed that the GT-R is at a disadvantage at first, but its tuning upside upstaged the Porsche.

"The 2.6-liter GT-R is no good unless you have [tuned] it to earn power," one said. "Honestly, the [911] Turbo," said another, "it is difficult to line up shoulder-to-shoulder with the GT-R at speed, even if you tune considerably."

Still, one Porsche sat above everything else. Yoshida, the team chairman, took special steps to ensure his Turbo would never be beaten. He spent years perfecting the car in the back of his shop, pouring millions of yen into the development of new parts and commissioning a Tokyo engine builder to remake the Porsche's six-cylinder with a massive turbocharger and more than 600 hp. The rear seats were discarded to make way for a roll cage, and he stretched the car's purple bodywork tastefully, the front bumper pulled nearly flush to the ground. Low-drag mirrors topped the doors, and an aircraft-style NACA duct sat in one of the side windows, forcing cool air into the engine with minimal penalty in top speed. Dotted with subtle stickers that made its Mid Night association clear, the "Yoshida Special" was the stuff of legend.

The cars were getting more extreme, and the team was becoming more difficult to hide. Mid Night members were rumored to run headlights-off to avoid detection, and to wear racing helmets on public roads—the latter not just for safety, but to hide their faces. And though many saw the team as a menace, it became a phenomenon. Mid Night's exploits would go on to inspire countless pop-culture sensations, from manga and anime to blockbuster video games like *Midnight Club* and movies like *The Fast and the Furious*. And at the forefront of each, always, was the GT-R.

Since its 1989 launch, Nissan's all-wheel-drive wonder had romped to success in nearly every form of motorsport around the world. But as tales of its exploits on those darkened Tokyo streets began to spread—whispered at first, then printed and broadcast and filmed—the car known across Japan for outrunning police and shattering speed limits grew only more famous.

No one was more surprised by the popularity of the R32 GT-R than Nissan. From day one, the public was enamored, but Nissan executives at first insisted the model would be sold only at home. When company offices abroad were flooded with callers begging to place a deposit, they were forced to change tactics. According to an Australian newspaper, one local racing champion "pursued a Nissan PR man around the pits at Bathurst" doing everything but waving money in his face. Meanwhile, in Japan, where the car was priced highly but within reach, hardworking businessmen often stretched to make the numbers work.

A Nissan employee and superfan named Hiroshi Tamura was one such buyer. Born and raised in the shadow of Nissan headquarters in Yokohama, a young Tamura had been in the stands at Fuji Speedway in 1972 when a Hakosuka had blown the doors off the competition in the pouring rain. "I was at the first corner," Tamura told me. His family had good seats, close enough to get hit by chunks of rubber and pavement from passing cars. Tamura worried about losing an eye. But he never left his seat. He was hooked: "I wanted to go to Nissan. I said I have to create Skyline."

Tamura was drawn to more than just Nissan; he became addicted to speed. As a teenager, he found himself with a driver's license and lots of free time, so he bought a motorcycle and took to the highways around Yokohama. One day, he lost control, flying over the handlebars and landing face-first on the pavement. When Tamura awoke, he was in a hospital bed, immobilized by a protective brace and with nothing to do but look up at the room's bright white ceiling. He couldn't hold books above his head to read or move his neck to watch television. For six weeks, all he had was free time. And that ceiling.

"Life is short," Tamura said to me, remembering that long and painful period. If anything, the crash taught him to go faster. "I thought about how you can spend a high-concentration life with peak power and energy," he said. "That became the life work for me. Always maximum speed."

Tamura recovered, and in 1984 he accomplished his goal, joining Nissan as a materials researcher. But the reality of corporate life soon sapped his spirit. Tamura had to follow orders; the young dreamer had to conform. By the end of his first day, Tamura had grown bored with corporate life. He trudged through more days, then months, considering quitting more than once. The whole point of working for Nissan had been to get his hands on cars like the mighty Hakosuka he witnessed blasting down the track; now he was stuck in a lab.

Two years in, Tamura received an interesting tip. Sakurai-san, father of the Skyline and the brain behind the MID4 and the MID4-II, was being tapped to launch a Nissan subsidiary. The new company, Autech, would produce specialty vehicles and conversions. Some of those vehicles were for industrial use, modified shipping vans or work machines based on standard Nissan models. But some would be low-production sports cars made to push the envelope. These projects would need hands-on treatment, passionate managers and—Tamura noted this with particular interest—test drivers.

It was a risk. Even though Autech was technically a division of Nissan, it was a step off the corporate ladder, and the move would pull Tamura from a carefully designed system he had already invested years in. He could lose his place in line for advancement, and the future of Autech was uncertain, with no guarantee that his old job would be waiting if things fell apart. And yet for Tamura, the opportunity seemed a no-brainer. He made the switch. Three years later, the R32 GT-R made its debut. Tamura took out a bank loan ("a big one") and bought one of the earliest cars, a Gun Grey Metallic model. As delivered, it made around 300 hp. But it wouldn't stay that way for long.

Before he was Nissan's prized test driver, with his famous three-finger driving technique, Hiroyoshi Kato had fallen in love with cars thanks to a book. As a boy in the mountains of Akita Prefecture, he discovered the 1962 spy novel "Black Test Car," by the journalist Toshiyuki Kajiyama, and was thrilled by its tale.

"Black Test Car" is about two competing car companies who are each preparing to launch a sports car, and the risks they will take to sabotage each other. The book was a best-seller when new, spawning a film adaptation and two spin-off detective mysteries, "The Black Report" and "Black Statement Book."

Though the original book and the movie are ostensibly about cars —at least, enough to convince a teenage boy to pursue a career in them—they were really, as the site Asian Movie Pulse would later say, a "deeply engaging and unrelenting experience of espionage, greed and corruption." Automotive enthusiasm sat at the core, but everything atop had been aimed at a broader audience.

Writing can play an important role in bridging cultures. It was Dutch books, after all, first brought to Japan in the 1700s, that had helped an isolated country keep pace with the outside world. And as Japan became a global leader in exported goods, books would lead the way in spreading Tokyo street-racing around the globe.

In the U.S., long before the general public had heard the phrase Racing Team Mid Night, a swath of the population had grown familiar with what the team represented. In Japan in 1990, the writer and illustrator Michiharu Kusunoki published the first edition of a story he called *Wangan Midnight*—a thinly veiled reference if ever was one—in a manga magazine called *Big Comic Spirits*.

Wangan Midnight told the tale of a teenager named Akio Asakura and his red Nissan Fairlady S30, and of his tense rivalry with the driver of a black Porsche Turbo, a doctor named Tatsuya Shima. The Nissan was named "Devil Z" and the Porsche was called "Blackbird." The tale centered around Akio's relentless desire to take down Blackbird in a race and be crowned the top racer in Tokyo. The men were not teammates, but anyone in the know would have recognized the red Nissan as a tribute to a famous one that had traded hands among Mid Night members over the years. The Porsche, of course, was a tribute to the famous "Yoshida Special" of the boss himself.

Manga has long been hugely popular in Japan, and American awareness of the art form was rising at the time. Just as *Black Test Car* had inspired a generation 30 years prior, *Wangan Midnight* did the same. Kusunoki reportedly knew members of Mid Night and had even received their blessing for his work. None of them likely imagined that *Wangan* would become wildly popular, running for 42 volumes and 28 years while spawning a number of films, television series, and video games in its wake. Regardless, the secret was out, and there was no going back.

WANGAN MIDNIGHT WAS the first proof that there was an audience for entertainment depicting the 1990s Tokyo car scene. But the series never fully cracked the international market. That would take a different manga, one with a humble Toyota, a lot of sliding, and some tofu.

It was called *Initial D*. Written and illustrated by Shuichi Shigeno, the story had more of a heroic arc than its *Wangan* predecessor. The main character, Takumi Fujiwara, is a lowly delivery driver at his father's struggling mountaintop tofu shop. He takes orders every night, driving his underpowered, rear-wheel-drive Toyota Corolla to customer homes at the bottom of the mountain. After years of this, Takumi develops an interesting style: He attacks sweeping corners at high speed, pointing the car's nose toward the inside and sliding the rear wheels outward, creating a controlled fishtail.

Drifting.

Takumi's remarkable skill is eventually discovered by others. An underdog in an underdog car, he is challenged to face other drivers, toppling one after another. This goes on for 48 volumes.

Initial D was an immediate hit, and it's credited with popularizing the drifting style that would eventually find its way to the States. When Option magazine founder Daijiro Inada organized drift exhibitions, they drew enormous crowds and led to the creation of the Formula Drift (a.k.a. Formula D) competition series.

To date, more than 55 million copies of *Initial D* have been sold globally. While the US had its own distribution, the books are now out of print, and examples in good condition are hard to come by. In late 2022, I spoke to an 18-year-old Los Angeles enthusiast who had stumbled onto 39 of the 48 volumes in a local Goodwill store. He bought them all for $34 and was trying to sell them on Facebook Marketplace for $2,000. "I don't think I'd go under $1,800," he told me.

Initial D fans go hard. They gobble up licensed merchandise and wear out old VHS tapes they watched as kids. Some have even built full-scale working replicas of the fictional Fujiwara storefront. But the main way fans pay tribute is by customizing their cars to resemble their favorite models from the story. The main character's Corolla, a model known as the AE86, features an iconic black-and-white paint scheme that enthusiasts call "Panda style." Japanese characters on its doors translate roughly to "Fujiwara Tofu Shop (Private Use)." The modest Toyota starts out mostly stock. But as the story progresses, Takumi modifies it to take on bigger and badder rivals. By the end of the series, the car has a carbon-fiber hood, a roll cage, lowered suspension, and popular RS Watanabe wheels.

Vincent Chan is one of those who take *Initial D* seriously. Born in Hong Kong, Chan moved to the U.S. with his family as a child and was exposed to the anime by his brothers as a teenager. Through the years, he managed to collect all the books, first in Japanese, then in English, and then again in his native Chinese. Chan also owns a near-perfect replica of Takumi's Panda AE86, down to the cage and Wats wheels. But that's not all.

One weekend evening in Los Angeles, I drove up the 605 freeway and exited in the town of El Monte. Nestled in the San Gabriel Valley, El Monte's streets were a hotbed for illicit racing in the 1990s. Located roughly 20 miles east of downtown L.A. and blessed with a relatively sparse population, the area let street racers fly under the radar. It was a decent distance from main thoroughfares, and if a quick escape was in order, highway access was easy. With a sizeable Japanese community of its own, the "SGV" also had supermarkets that carried Option magazine and other sources of car-nerd inspiration. These days, the valley is a popular spot for car meets, and I had come to visit one of the reasons why.

Here, on the corner of a beige strip mall, sharing walls with a

FedEx Office, stands one of those real-life Fujiwara Tofu Shops. From the outside, it looks like any other nondescript Japanese restaurant. But for *Initial D* fans, one look at the sign above the door—Japanese characters with the English words "Fujiwara Tofu café" printed underneath in parentheses—makes it clear this is something different. Inside, just about every square inch of the place is plastered with *Initial D* paraphernalia. Murals of original illustrations cover the walls; glass cases house the books, dioramas and *Initial D*-branded Chuck Taylor sneakers sit on shelves. You can slide into one of two *Initial D* arcade racing simulators and test your own skills driving sideways down the touge. Above the counter, a white and yellow overhang is draped in flourishing ivy, just as in the books.

Chan and his girlfriend Cheri Kyoo opened the shop in early 2022. They chose the location for its large parking lot (for holding car meets) and proximity to the highway (for quickly scattering car meets). The fact that the storefront stares directly into a Starbucks didn't factor in; they don't consider the coffee giant a competitor. Anyone who comes to Fujiwara is looking for something specific, they say, be it a fun night with fellow car people, a heaping whiff of nostalgia, or the chance to live out a childhood anime fantasy.

On the night I visited, the shop was crowded. Fujiwara was holding its first annual holiday party and toy drive, and enthusiasts were out in force. Parking was scarce, the lot overtaken by JDM imports, sports cars modified for performance, and luxury cars that had been lowered, or "stanced," nearly to the ground. A row of three pristine Mark IV Toyota Supras occupied primo spots. Mitsubishi Galants with aftermarket body panels and Mazda RX-7s shared space with Honda S2000s. A second Panda AE86 was parked out front next to Chen's, and there was a line out the front door for sampling specialty soymilk drinks and tofu-pudding desserts. (Unlike the fictional shop, Chen and Kyoo don't actually sell noodles.)

A few weeks later, I returned for the store's one-year anniversary party. This time, it was even more packed. A local business that sold diecast model cars had set up a tent with a toy racetrack. The parking lot held an even more impressive array of cars than before, plus a full-size stage blaring Eurobeat, the fast-paced anime soundtrack of choice, while Japanese culture diehards performed choreographed dances.

A group of Mitsubishi 3000GT owners had congregated in a corner of the lot, parking together. One, Alex Serrano, showed me the ins and outs of his custom-built example, which had been painstakingly decorated and modified to honor the memory of the late basketball player Kobe Bryant. Serrano told me that he knew Fujiwara would be a good spot as soon as he heard it was opening. "Everybody in the car scene has seen *Initial D*," he said. "I knew it was going to attract a lot of people... This shop has the arcade, the music and the AE86 outside. If it was a little closer to the canyons, it'd be even crazier."

One thing I didn't see much of was GT-Rs. But that, Chan told me, isn't because *Initial D* fans don't like them. If anything, he said, they revere the Nissan, and he hopes to own an R32 one day himself. Like American enthusiasts in the 1990s, Chan and his friends view the GT-R as a kind of unobtanium. They would all jump at the chance to have one, he said.

FOLLOWING the success of *Initial D*, other forms of entertainment rooted in Japanese street racing and motorsport found their way to U.S. shores. One of the most significant arrivals was that of *Gran Turismo*, a video game for the original Sony PlayStation console, in December of 1997.

Gran Turismo had been shopped around for years before its Japanese developer found a partner willing to bring it to market. Software executives of the day believed that racing titles had a hard sales ceiling, particularly when those titles were built like *Gran Turismo*, which passed on wild theatrics in favor of a more realistic, simulation style. To their surprise, the game took the world by storm. It took half a decade to make and had almost been permanently shelved during development, but *Gran Turismo* would go on to sell more than 10 million copies and become the best-selling disc on the original PlayStation. Seven sequels followed, each selling well, across all five versions of the PlayStation.

The original *Gran Turismo* featured hundreds of cars that a player could choose to drive. That volume was part of the appeal, a massive selection next to similar games of the time, which often had no more than 20 to pick. With a Japanese developer and a focus on JDM cars, *Gran Turismo*, by contrast, had 12 different versions of the GT-R alone, including a host of limited editions. It even had the most desirable models of all: the 400-hp R33 400R, and two versions of the hyper-limited R33 LM, one each in road and racing trim. Later games would feature GT-Rs modified by Mine's, the tiny but infamous tuning shop.

Another of the game's prime draws was that it let you modify your cars. This, of course, suited the GT-R particularly well. With a few clicks of a button, you could tune an engine, add a sports muffler, throw on some racing tires, and remove weight. (Who needs air-conditioning or sound deadening in a video game anyway?) With a few minor upgrades, your two-door Nissan would transform into a fire-breathing, record-setting beast that stuck to the ground in corners as if pulled there by magnets.

Gran Turismo was a revelation, and the GT-R was its star. When the game made landfall in the States, it sent out a shockwave. Outside of the street-racing, Option-reading set, few people in the U.S. even knew the car existed. Media coverage in America had been limited at best; why waste ink, editors thought, on something that would never make it here anyway? But all of a sudden, hundreds of thousands of Americans were introduced to the GT-R experience.

"Here's this Nissan, and it's beating all these other cars," Sean Morris said, remembering the game's public reception. Soon, he said, people began asking an obvious question:

"Why can't I have it?"

As GT-R MADNESS was starting to build momentum, Bill Gates was growing impatient. He had waited years for his Porsche 959 to enter the country legally. Ten years on, into the mid-1990s, it still sat somewhere at the Port of Oakland, collecting dust.

Gates had watched other titans of industry figure out ways around the problem. A San Francisco businessman converted his 959 to racecar specification, then brought it into the country (and never raced it). Newspaper mogul Otis Chandler placed his in a museum and never drove it.

Gates, however, wanted to drive. His importer, a Northern California Porsche specialist and retired racer named Bruce Canepa, was looking to make a practice of helping wealthy clients secure and upgrade their cars. At first, Canepa tried to establish his company, Canepa Design, as a federally recognized manufacturer, a status that would have given him the authority to work through the import process. Regulators, he said, "stonewalled" that plan because of the 959's reputation. Gates wondered if they should simply buy several 959s and pay for the model to be crash-tested and certified by NHTSA, but that didn't pan out. Paul Allen, the Microsoft co-founder whose car had been sitting next to Gates's in the impound next, finally gave up. He got his 959 back the easy way: He moved to Europe and took it with him.

Unable to work within existing legislation, Gates and Canepa settled on a plan—they would make their own law.

Canepa called a Washington D.C. lawyer named Warren Dean. Together, they recruited even more high-powered individuals who wanted to drive a 959 in the U.S., including the fashion designer Ralph Lauren. Dean came up with a rules package he thought the government might get behind. He called it the "Show or Display" exemption.

The requirements were simple. An individual could import a noncompliant specialty collector car before it was 25 years old if: The model in question had been produced in fewer than 500 units; it was not currently in production; it had never officially been sold in the

US; it met EPA emissions standards; and it was driven fewer than 2,500 miles per year.

Basically, with the right connections and a mountain of paperwork, a person could arrange to drive an expensive, illegal toy as much as 20 years before the general public, so long as they didn't drive that car too much.

Dean set about trying to get the exemption passed. It took two years, but in 1998, President Bill Clinton signed a version of it into law. Regulators drafted an early version of the legal language two years after that. Canepa set about modifying the 959 emissions system to meet EPA standards, developing a winning set of parts and safety equipment after only a few hiccups. (The fact that his work also happened to increase horsepower from 450 to 575? Some called it a happy accident.) Gates and Lauren both had their cars shortly after, and Canepa rapidly received more than a dozen orders for similar conversions.

The Show or Display era had begun. The exemption made getting around the 25-year rule possible, and it opened the door for certain notable cars to enter the country long before they could have previously. Be it a 200-mph Porsche or a some dreadfully slow Toyota, if the car you had always wanted was never made for America, you finally had a glimmer of hope. Show or Display was not a panacea, though, and it did not rescind the 25-year rule or reduce the punishment for its violation. Most important, as many later found out, it would not keep you out of trouble.

CHAPTER 9

Remember Andres Diaz and Nicole Chiong, the Miami couple who founded Soho Imports and were arrested on charges of fraud?

No criminal enterprise is entirely ordinary, but some details of Soho's operation were downright wacky. Diaz and Chiong were bringing in, among other rare vehicles, R33 GT-Rs and Nissan Silvia S15s. As neither model had originally been sold in the U.S., Soho had to present those cars to customers as being properly converted to federal regulations.

Yet there was no evidence that Soho had done any conversion work. Not only that, there was no evidence the cars would have been legal even if they did. At the time, some but not all R33s had been made legal through NHTSA exemptions, but that particular R33 didn't qualify. The S15, for its part, had no such exemption. Sean Morris wrote a blog post in 2014 noting that, among other inconsistencies, the documents submitted by Soho appeared to have a fraudulent stamp from the Florida Region 10 DMV office, the one responsible for policing Dade County, where Soho did business. Soho Imports wasn't even listed with the government as a Registered Importer, a requirement for any firm trying to bring in cars before the 25-year rule. There was nothing that indicated Diaz and Chiong were able to do what they were doing. It appeared they had just kind of... done it anyway.

That wasn't even the most confusing part. What really befuddled investigators, when they started digging, was why a Florida company was bringing in so many Japanese-market cars with titles approved by the state of Vermont.

Here's how investigators alleged it worked: To obtain cars, Soho Imports would send money via wire transfer to partners in Japan. The arrest reports for both Diaz and Chiong indicated that Japanese bank accounts had been wired a total of $600,000, enough money to support the idea that Soho bought cars in bulk. To bring those cars into the country, the couple simply bypassed Customs.

Neat trick, right? It's not as difficult as it might sound. The Safe Ports Act of 2006 mandates that officials inspect each and every shipping container that enters the United States through the use of noninvasive technology such as X-ray scanning. According to the American Journal of Transportation, however, the reality is much less reassuring, with only about 3.7-percent of containers being inspected annually. Some sources claim it's even lower, around 2.5-percent or less. The number of containers inspected globally is near 1-percent, with the vast majority of those being scanned through radar, not opened and rifled through.

Containers do get physically inspected, but the procedure is rare. It's also expensive, and the importer gets stuck with the bill regardless of whether anything nefarious is found inside. (Multiple GT-R owners told me they have had containers physically inspected, at thousands of dollars in expense. None of those inspections turned up illegal vehicles, at least according to them, anyway.) Long story short, if you're playing the numbers game, bringing in lots of cars each year, you're unlikely to get scanned at all. This is likely how Soho got its hundreds of cars into the country.

Once the cars were in the U.S. and snuck past Customs, Diaz got to work. This was no longer the world of gray market conversions, after all—they were black market cars, through and through.

In order to sell those vehicles in Florida, they needed to be properly titled and registered by the state. Otherwise, buyers would be tipped off that the cars weren't legal, and potential buyers would say "No thanks." The problem was Soho could have never tried to pass the cars off to state officials as recent imports, though, since that would have triggered what Florida calls a "dealer license alert inquiry." At that point, the state's Motor Vehicle Field Operations team would have inspected each vehicle, which would have meant taking a deep look into how Soho Imports operated. Of course, they would immediately notice that Soho wasn't a Registered Importer and had no standing to import these vehicles.

So Diaz tried something new. Rather than presenting the cars as foreign imports, he claimed they weren't imports at all. Soho's offerings, he said, were already legally in the United States.

In order to "prove" this, prosecutors alleged, Diaz drew up fraudulent documents. He fudged the required signatures and stamps, then faked authorization paperwork from the Department of Motor Vehicles Enforcement and Safety in Vermont.

Vermont is best known for fall colors and Ben & Jerry's ice cream, but it also had the most lax vehicle-registration laws in the country. Each year, the state earned roughly $3 million by registering vehicles for people who didn't live within its borders. If you wanted a Vermont plate and a Vermont title, Vermont regulators didn't need to interview you, and they didn't need to see your car in person. The practice ended in July of 2023, but it earned the Green Mountain State the nickname of "America's DMV."

Vermont, unknowingly, became Soho's DMV too. The faked documents made it appear as though the state issued hundreds of titles, sight-unseen, to vehicles that had actually been illegally imported. Duly armed, Diaz could obtain legal Florida titles by claiming his company's cars were being brought into Florida, not from Japan, but as interstate transfers from up the Atlantic coast.

Soho's investigators had seen shady characters try to sneak cars into Florida dozens of ways, but they hadn't seen this. (One investigator called Diaz's scheme "...a new method of presenting fraudulent out-of-state titles for imported vehicles.") Soho had one more hurdle to cross, though: To convert Vermont titles to Florida titles, it had to have the cars inspected. Miraculously, those investigators thought, all 348 vehicles had been authorized by the same two individuals. One Miami Beach officer had verified that all the VIN plates matched the Vermont titles. The other official, a member of the Motor Vehicle Field Operations team, signed the vitally important HSMV 84044 form, an affidavit for application of title, for every single car.

Investigators spoke with both the Miami Beach officer and the operations official to get to the bottom of things. Soon, they say, it became clear those people actually had no involvement at all. Their signatures were forged. The public notary who verified the signatures was Nicole Chiong.

The charges levied against Soho Imports pertained to vehicles imported between November of 2014 and October of 2020—348 cars in just under six years. But the Florida Department of Highway Safety and Motor Vehicles had issued Soho its dealer-license number in 2011, and experienced vehicle importers began suspecting questionable goings-on in 2012, prior to the scope of the investigation. It's possible that more Soho vehicles are out there. Many more.

ON THE MORNING of March 7th, 2022, investigators showed up at Diaz and Chiong's home with a search warrant. They seized electronics, documents, and a fake Florida Region 10 stamp. In the garage they found two vehicles, a 2017 Cadillac and a 2019 Lamborghini. Both were stolen, with their factory VIN plates replaced by fake decals, and the Lamborghini had been repainted. (The VIN plate, a literal metal plate riveted or screwed onto every vehicle, is stamped with a unique alphanumeric code that allows for positive identification during everything from theft recovery to accident reporting. It's basically a car's fingerprint, and messing with it violates both state and federal law.)

When investigators reviewed messages on Diaz's phone, they found "lengthy conversations about illegally importing vehicles in parts for reassembly in the United States after fraudulently bypassing Customs." They also confirmed that Chiong had personally bought blank versions of a Manufacturer's Certificate of Origin, a document used to obtain a title and that can only legally be provided by a car's manufacturer or its authorized representative.

By their accounts, Diaz and Chiong had, through a coordinated effort over multiple years, violated importing laws, bypassed requirements for titling and registration, and impersonated state officials. They had forged documents—which were then illegally notarized by Chiong—and then presented those documents as real to the Department of Transportation, U.S. Customs, and the EPA.

The funny thing is, when government representatives reviewed that 348-vehicle list, they discovered that many of the vehicles on it were already 25 years old. The cars were already legal to import, title, and register. Soho could have brought them into the country and sold them without a problem.

It's hard to consider all this without coming to one reasonable, tempting conclusion: Diaz and Chiong didn't commit forgery because they had to. They simply thought no one was watching.

Soho Imports had never been aggressive with its online presence. Evidence of the company's marketing is virtually nonexistent; if Diaz and Chiong advertised, they left almost no trace of it. Instead, the business operated below ground, in a fashion best described as "if you know, you know."

In a way, this was a throwback to the original American Skyline underworld of the early 2000s. Back then, you had to know how to break the law simply to be in the community. And as a frequent presence in the South Florida JDM scene for more than a decade, Diaz and Chiong knew exactly how to reach people without attracting the attention of the general public. As one seasoned importer explained to me, "Soho didn't reach anyone who didn't already know they were there."

Within days of the couple's arrest, the Florida Highway Patrol circulated a letter intended to reach owners of cars that the company had imported. Due to the investigation, the letter explained, the titles and registrations of all Soho-imported vehicles had been "cancelled/revoked," and those cars were no longer legal to drive on public roads. Not only that, but the affected vehicles were now perpetually ineligible to receive a new title—not just in Florida, but in any state in the country, "regardless of any corrective measures taken."

The letter offered three possible courses of action: never drive your vehicle again; export your vehicle to another country; or surrender your vehicle for immediate seizure. (Importers told me that because exporting your vehicle means turning it over to U.S. Customs, the second and third options were essentially the same thing.) All of this information, the Highway Patrol explained, was simply being relayed, passed down from the Department of Homeland Security.

The collective mood of those owners at this point is best described as panic. Attention from the state was frightening enough on its own, but if the feds were involved, seizure was a very real possibility. Years earlier, Customs and Border Protection had seized a running and driving R33 GT-R from a South Carolina company called All JDM Motors after discovering the vehicle hidden in a shipping container. GT-R enthusiasts regularly told me stories of cars stuffed into shipping containers and surrounded with paper towels to hide it, or trailered across the border from Canada with paperwork stating the car was actually a U.S.-legal 240SX. Hopefully, they thought, Customs agents wouldn't know the difference. One story, vouched by multiple GT-R long-timers, involved a car that was literally sawed in half, down the middle, and welded back together once safely across country lines.

The owner of one R33 GT-R in the Midwest knew their car was illegal, but stated in an email to Jalopnik.com that he "never thought the feds would show up in Ohio of all places lol."

For one reason or another, Florida has been a hotbed for this sort of thing. In 2018 alone, a business there called Black Ops Performance closed after officials seized an R34 Skyline GT-R in the middle of a Daytona Beach car show, and the owners of All JDM Imports abruptly left town after attempting to use three Skyline GT-Rs as collateral for a loan to pay down their debts. If it seems like so many suspect importers stay unnoticed, it's partly because it's difficult to keep up with all of the companies undergoing vehicle seizures at once.

FALSELY APPLYING for a motor vehicle title in the state of Florida is a third-degree felony, punishable by a maximum of five years in prison. The same goes for "uttering a forged document," as Diaz and Chiong allegedly did with those title-affidavit forms. Diaz was charged with another third-degree felony for forging the names of an officer and regulator, and Chiong faced her own third-degree felony for notarizing each document. Each faced additional third-degree felony charges for using their cell phones to facilitate crimes.

Then there were the stolen cars. Possessing the stolen Cadillac, with its fake VIN "plate" and a street value from $20,000 - $100,000, was a second-degree felony punishable by up to 15 years. Possessing the stolen Lamborghini, repainted and re-VIN'd and valued at more than $100,000, was a first-degree felony. For that, the maximum sentence was 30 years in prison. A racketeering charge under the Florida RICO Act tacked another first-degree felony onto the list.

Diaz and Chiong were individually facing hundreds of years in federal prison. The possibility of living the rest of your life behind bars can be difficult to comprehend. There's no easy way to explain away a pattern of forgery, fraud, theft and the impersonation of state and local officials. On the other hand, the criminal acts themselves can be boiled down to skirting a rule that even proponents admit is somewhat arbitrary. Maybe even unnecessary.

Was this a case of career criminals perniciously exploiting people and not caring who got hurt in the process? Or was it a crime that was bound to happen, given the demand for JDM vehicles bottlenecked by a law that no one seemed to believe in anyway?

Violators of the 25-year rule tend to find a soft landing, sometimes paying a small fine, escaping prison on probation, or simply floating away with the wind, never to be heard from again. Because of its size and scope, the Soho case was different. Importers and enthusiasts I interviewed tended to swing to one side or the other: Diaz and Chiong would either get a slap on the wrist and wriggle away, they said, or the two would spend the rest of their lives in prison.

Whichever outcome they felt more likely, no one was very confident in their answer. There just weren't many examples of the government enforcing the 25-year rule to the fullest extent. One case, though, kept coming up, again and again, as an infamous example of someone who pushed the feds too far.

GRAN TURISMO ARRIVED in American stores just in time for the 1997 holiday season. And as the PlayStation game began to fly off shelves and warp young minds, a small corner of the car industry was working hard and fast to bring in another Japanese import however they could.

The Show or Display exemption, spearheaded by Bill Gates, didn't yet exist. That process was designed to bring uncommon foreign-market cars into the country for permanent and ordinary use. But there was another way in, so long as you didn't care about the "permanent" or "ordinary use" parts. It was called Temporary Importation under Bond, or TIB, and it fell under the jurisdiction of U.S. Customs.

The TIB process was designed for the short-term, duty-free importation and use of goods that are destined to either be destroyed or shipped back out of the country. To qualify for a TIB, an object must fit into one of a handful of categories specified by Customs, and it can't be intended for American sale. After that, you simply post a bond and promise to either export or destroy the item within three years.

Foreign automakers often take advantage of a TIB to bring in noncompliant show or test cars, but the process is also used for everything from valuable trade tools to breeding animals and priceless fine-art paintings brought in for display. It's also used for vehicles brought in for crash testing.

That last part was just the opening that a pair of young Californians needed. Hiroaki Nanahoshi was born in Japan and spent his teenage years in the U.S. In the late 1990s, he joined forces with another SoCal local named Ken Takahashi. Both Nanahoshi and Takahashi were in the export business, locating and purchasing desirable American vehicles and shipping them to buyers in Japan. (Shockingly, one of their main cash cows was full-size vans, chiefly the Ford Econoline and Dodge Ram. The Japanese love hulking American machinery.) As the Asian markets tanked and the Japanese economy struggled to find its footing, Nanahoshi and Takahashi decided it made more financial sense to reverse the flow, and sell Japanese cars to Americans.

They found a backer, a wealthy Japanese businessman from one of Nanahoshi's previous dealings, forming a company called GT Autohouse in September of 1997. A few months later, they changed the name to MotoRex. Nanahoshi, then barely 25 years old, and Takahashi specifically intended to bring in Skylines, including GT-Rs, for U.S. sale. They knew it would be tricky—the IVSCA, or 25-year rule, had been in effect for almost a decade and was widely understood. The R32 GT-R was then only eight years old; the R33 was still on sale in Japan; the R34 wouldn't come out for another few months. But Nanahoshi and Takahashi weren't worried about that. They had a plan to make GT-Rs legal: They were going to crash them.

Crash testing the cars was the first step to getting them certified for U.S. roads. Microsoft founder Bill Gates had proposed the idea of funding a series of Porsche 959 crash tests when his personal car was stuck in federal impound all those years. The idea hadn't panned out, but for MotoRex, it seemed to make sense. Skyline GT-Rs were called Skylines for a reason—the model was built on the bones of Nissan's affordable, family-friendly Skyline coupe and sedan. Skyline coupe models used the same basic structure and as the GT-R, minus most of the expensive performance equipment. Nanahoshi and Takahashi figured they could procure a couple of lesser Skylines on the cheap, pay for those cars to be crash-tested and federalized, and then use the newfound certification to import high-powered, high-ticket GT-Rs.

It was possible, it turns out, so that's exactly what they did. By 1998, the two partners had leased an office space in—where else?—the South Bay, in Gardena. A collection of Skylines, both GT-Rs and the lower-powered, rear-wheel-drive GTS model, were brought into the country. The cars were fitted with three catalytic converters (Three! Belt and suspenders!), to make their exhausts blow clean enough to satisfy emissions regulations. Then they were sent to a Maryland importer and conversion company called JK Technologies.

Once there, the cars met their fate. Which is to say, a few engineers in a large building ran several Skylines into very solid objects at decent speed, and somewhere, as the saying doesn't go, an angel lost its wings. A safety-equipment and testing company called MGA Research Corporation conducted the tests and analyzed the results. Its report indicated that, despite having never been engineered to pass the relatively strict U.S. crash standards, the Japanese-market cars held up reasonably well. MGA even found that some components, such as the tail lamps, the power windows, and the roof, passed as they were—no modification needed. Other parts, like the airbags and rearview mirror, were replaced with items from other compliant vehicles. And still others, like the Skyline's door structure, seatbelts, and fuel system, were modified by MGA Research before testing and found, in post-test investigation, to have met standards.

MotoRex used the MGA report to file a petition with NHTSA. In that petition, Nanahoshi and Takahashi asked that 1990-1999 Skylines and GT-Rs be permitted to enter the country on the grounds that those cars could be converted to meet federal standards. Believe it or not, NHTSA agreed. In June of 2000, the agency wrote a letter to MotoRex stating that Skyline GTS and GT-R models from the requested model years were "eligible for importation into the United States because they have safety features that comply with, or are capable of being altered to comply with, such standards."

MotoRex and its young founders had somehow danced their way through a minefield of regulations imposed by the IVSCA, the Federal Motor Vehicle Safety Standards, U.S. Customs, NHTSA, and the EPA. They had tackled a set of laws designed specifically to keep vehicles like the Nissan Skyline GT-R out of the country, and they had won. It was a stunning victory. Even better, they were protected from competition: NHTSA agreed to keep confidential the list of modifications that MGA Research had performed to bring the cars to compliance. No other importer would be able to duplicate what MotoRex had done unless they went through the trouble of importing, outfitting and crash testing Skylines themselves. A tiny shop in Gardena now had a monopoly on the American Skyline market.

ONE OF THOSE Honda tuners from Torrance who grew up around the street racing scene was a Japanese-American named Kenji Sumino. In 1995, armed with his prized Honda Civic, Sumino had made the two-hour drive up to Palmdale to test his drag-racing skills at the Battle of the Imports. There, in the desert outside L.A., he saw Daijiro Inada and Keiichi "Drift King" Tsuchiya, legends he had grown up reading about while working as a stockboy at the local market and thumbing through issues of magazines like Option. Sumino was the most fluent Japanese speaker in his group of friends, and they prodded him to introduce himself and say hello. But he was too nervous. "I was starstruck," he told me.

Representatives from Trust/GReddy in Japan had flown out to attend the show, and they had brought a special gift. Parked next to their booth was a bright blue R32 known as the SROC Skyline GT-R.

The SROC was Trust's demo car, stuffed with aftermarket parts to entice customers, and it had been trekked up and down Japan and beyond. Even though the GT-R wasn't available in the U.S., Trust wanted to expand into the country's vast aftermarket and thought showing the car would earn some attention. It was the first GT-R Sumino had ever seen.

By happenstance, a few months later, Sumino found himself in a job interview for the position to lead Trust/GReddy's U.S. expansion. He was offered the job on the spot, resigning almost immediately from the aerospace company where he worked. A few weeks later, Sumino was on a plane to Japan, headed off to begin hands-on training. His first project was to follow up the R32 SROC demo car with an R33 version. The knowledge he would bring back to America would help GReddy (as it's still known in the US) make inroads into stateside garages.

Years after his return, in 1999, having successfully established the brand and finding himself with a little extra cash, Sumino called up MotoRex and inquired about getting a GT-R of his own. He headed up the freeway to Gardena, where he noticed a young go-getter who seemed to know everyone and everything connected to importing Skylines.

That was Sean Morris, the New Zealand-born importer with an encyclopedic mind who would go on to run Toprank. Morris was then only a few years out of the Navy and had recently parted ways with the family business ("I told my dad to go fuck himself," he told me) and he had found his way to a job at MotoRex. From the jump, Morris was sent to JK Technologies in Maryland, to monitor crash testing, then to Washington, D.C. to meet with federal regulators. Once home, he began working with G&K Automotive Conversions in Los Angeles, arranging emissions testing. (Years later, both JK and G&K would work with Bruce Canepa to do the same for Porsche 959s.)

Morris kept himself busy, building a habit of always having somewhere to go, someone to see or some law to decipher. His industriousness paid off big-time for MotoRex: one of Morris's contacts was

Coleman Sachs, Chief of the Import and Certification Division at NHTSA, who had personally signed off on the decision to approve Skylines for import. It was Sachs who assigned a Vehicle Eligibility Number, VCP-17, to 1990-1999 Skyline models in January of 2000. Once the cars had a VCP, Morris got to work.

Over the next three years, Morris and MotoRex imported and federalized more than 100 Skylines, the majority of them GT-R models. Firm numbers are hazy, but Morris now estimates the total at 111 cars—34 R32s, 62 R33s, and 15 R34s. Nor was the process quick. After a Skyline had been purchased and imported, it had to be shipped across the country for extensive conversion work and testing at JK and G&K, sometimes adding as much as $25,000 to the final cost, before it could technically be considered legal.

The small parking lot and garage at MotoRex began to overflow with cars. Word got out that, if you wanted to see your first real-life GT-R, all you had to do was drive past this Gardena business park, where you'd get an eyeful. Prospective customers started calling, attempting to find a way onto the waiting list even if that meant plopping down a deposit before the company had located them a car.

GT-Rs were coming in, conversions were getting approved, and sales were happening left and right. But the profits were hardly enough to cover the astronomical costs. Plus, the time it took to convert and certify cars caused a massive backlog. And while MotoRex had received approval to import 1990-1999 GTS and GT-R Skylines, they had actually converted and crash-tested only 1995-1998 R33 models.

It's important to remember that all second-generation Skylines, R32, R33, and R34, are mostly identical under the skin. "The chassis are very similar from beginning to end," Morris told me. "The wheelbase changes a little... they change the wheels and headlights and tail lights, but a lot of the main structure is very similar. Evolutions, not revolutions."

MotoRex assumed that similarity was enough of an umbrella to cover everything. It was one of many decisions that would come back around in unexpected ways, and that would ultimately turn it into, as one blog later put it, "an epic of fast cars, easy money, and criminal activity." But there were still moments of glory ahead.

ONE OF MOTOREX'S first customers was an American named Craig Lieberman. A lifelong drag racer and enthusiast, Lieberman owned several imported sports cars and had his eye on Skylines. At one point, MotoRex loaned him a black R34 GT-R to drive around while deciding whether he wanted to buy the car. While making up his mind, he loaned it to the actor Paul Walker for several months.

In 1999, Universal Studios retained Lieberman as a technical advisor for an upcoming film about illegal import racing. The script was based on an article about the L.A. street scene that had first been published in Vibe magazine, and the studio needed help procuring the right cars. Lieberman brought several of his own to the set, including a Mark IV Supra and the black R34. He also invited MotoRex to bring any interesting vehicles they had lying around.

MotoRex did have one. Stashed in a back corner of the Gardena garage was an R33 GT-R the company had been holding onto. Still unmodified and wearing its factory white paint, the R33 had once been destined for the crusher. MotoRex had planned to use it as a sacrificial lamb, a TIB import for crash testing. Once the company had crash-tested its first few R33s, however, NHTSA had decided anything further was overkill. They spared it.

Now the company had a GT-R that it didn't need and couldn't sell. So they sent the car on a world tour of sorts. The tuning company HKS plastered the R33 with stickers and installed its most current performance parts, then displayed the car at booths and shows around the country. Later, a motorsport team called UPRD Racing slapped on its own livery, added an exhaust and race tires, and put rally-racing driver Rhys Millen behind the wheel for the annual Pikes Peak hillclimb race in Colorado. Millen, who had never driven a right-hand-drive car with a clutch pedal, learned to shift with his left hand on the first day of practice. Then he won the event and set a new course record. (He would later become a Formula D champion.)

When Lieberman called, MotoRex's extra R33 wasn't scheduled for anything. They put the GT-R on a trailer and sent it to "audition" for a role in the film, which had a working title of "Redline." The producers liked the car, and they reportedly asked for more identical R33 GT-Rs in order to build a bigger story arc for it. But MotoRex was still in its infancy, and importing more R33s in the required time wasn't possible. Universal held onto the car to see if they could work it into the movie.

Months later, when the GT-R returned to MotoRex, it was hardly recognizable. The production team had gone to town on the looks. Not only was the R33 (again) wearing a new set of stickers, its white bodywork had been repainted a bright yellow. (Morris and the crew nicknamed it "Big Bird.") MotoRex loaned the car out again for display purposes and waited to see what would come of the film, which was apparently about a gang of thieves who stole VCR and DVD players.

That film, starring Paul Walker and Vin Diesel, would later be retitled *The Fast and the Furious*. Its June 2001 release kicked off one of the most successful movie franchises of all time. Reviews were mediocre—Roger Ebert said the movie "doesn't have a brain in its head"—but the critics didn't matter. What mattered was the impact, which was immediate. Kenji Sumino, the head of GReddy in America, remembers people calling his office to ask if he could make their exhausts shoot flames like the ones in the film. *The Fast and the Furious* thrilled audiences, earning $40 million in its first weekend and quickly becoming the number-one film in the country.

Just as in *Wangan Midnight* and *Initial D*, the GT-R didn't have a starring role. Walker drove a bright-orange Supra, and Diesel had a jet-black Pontiac GTO. The bright yellow R33 appeared sparingly and belonged to a bit character named Leon who mainly looked out for cops and never got to race. (That was that for poor Leon, who wouldn't reappear in any of the movie's nine sequels.)

Though the GT-R had a minor credit, the sheer reach of *The Fast and the Furious* would soon catapult the car into the nation's consciousness. You couldn't buy one, but you could read about it in Option, or play it in *Gran Turismo*, or watch it on the big screen. And word was, a tiny garage hidden in Gardena that was full of them—they could bring one into the country for you! The feds had even approved it!

Paul Walker was seen driving one on the street. A tuner magazine called *Sport Compact Car* put a MotoRex R34 GT-R on the cover next to the headline, "It's Here, It's Legal, We Drive It."

If you knew, you knew. And you lost your mind.

THING IS, the Skyline wasn't legal. And MotoRex wasn't built to last.

Sometime in 2002, Nanahoshi's partners had begun growing suspicious of the man they called "Hiro." He had hatched the original plan to bring Skylines into the country, and against all odds, it had actually worked. But Nanahoshi was worrying the team. His accounting methods were questionable, and customers were getting rowdy. More and more had started calling MotoRex demanding to see their cars or get their money back. Nanahoshi also liked spending a little too much time and money at high-priced hostess bars around the South Bay, acting like some wheeling, dealing magnate.

Along the way, MotoRex had also fallen out of favor somehow with federal regulators. The very people that had helped them navigate the importing process in the first place had suddenly switched course, retracting VCP-17 and replacing it with a new eligibility number that only applied to certain R33 GT-Rs. For MotoRex, this was nearly a death blow: There was nowhere near enough demand for the R33 to support the company, and it was sitting on R32 and R34 GT-Rs that couldn't legally be delivered, their angry owners demanding the cars they were promised.

MotoRex employees began to suspect that Nissan itself had pressured the federal government to keep GT-Rs out of the United States.

Most American enthusiasts were oblivious to MotoRex's troubles.

They knew only how the company had been glorified in media. A 2003 *Popular Mechanics* article cited MotoRex as an importing authority. A 2005 story on the website *Edmunds* (full disclosure: Edmunds is my former employer) carried the headline, "How to Get One of the Most Desirable Sports Cars in the World." After MotoRex gained approval to import Skylines, it said, the company had been "applying what it's learned to producing DOT-approved Skyline GT-Rs ever since." The story mentioned the car's role in *The Fast and the Furious* and noted that Paul Walker had purchased one of his own.

"And if Paul Walker can get one," it stated, "so can you."

By the time that article went live, MotoRex was already speeding toward collapse.

THE 25-YEAR RULE was hard and fast, but people still brought Skylines into the country. There are likely hundreds of illegal Skylines parked in the United States right now. One person who currently owns an illegal R34 GT-R, speaking on the condition of anonymity, estimated there are at least 100 illegal R34 GT-Rs in California alone. Whether it meant covering up a car on a trailer and fudging paperwork, producing sophisticated forgeries, or even bringing in a GT-R from Canada under the government's one-year visitor "grace period" and then—whoops—conveniently forgetting to return it, those who really wanted a Skyline in America found a way.

One of the most common was exploiting the "kit car" policy.

The kit-car policy is an EPA exception to the 25-year rule. Kit cars are homebuilt vehicles often comprised of parts from multiple different sources—a Ford with a Chevrolet engine, a Toyota truck with an electric Tesla powertrain, and so on, in any combination you can imagine. In particular, the kit-car policy lets a person legally import a vehicle's frame or one-piece body without an engine, transmission, or other running gear. It also allows for the importation of individual parts, including that very same engine or transmission. As those parts don't add up to a vehicle on their own, the EPA doesn't regulate them.

The kit-car policy, the agency says, does "not apply to regular production vehicles offered for importation." Basically, you can't use it to bring in a complete noncompliant car. But the suspension parts of an R34 Skyline GT-R? Or that car's trunk and front bumper? Sure, the government doesn't care—it's just parts, after all.

The catch was, you absolutely, explicitly, without-a-doubt could not separate a vehicle from its engine, ship both the car and its engine into the country separately, and then reunite them once they arrived. That would recreate the original car. Of course, that's exactly what people did.

In 2007, Daryl Alison was a deputy in the Orange County Sheriff's Department and a noted car enthusiast with loads of cool rides. In his spare time, Alison founded and ran a collection of automotive businesses. One was an Orange County garage called Kaizo Industries. *Kaizo* is Japanese for "rebuild" or "modification." Based in Costa Mesa, just a stone's throw from the ritzy coastal enclave of Newport Beach, Kaizo dealt in the importing and sale of JDM vehicles. Which of course meant Skylines.

Publicly, Kaizo claimed to import Skylines, particularly the R34 GT-R, for the purpose of bringing the cars up to federal standards—conversions featuring "strengthened seatbelt mounts and reinforced body shells," according to the auction house Bonhams—and releasing them for sale. Privately, Kaizo did none of that. Instead, it imported entire cars in pieces. A body shell would arrive in one container, stripped of its engine and other driveline components. Everything else would come in another container.

Kaizo wasn't the only shop bringing GT-Rs into the country in pieces. But typically, the others stayed under the radar from regulators by swapping in parts from different vehicles. That way, even if you were mating an R34 Skyline GT-R to an RB26 engine and transmission of the correct specification, at least it wasn't the exact pair Nissan installed at the factory. Alison was more brazen. Kaizo simply stuffed the car's original factory parts back into the vehicle they came from, as it was originally built. What's more, there was none of the promised conversion work required to bring the vehicles into federal compliance. The cars rolled onto American roads exactly the same as they had been in Japan. Which made them not just illegal, but blatantly illegal.

Not that the company didn't try to cover its tracks. For instance, Alison rebadged and titled some cars not as Nissans, but as "Kaizo" Skylines or "Nissani" Skylines. (The latter was the name of one of Alison's other businesses.) To make the paperwork line up, Kaizo simply committed a state and federal crime: It had the cars' VIN plates removed in Japan, and replaced them with new Kaizo or Nissani ones made in-house, before shipping them into the Port of Long Beach.

This worked for a while, and Kaizo carried on selling vehicles to the public. Cars it had sold were often noticed cruising around on Southern California highways, where driving an instantly recognizable Nissan silhouette is a great way to attract attention.

"The chassis can be registered as a kit car," one poster wrote, referencing Kaizo, on the GTRLife internet forum in early 2008, "but getting a smog exemption [sic] sticker in California is the tricky part... I guess if you really want an R34 in the States, this would be the best way of going at it." Another poster on the same forum claimed that Kaizo had quoted them $80,000 for an R34 GT-R—just the shell, no driveline.

Once again, the Skyline came into contact with Hollywood. Around the same time, Universal Studios contracted with Kaizo to provide Skyline GT-Rs for the third *Fast and the Furious* sequel. Alison personally delivered several vehicles to set, including his own personal GT-R, another GT-R he had already sold to Paul Walker, and a third one, in dramatic Bayside Blue paint, built to Walker's specifications. In particular, Walker had requested that every sticker on the car be removed. He chose several specific aftermarket parts to be installed, including new wheels, a new body kit, a new hood, a new suspension, and a new exhaust. He had the pedals and steering wheel swapped out, had a roll cage built, and he had an aftermarket seat fixed to his personal driving position. Last but not least, he had the rear seats removed, a new center screen installed, and the engine tuned to 550 hp. Kaizo still legally owned the car, and the actor already owned another, separate R34 GT-R, but for all intents and purposes, the Bayside car was Walker's. It became almost universally known as "the Paul Walker GT-R."

The movie, simply called *Fast & Furious*, was released in March of 2009. Widely panned by critics—a *Variety* writer called it "by far the weakest" of the franchise—it did feature the Kaizo Bayside car, which only served to elevate the legend. In one scene, Walker's character selects the car from a lineup as his personal project. It's followed by a montage of him installing parts and turning wrenches to bring the package together, then two extended chase scenes—one where Walker throws the GT-R into big drifts in traffic, and another in a mine shaft, where he weaves it around wooden support beams before jumping off a ramp to safety.

The movie made Bayside Blue R34s even more desirable than before, and that shone light on Kaizo. Magazines ran feature articles on the tiny garage in Costa Mesa that sourced the now-iconic car. (Physical copies or scans are difficult to find, but owners I spoke with paraphrased the headlines as, "Want an R34? Go to Kaizo.")

It was all a triumph for Alison and a boon for his business. Simultaneously, it was the worst thing that could have possibly happened. "He was saying they were kit cars," remembered Sean Morris, during one of our long interviews in the Toprank lobby. "But then he had them in *Fast & Furious*, and there's articles about it, and now you're rubbing the government's face in it."

Morris ran a series of blogs in 2009, backed by findings later revealed in a civil lawsuit, that documented the fall of Kaizo's house of cards. On June 4th, just three months after the film's release, federal agents from Immigration and Customs Enforcement swarmed Alison's business with search warrants. They took records, electronics, and three vehicles, including the Walker screen car.

By July, Kaizo's website was no longer online and JDM enthusiasts were warning one another that DMV offices in multiple states were reviewing records and scheduling inspections of suspect vehicles to ensure proper documentation. According to multiple sources who requested anonymity, this set off a frenzy, as GT-R owners across the country began moving their vehicles to distant locations. The movie had shined a very bright light into a dark corner.

Kaizo dissolved as a corporate entity on August 1st. By then, federal agents had visited owners of Kaizo GT-Rs in person to ask questions and take photographs documenting their vehicles. Some owners reported receiving letters from the Department of Justice directing them to surrender the cars or export them within 60 days.

In October of 2010, the government charged Alison with multiple federal crimes: smuggling; conspiracy to defraud the United States; violating the Clean Air Act; making false statements to an agent of the federal government in relation to a federal matter; and international money laundering. The conspiracy charge and false statements charge each carried a maximum penalty of five years in prison. The smuggling and laundering charges held a max of 20 years each.

The Clean Air Act part wasn't as cut and dried, as the Act doesn't specify punishment for violations outside a maximum fine for each instance. But given that the maximums are $45,268 for each noncompliant vehicle or engine, and given how doggedly the EPA had pursued Albert Mardikian, the gray-market conversion-shop owner, in the 1980s, it didn't look good.

Rather than risk federal trial, Alison plead guilty to all charges. Authorities raced to the press to emphasize the seriousness of his crimes. "While many car buffs scoff at enforcement of vehicle import laws—to be clear, these are not just technical violations," a Customs special agent told the *San Clemente Times* in 2010. He promised a heavy hand.

Four months later, Alison received a $1,000 fine and 24 months' probation.

AT FIRST, during the initial Customs raids and vehicle seizures, Sean Morris had publicly advocated for Alison and Kaizo. He pointed out inconsistencies in the language of the EPA's kit-car policy, arguing that if Kaizo was recognized as a manufacturer, then it was protected from certain importing laws.

"We appreciate it, big, bad, Kevlar-clad, gun-toting agents, going after car owners with [things] dangerous... as a speeding ticket on their record," he wrote on his blog in 2009. "We appreciate the use of your budget in these times of 17% unemployment in California, and the inability of the California legislature to even keep the Department of Motor Vehicles open on Fridays."

Later, though, Morris changed his tune. After a couple of years in Customs custody, the Bayside car from *Fast & Furious* ended up in the hands of Manheim, the automotive auction company. Ahead of a live sale in San Diego, Manheim hired Morris as an expert to inspect the car and verify its origins. During the inspection, a team of lawyers watched his every move. Morris knew exactly where to look first—when he checked the VIN plate under the hood against the serial number stamped into the engine, the digits matched. It was the same pair that had been mated to the car back at the factory in Japan, when the car was first built. In other words, there was practically no difference whatsoever between the "Kaizo" GT-R and the original Nissan.

"It really wasn't a kit car," Morris said. "It was disassembled specifically for the purpose of evading the importation laws."

The "Walker" movie GT-R continued to have a crazy ride. Forced to leave the country, it found a buyer in Germany, where it stayed for roughly a decade. A museum called Munich Motorworld kept the car on display until a company called GT-A International announced that it would sell the car at auction. After more than a year passed with no sale, the fine-art auction house Bonhams included the car in a week-long sale in Spring of 2023. After days of watching bidders outdo each other, an auctioneer dropped the hammer. The nearly $1.36-million final price was touted as a "new auction world-record" for a Skyline GT-R. The previous record-holder, an R34 sold in 2022, had brought in more than $577,000, less than half as much.

One-point-three million dollars for a GT-R. And an interesting record-holder, to boot, given that Morris calls the driving experience of this particular car "nothing special." There are more powerful Skyline GT-Rs, faster ones, ones more decorated on the racetrack. But none are more closely associated with Walker and his movie franchise, and that—plus a litigious backstory—apparently counts for a lot.

Here's the funny thing: The previous record-holder was also a Paul Walker car, also Bayside Blue. The actor drove it to help promote earlier *Fast & Furious* movies. It's the one Craig Lieberman lent him in the early days of the franchise. And it has its own litigious history: It's a MotoRex car.

CHAPTER 10

After leaving HKS and putting Fujisan in my rearview, I drove back onto the Tōmei Expressway, heading east toward Atsugi around 40 miles outside of downtown Tokyo. Atsugi is moderate in size, home to about 225,000 residents, a company town headlined by the Nissan Technical Center. Nissan's global headquarters in Yokohama is where decisions are made and passed down, but the NTC in Atsugi is where many of the company's products are actually developed.

Nissan has always enjoyed a breadth of engineering talent. In fact, it has sometimes caused trouble at the company. In their 2022 book *Boundless*, authors Nick Kostov and Sean McLain described the brand in the late 1990s as "more focused on building cars its engineers found interesting and impressive... than those that an average consumer wanted."

This was true, but the dedication and passion of the company's development team was also one of its greatest strengths. One of the most famous examples is Hiroshi Tamura, the young hotshot who had been bored with his first job as a Nissan materials researcher and left for a career at the company's Autech subsidiary. At Autech, Tamura helped launch one-off specialty performance cars before returning to work in Nissan's marketing department. But that bored him, too. He resented the way marketing employees talked dismissively of the customer and boasted of knowing what was best for them. On a whim, looking for hands-on experience with buyers, he asked to join the sales team at a Nissan dealership. In just two short years, he became the company's top salesman in Japan. When Tamura returned to the home office in the late 1990s, he was named product planner for the R33 GT-R, going on to then serve the R34 in the same capacity.

All of that paled, however, in light of the man's home life: Tamura *was* a GT-R customer. Years into his career, he remained as much of a diehard as anyone within Nissan, and he had chased his own version of the lifestyle for a decade, simply because he loved it. He still owned the 1989 R32 he bought new, the one that had required the big bank loan. The car had become a long-term project, not that the average commuter could tell. Where most tuned GT-Rs of the period shouted their intentions, all massive wings and scoops, Tamura's R32 was relatively demure. It looked nearly stock.

This was a car of small but significant touches. Tamura had switched out the stock five-speed manual transmission for a Getrag six-speed manual, and he had installed a flat tray beneath the body to smooth airflow. Crucially, he had added an active differential that could shuttle drive torque from one rear wheel to another based on which needed traction the most. The only eye-catching exterior change was a gleaming silver sticker on each bumper, front and rear. Each decal was cocked at an angle and lettered with those infamous words: Mid Night.

The man who had once been strapped to a hospital bed had made good on his word: He had no interest in the parts of life that don't make a difference, and he had no time to waste. Especially on certain highways.

AFTER TWO HOURS on the road, I arrived at the NTC campus in Atsugi, weary from a long day of travel. As a result—or at least, I'd like to blame it on that—I pulled into the wrong entrance, trying in vain to explain to corporate security just who this *gaijin* in the GT-R was, as well as where I was headed and who I was supposed to meet. After an extensive back and forth, we finally established that I was a legitimate invited guest, just in the wrong spot. I turned around and circled back to the other end of the property, made it through another set of gates, and followed directions to the guest parking lot. And that's when I saw it in the mirror.

Even at a distance, I recognized the low-slung profile. The gunmetal grey paint. As I drove on, leading the way, we followed weaving roads around the *sakura*-lined NTC campus, eventually passing through a tunnel. The car behind me accelerated, closing the gap, and I could just make out in my mirrors the slightest hint of an aftermarket hood and bumper. The car looked ready to pounce.

I turned into a visitor's area and drove to the top level of a parking garage. A new Nissan Z sports car sat there, the modern successor to company icons like the 240Z and 300ZX, parked and waiting for us. Even static, the Z had definite chemistry with the GT-R I was driving, but it paled in comparison with the car that followed me in.

It was an R32. But not just any R32—this was the GT-R of Hiroshi Tamura himself, the famous one, painstakingly modded and evolved over the past three decades. I parked my borrowed R35 alongside for a photo shoot, GT-Rs new and old, sakura in bloom all around, and I pored over the older machine. It had been outfitted with massive brake discs and the wheels from an R34 GT-R. The front bumper wore the logo of the tuning company Pent Roof, which borrowed its name from the pitched-style combustion chamber in the RB26, its prominent sticker wrapping around the car's front lip. Almost like a warning.

Two parts, however, outshone the rest. They were, of course, those crooked silver stickers: one on the front bumper, faded from years of sun and speed, and another on the rear, more legible.

"Mid Night Car Speciall," each read, with two Ls. The real deal.

Tamura-san appeared, bounding over on his toes from a corner of the garage, having seemingly sprung from the cherry blossoms. He was rail-thin, with a taut face and a warm smile, in a tailored and denim-colored wool suit, a green tie, and color-coordinated green leather Negroni driving sneakers. Impeccably dressed as always. I marveled that someone could pull that look off, but with the confidence of a rockstar, he did.

We said hello, and casually, he dropped a question: "Do you want to drive?" And then, almost unbelievably, he was offering me a key, the key to his personal car, while smiling. But I had an answer ready: I was in Japan to research, to observe and learn. And once-in-a-lifetime opportunity or no, I absolutely did not want to drive a priceless artifact on unfamiliar streets.

I thanked Tamura-san profusely and declined as politely as possible. Secretly, I wondered whether I would regret the decision later that day, or in a week or a year. (I'm relatively certain I will at some point.)

My begging off didn't seem to offend Tamura-san too severely: He offered to take me on a ride. I opened the passenger door and dropped into the left-side seat. Immediately it became clear that there is almost nothing normal about this GT-R. The glove box in front of me hung open, but instead of an empty storage compartment, it held a collection of gauges. Four white-faced dials with green GReddy branding stared back at me, built into the glove box to keep an eye on the internals: engine temp, oil temp, water temp and turbo boost. This is about to get serious, I thought. I buckled up. The seats were fitted with five-point harness seatbelts that had to be pulled around both hips and over your shoulders to latch, connecting in a locking mechanism near your belly button. Belts of this type are normally reserved for hard-core race cars—well, race cars, or the personal pride and joy of a Nissan executive.

IN THE EARLY years when Tamura first bought this GT-R, the Japanese car scene experienced rapid transformation. Tuning was hot, and the streets were flooded with homegrown sports cars customized into fire-breathing supercars. But the foundation on which this culture was built began to crack. Nissan had long been less financially stable than its rivals, and the fast and loose economy of the 1980s was gone. Japan's massive financial success had been revealed to be a bubble, driven by overvalued real estate and easy credit. The nation had also painted itself into a corner by carrying a national debt 2.5 times its gross domestic product, a relatively massive offset. (The U.S. national debt historically hovers around 1.05 times its GDP.)

Japan's stock market, the Nikkei 225, lost 46-percent of its value in less than a year. Nearly 150 years after Commodore Perry, the country's once self-sufficient society had become almost completely dependent on imported goods, paying for them with export revenue. When those markets dried up, Japan was left completely exposed.

At the same time, Racing Team Mid Night was facing its own troubles. Though born in the underground, Mid Night had become wildly popular with the public. The undisputed top team on the streets, they also conducted sanctioned high-speed runs at Yatabe, stress-testing various tunes and aftermarket parts. (One Mazda RX-7 allegedly owned by a Mid Night member sported gauges built into the glove-box so passengers could easily transcribe speed and engine performance during testing.) While its drivers remained largely unknown, their faces hidden under helmets, Mid Night's cars became stars all their own. The 300-kph milestone, about 186 mph, had once taken intense grit to surpass. But now Mid Night cars were blowing by it with ease. Some GT-Rs surpassed 320 kph—198 mph.

On the street, up-and-comers roamed around looking for Mid Night members to challenge. Taking a victory against a Mid Night driver could do wonders for a reputation. Actually joining the team was no longer as appealing as it had been in the beginning—most potentials would either balk at the year-or-more waiting period, or find the strict hierarchy unnecessarily old-school. Some tried the easy route, printing their own copies of the vaunted Mid Night stickers and windshield banners. When the club officially copyrighted the design and promised to shun anyone caught in violation, the wannabes simply created teams with similar names.

Mid Night was coming under attack. Its original group of members was also aging out of the risks of high-speed night racing. The ones without families and children were concerned for their careers; a public arrest would have been humiliating for a rising executive. Amid economic uncertainty, they were being asked to race against tuned supercars that grew more powerful with every passing day, and against drivers that were extremely motivated to make a name or themselves. Drifting was rising in popularity, anyway, they figured, and it seemed ready to take the baton and move Japanese tuning culture forward.

For years, one story circulated as the real reason behind Mid Night's demise. It was whispered across garages and meets, shared in internet forums, even printed in some magazines. It held that, one night in the late 1990s, club members entered into a race with bosozoku on motorcycles. They flew down the Wangan for some distance, carrying on wheel-to-wheel at breakneck speed, then suddenly came upon stopped traffic. As the story goes, there was nothing the racers could do to stop, and so the drivers crashed. Several innocent civilians were rushed to the hospital. The bikers fell and were killed. Because they had broken their promise to never endanger the public, the legend goes, the club's members agreed to immediately disband.

Of course, there are several details that don't add up. Mid Night's strict moral code was well known—after all, it was that code that had separated them from minor teams and loosely organized speed hooligans and led to the group's notoriety. Among the team's rules was a rigid adherence to club procedure when organizing races—they had a way they went about doing things, and spontaneous speeding in order to show up some bikers was not it. Moreover, Mid Night members would never have participated in a race against bosozoku, as it would have given the police and the public more reason to lump the two groups together.

Finally, and perhaps most important, for a story that centers on a massive and grisly accident on a public highway, the tale is remarkably difficult to verify. It's always passed along without specifying where the race occurred, or when, or which cars were involved. Most sources say the crash took place in 1999, but according to a YouTube sleuth account, an anonymous Mid Night member referenced a similar story during an interview in 1995. Like so much of the group's history, its fade from prominence is shrouded in half-truth, part-truth, or obvious no-truth—and perhaps all of that on purpose, to keep people guessing.

Most likely, the era in which Racing Team Mid Night had grown and blossomed had simply passed. Cars were getting faster and faster. Drivers were getting more daring. Original members were maturing out of street racing. From day one, the club existed under a pressure that it couldn't withstand forever. Perhaps, rather than wait for something terrible to happen, they simply let the public imagine that it already had. The legend was just getting started, but the reality —and a chapter of Japan's underground car culture—had come to an end.

OF COURSE, my first meeting with Tamura had actually come in the United States. He had traveled stateside about a month before my visit to Japan, when he attended that Toprank meet with the cruise to the brewery. The Texas drag-racing competition he had visited just before, TX2K, was held outside of Houston.

Drag racing is known for its American roots. Muscle cars have traditionally dominated that scene, Detroit names like Mustang, Camaro, and Challenger. At TX2K, however, two cars are ubiquitous: Lamborghini Gallardos, sold from 2004 to 2014, and R35 GT-Rs. Each machine, though high-priced when new, can now be bought used for relatively cheap, and their stout frames can handle tremendous amounts of force. The Gallardo and the R35 are also blessed with engines that can readily accept tuning and lots of turbocharger boost. (The Lamborghini didn't come with factory turbos, though the Nissan did.) Long story short, it's become normal for the TX2K championship to come down to contenders boasting 2,000 hp or more.

Tamura went to Texas with a team from Toprank, including Sean

Morris, Brian Jannusch, and Yaska Kosuge. After the competition, the group returned to California and that cruise. At the brewery that night, Tamura had thanked the group for coming, giving a short speech about the virtues of the close-knit GT-R community and why the relationship means so much to him. People stayed for an hour afterward to chat and take selfies with Mr. GT-R; one attendee produced a three-foot long aluminum Nismo strut brace and asked Tamura to sign it.

The meet was not an anomaly. Tamura and Toprank have organized many like it, giving U.S. enthusiasts an opportunity to meet one of their heroes, and giving Tamura a chance to connect with a side of GT-R culture he couldn't possibly see from behind a desk in Atsugi. "I love that guy," said Larry Chen, the motorsport photographer. When Chen first bought his red R32 GT-R, he had attended a similar Toprank event, asking the cult hero to sign his car's center console. Years later, now that Chen is the hired shooter at factory launch events for the Nissan Z and R35, he and Tamura have worked together somewhat regularly, but the shine hasn't worn off. Chen told me that he looks forward to Tamura's infectious attitude. "He's like a cartoon character," he said, smiling.

In Japan that day, I asked Tamura why it's important for him to take trips like the one to Texas, a journey with little obvious value for his role as the GT-R brand's product planner. He responded by listing nearly two dozen other countries he has visited as part of a worldwide fact-finding mission.

What was he searching for?

"My teammates' smiles," he said. "Customers' smiles. Everybody's smile. And your smile, your energy. People cannot keep up a smile sometimes. They are upset or crying or sad, and it's okay. But in everything, people always have a biorhythm. That's life. It's about Ryan and me. Our relationship is important. Larry Chen, Dai Yoshihara—my friends! You were there, so you know that. That's my happy place for a life."

What the GT-R provides for owners, he says, through the car itself but also through a sense of belonging to a wider culture, is a pleasurable life.

"Too much we focus on a gadget or product. But it doesn't matter. Someday the product will not exist, it will be finished. Over!" He slammed a fist into his hand. "Our memory, or story, is always keeping your energy or heart. It's an important message for life. Cars are not what matter. To the customer, his heart, his young heart, is keeping inspiration to spend a life doing something. If he selects GT-R or Z, I'm super happy. That's my goal."

NISSAN HAD BUILT the groundbreaking R32 Skyline GT-R in 1989 on the back of a boom economy, one that allowed its research and development department near-limitless budgets. But as the 1990s ticked on, it became clear that market wouldn't last. The money had evaporated.

The R33, the R32's successor, had suffered. The newest Skyline had been made to share a platform with the company's cushy Laurel sedan "to save money," as the Australian magazine *Wheels* said in 1995. The model's "tortuous evolution," the magazine wrote, "hints at the turmoil within Nissan, which is still reeling from the collapse in sales and profits following the bursting of Japan's bubble economy. And its dimensions—longer, wider, taller, and heavier than the old car—are not clever in a business where, increasingly, smart car companies are finding less is more."

By 1997, things had gone from bad to worse, and it wasn't just Japan. Across nearly all of Asia, developing countries had spent the latter half of the 20th century receiving cash infusions based on foreign investment. Those infusions allowed those countries to build toward middle-income lifestyles for their populations, but the growth was based on valuations that turned out to be bogus. The data that had shown Japan's market cap as higher than that of even the United States turned out to be a façade.

The purse strings of those Asian countries were typically

controlled by a select few people at the top, politicians or bureaucrats who had spent wildly during the boom while neglecting to set up effective regulation. In some cases, that regulation was virtually nonexistent. In fact, it had been government over-involvement in the dealings of some companies, particularly within the automotive industry, that had allowed for such quick growth and status inflation. Japan's Ministry of International Trade and Industry, or MITI, had essentially been in control of the economy since America had de-occupied the country in the 1950s. Propping up the auto sector behind the scenes in order to grow exports, MITI was a key factor in Nissan's explosive growth; a Toyota executive once claimed that the Japanese government had, through MITI, funded 100-percent of the development of its famous Prius hybrid system. That claim was quickly shot down by higher-ups, but it furthered the perception that Japan's government was choosing the country's winners and losers in business, and that the nation's automakers would have trouble standing on their own in tough times.

Sure enough, when things started to go south, there was no safety net. When the Japanese economy crumbled, Nissan was left exposed and in serious trouble. The company's balance sheet showed $22 billion in debt by 1998. (By contrast, Ford Motor Company had a similar amount in cash on hand at the time.)

Nissan had spent decades expanding its production capacity, but the economy had forced its factories to slow. Economists call this a "growth recession." And for every day those factories sat idle, the company lost money. In the rest of the world, other major automakers were operating at around 75-percent to 80-percent of capacity; Nissan could only afford to run at 53-percent. To save money, executives had gone so far as to shut off the air-conditioning and the elevators at the Yokohama headquarters.

The Japanese government recognized the problem and tried to encourage growth. Throughout most of the 1990s, in an attempt to spur consumer spending, interest rates across the country were reduced to zero. Still, it wasn't enough. The growth recession was flirting with becoming a growth depression, and the state of the economy created, in the words of the Pulitzer Prize-winning economist Paul Krugman, a "sense of fatalism and hopelessness" among the population.

The hits kept coming. Nissan tried to raise money from Japanese banks, but in 1998, the American credit-rating agency Moody's downgraded the company's score, making credit more difficult and expensive to obtain. After much effort, Nissan was able to secure 100 billion yen, or about $817 million, from state-run banks. Management tried to spin the deal as typical of loans arranged by Toyota and Honda. But the truth was, Nissan was far more desperate.

Executives put the loan to use immediately. Nissan couldn't afford to use the money to chip away at its debt, as rival automakers had. Instead, the company needed the 100 billion yen to keep its production lines moving at all. Meanwhile, over the past two decades, the company's share of the auto market in Japan had fallen from 33-percent to 20-percent. In the same period of time, Toyota's share had risen from 39-percent to 41-percent.

"Japan was in poor shape," as one analyst put it at the time, "and Nissan was the poorest."

TAMURA HAS NOT ALWAYS HAD A "SUPER happy" life. When he was only 13 years old, his younger brother passed away unexpectedly. The loss crushed his family's spirits. Tamura struggled to watch his parents cope with the pain. His mother became a recluse; she stopped working and could not bring herself to care for Tamura and his surviving brother, then just 5 years old. It fell to Tamura's father to provide everything, and the stress got to him. When Tamura's father was home, the two butted heads. When the father was out, the sons were left virtually unsupervised. Tamura declined to go into detail, but said that around this time he began to get into trouble.

He does not place blame directly on his parents for the motorcycle accident he suffered as a sophomore in high school, the one that nearly killed him. But he does believe that blasting around on a bike at breakneck speeds was a subconscious act of attention-seeking. A recklessness, which he admits was born of his own unprocessed grief, that set him on the path to staring at the ceiling of a hospital room for six weeks.

A second heartbreak arrived after Tamura reached adulthood. The loss of his brother and his brush with death on two wheels had molded him into a young man determined to live his passion, to not waste a minute of life. He enjoyed music; he enjoyed food; he graduated from Tokyo Metropolitan University with an engineering degree. But when he and his then-wife welcomed their first child, Tamura was forced to watch as his baby fought for her life in the intensive-care unit. It was not enough. When she passed, he said, he felt broken.

"The tears dropped so big," he told me. "It was the first time and last time I've cried like this. Like a super-cry."

That, more than the loss of his brother, more than nearly dying, is what set Tamura on his current path. There would be no more compromises, he decided, no more wasted time. He vowed to spend his life at "peak power, peak energy," as much as possible. He imagined what his daughter would want him to do, what she would tell him if she could.

"I realized I have to live my life," he told me. "She would have wanted to say, 'I cannot make time on this planet. But you get to own your story. You get to own your stage.'"

BY THE TIME the R34 came around, with Tamura a top manager on the project, Nissan was awash in red ink. The company rolled out the final version of its second-generation Skyline GT-R in January of 1999, just weeks after reporting a staggering $22 billion in debt. Nissan was still the second-largest car manufacturer in Japan, and perhaps the most beloved, but without cash on hand, its executives were aggressively lobbying the government to flood banks with funds that could be lent out at favorable rates. This money, they insisted, would be used not for debt, but to simply keep the company going. The launch of a low-margin, high-ticket performance car was hardly top priority.

But at least the company had gone ahead with it. As a result of the tightening economy, the GT-R's main rivals—the Toyota Supra, the Mazda RX-7, the Honda NSX, the Mitsubishi 3000GT—had been left to rot, sitting in showrooms with no significant updates, or killed entirely. For Nissan, plowing ahead with a new Skyline was part heart, part staying the course. Like the R33, the R34 shared much under the skin with the R32. Using roughly the same equipment over more than a decade of production helped amortize R&D cost, and ending the GT-R early had never been an option. What management couldn't do was throw money at the car left and right.

The R34's engine was a prime example. Nissan engineers had originally planned to give the third modern GT-R an all-new powerplant, in the form of a twin-turbocharged V6. Since the days of the Hakosuka, GT-Rs had worn their six cylinders in a straight, or inline, configuration. Inline-sixes sound good and offer remarkably smooth power and torque, but they tend to be long and heavy. V6 engines feature the same cylinder count in a "vee" shape, with three cylinders on each side of the vee. They rarely sound as nice as an inline-six and their geometry produces slightly more vibration, but the benefits—namely the layout's compact size—are usually worth it.

With no other changes, switching to a V-6 would have given the GT-R road car a lighter driveline, a lower center of gravity, and better weight distribution from front to rear. Nissan had tested the VQ in R34 prototypes extensively, and engineers were happy with the combination. The catch was, tooling up to build a new GT-R engine would have meant constructing an entirely new production line at the company's factories. In a cash-strapped time, the discussion was a non-starter, and the idea was shelved.

Unfazed, the engineers laid out the R34 with their usual ambition. Resigned to beefing up the trusty RB26, they gave it a pair of new Garrett turbochargers, the shaft of each turbo mounted in ball bearings for quicker spin-up and a 50-percent reduction in friction over the turbos on the R33. That change improved low-end torque and helped reduce turbo lag, i.e., the delay between throttle input and engine response. A new intercooler helped reduce the temperature of the air the engine breathed, aiding power, and a host of small improvements helped reduce emissions. All told, the R34's RB could respond quicker and run faster and cooler for longer stretches of time. And they weren't done yet.

Compared to the R33, a car known for its stability, the R34 was shorter. It was wider. The new proportions made it look squat and ready to pounce. It resembled the kaido racers that the hashiriya had used to slice up mountain roads in the 1980s. The shape was diabolical, purposeful, and clean, the best of R32 and R33 mashed together into something utterly and wonderfully new.

Trapped in dire financial straits, as its main competitors dropped out one by one, Nissan had just made its flagship sports car faster, lighter and more modern. Special editions followed in quick succession, including the more aerodynamic V-Spec, the carbon-fiber-hooded V-Spec II, the loaded and luxurious M-Spec, the race-inspired N1, and the one that combined them all together, the Nür. The R34 GT-R had the shortest lifespan of the second-gen Skyline GT-Rs, at scarcely more than three years. It also had the lowest production count of the three, sapped by weakening demand, slightly more than 11,500 units.

For U.S. enthusiasts, salivating over copies of *Option* magazine and fantasizing about merely seeing the car in person, none of that mattered. The R34 GT-R was alive and well, a breathtaking return to form. They would wait for it as long as they had to.

WE WERE CRUISING in his souped-up R32, me riding shotgun on the left and Tamura rowing through the gears on the right, when he turned and asked if I was familiar with "Stand Alone Complex." This is a popular spin-off television series based on the *Ghost in the Shell* franchise. (In addition to food, music, love and speed, anime is one of Tamura's obsessions.)

I am not familiar with it, I said, partly because it was half-true but mostly because I wanted him to explain in detail. So as the car growled back toward the entrance to the tunnel we had passed through earlier, he explained.

Stand Alone Complex, he said, is set in a futuristic time where humans have learned to incorporate mechanical and robotic parts into their bodies, blurring the line between flesh and machine. Many people walk around as a kind of human-robot cyborg because life is simply easier that way. They forget, Tamura said, what it even means to be human.

Of course, he explained, there is actually a clear difference. Even if the body is a hybrid organism, humans possess an intangible energy or spirit, one that can be stirred, creating emotion and passion and anger. Basically, we each have a soul that makes us who we are. In some ways, it's the only thing we truly own.

Tamura finished his explanation just as we arrived at the tunnel entrance. "Don't forget your roots," he said. "People is the most important thing. We are not machines. We are more emotional, and that is not a bad thing. People's relations, or people's smiles, that's my energy."

With that, he stabbed the accelerator with his right foot, pinning it to the floor. The car leapt forward into the tunnel, engine scream bouncing off the walls. He stayed in the throttle, lifting only to throw the shift lever up a gear. In that moment, the turbocharger's wastegate spit a visceral whooshing sound, like a hundred soda bottles opening at once. An instant later, he was back into it, the car wiggling beneath me, working to keep everything in line.

The engine built its furious roar again, shouting 9,000 rpm up against the tunnel until, finally, we were through to the other side, the noise spreading into open sky.

I looked to my right, at the driver's seat. Tamura was smiling wide, not quite giggling but definitely pleased, a man squarely in his comfort zone. He had probably performed the same feat dozens, if not hundreds of times before, for other passengers. I could see why—it works. I knew for a fact that, at least in that moment, I was no robot.

After the tunnel stunt, we left the gates of the NTC campus and headed onto the narrow roads of Atsugi. On those same streets where I had felt claustrophobic in the wider R35, its more modern body a few centimeters from curbs and walls at all times, the R32 felt perfectly sized.

We breezed through twists and blind corners. Inside the car, a lot was happening, but Tamura was not himself overly dramatic. He would smile or chuckle, but he did not white-knuckle the car down those roads. Instead, I noticed, he had a delicate touch at the wheel, pinching thumb and forefinger together to communicate with the car. Picture holding a steering wheel at 9 o'clock and 3 o'clock, not 10 and 2 as most of us have been taught, and keeping your pinky finger extended as if sipping a cup of tea. It is amazing to watch someone drive a car in anger, yet appear utterly unbothered.

Tamura's modifications, he said, increased the R32's weight from 1430 kilograms to 1530, but that's still 200 kilos lighter than an R35. He likes to hear the RB26's famous noises, he offered, staying within the engine's playful zone, where it feels the most lively, for maximum fun. We didn't always go fast, but the experience was theatrical. He seemed to especially like accelerating through turns, feeling the G-forces pull us from one side to the other, then letting off the throttle on straightaways, listening to the turbo flutter and the exhaust burble as we trotted along.

It was a relaxed, nonchalant way to pilot 600 horses over constricted pavement. But as I watched him navigate, I realized what I was seeing. It was that famous three-fingered approach, the delicate technique that allows for subtle adjustments, the one developed by Hiroyoshi Kato during testing at the Nürburgring.

I've ridden with professional racecar drivers who have a similar ease, emphasizing smoothness in input to gain speed in the corners. But watching Tamura at the wheel was more like watching someone read braille. His fingers were like sponges, collecting the tiniest movements, downloading information sent from road to steering wheel, then guiding the car from there.

A finely-tuned and extremely powerful car, not used to beat a road into submission. It was more like a form of self-expression. Even in the way he controlled it, Tamura made the GT-R his own.

CHAPTER 11

"There was one point, early on when I first started taking pictures, maybe in 2009. I was pushing and doing what I could but not really going anywhere. I wasn't putting as much effort into it as I needed to. And photography is just a hard industry to break into. There was a day where I thought to myself, 'I need to buck up and push hard, because there's an important date coming.'

"I made a decision to quit racing, and to quit autocross. I had a team meeting with all the people in my car crew, and I told them—I remember it very specifically—I told them, 'Look, I'm going to quit racing and I'm going to focus on taking pictures.' Because my goal was to be able to afford an R32 GT-R in 2014, when they became legal. And I'm glad I did." – **Larry Chen**

IN 2004, JDM culture in the U.S. was humming. The street-racing scene had been well-documented: *Gran Turismo* was the best-selling PlayStation game of all time; Rockstar Games had found a runaway hit with *Midnight Club* and *Midnight Club II*; and *The Fast And The Furious* had spawned a sequel, the two movies grossing more than $280 million combined. English-language magazines like *Super Street* and even *Motor Trend* now covered tuning in their pages. You no longer had to scour Torrance supermarkets for old copies of *Option* in order to follow the Japanese underground.

Racing organizers in both Japan and America caught onto the trend. In the former, the GT Association wanted to expand its Japanese Grand Touring Cars series, the successor to the JTCC series that the R32 GT-R had ruled a decade earlier. After a failed attempt to stage events in China, officials looked to America, with its many racetracks and its massive fanbase inhaling any scrap of JDM culture it could get its hands on.

The GT Association partnered with D1 GP, the Japanese drifting series, and began to plan a joint weekend event in the U.S. California was the obvious target, so event organizers struck a deal with California Speedway, an oval arena and infield course that regularly hosted NASCAR and IndyCar events. Crucially, the track sat in Fontana, a desert town at the base of a mountain range and roughly 55 miles east of Los Angeles—close enough to draw JDM enthusiasts from the city, but far enough to keep admission affordable.

JGTC air-freighted 10 of its premier competition cars across the Pacific. There were no GT-Rs (the R34 racing program had already come to a close), but fans were treated to a host of Supras, NSXs, and Nissan 350Zs, all with aggressive body kits and highly tuned engines. Those machines raced on both Saturday and Sunday, and at night, when their action was done, the D1 GP cars took to the track in a battle-style drifting demonstration that pitted a team of eight Japanese drivers against a team of eight American ones. The weekend drew an estimated 45,000 people.

Among the screaming fans was a 19-year-old kid from Santa Monica. Larry Chen had never been to Japan or seen an organized drift event in person, but he and his friends didn't need an introduction to the sport. Drivers like Ken Numora, Manabu Urito, Yasuyuki Kazama, and Keiichi Tsuchiya, a.k.a. the Drift King, were household names for Chen's crew, as famous and recognizable as any movie star. Particularly Urito and Tsuchiya, both of whom Chen had autograph his ticket. He still has it. "These people," he told me, "were our idols."

As a teenager, Chen found community in cars before he was old enough to drive. He never followed what he called "stick and ball sports," but something about motorsport naturally clicked. He and his friends would share drifting DVDs they had shipped in from Japan, and they'd go to each other's homes to watch dash-cam footage of Tokyo street racers they had illegally downloaded from the internet. They flocked to the local theater to see *The Fast and the Furious* on opening night, then ran home after to trick out their R/C cars. Chen printed out an image of an R34 GT-R on the family computer and taped it to his wall for inspiration. When it came time to submit his career ambition after graduating from high school, he wrote that his greatest goal in life was to own a 1999 Nissan Skyline GT-R in Bayside Blue.

Old episodes of the Japanese television program *Best Motoring* were a favorite in Chen's group, so the friends were well aware of the JGTC faces set to drive in Fontana. On the big day, Chen hopped into his modified five-speed Nissan Maxima and made the two-hour drive to the track in a caravan with his crew. Each person drove their own car so they could each enter the timed autocross competition held in the speedway's parking lot. (Chen's Maxima was so highly tuned that, when he drove around a corner too quickly, it would lift one wheel off the pavement. "I just pretended it was a Skyline," he said.)

It was a gorgeous California winter day, highs in the low 70s. The racing action went off as promised, and as the sun fell, the stage was set for a tranquil evening of ridiculous horsepower and wild driving. When fans packed the stands to watch the drift demo, it quickly became clear that Chen and his friends had terrible seats.

"Every time the cars would come around, everyone would stand up," he said. "And I would have to stand up too, because everybody was so stoked. People were yelling, 'Sit down!' but nobody did, because they [all] wanted a better view. This was such a big deal—it was the first time they were able to see these cars. Everyone was flipping out."

A budding photographer, Chen had strained to lift his digital camera above the crowd and capture clear photos. Digital cameras were not what they are today, and his 2-megapixel shots were less than inspiring. When he saw professional photographers maneuver right up against the track, shooting between holes cut into the chain-link fence, he vowed to himself that he would one day be down there with them. After the event, he scratched together $1,000 to buy his first DSLR camera, a Canon Rebel XT, and he began to take shooting seriously.

THE ONLY THING that saved Nissan was another car company.

All over the world, merger fever had struck the automotive industry. Ford had purchased Land Rover and Volvo, General Motors had partnered with Toyota, and Chrysler had combined with Mercedes-Benz. Still, at Nissan, the concept was met with trepidation. The Japanese are known for a national identity centered on pride and cohesion, born from banding together during hard years, that enduring of the unendurable. The economy being strong on its own terms was deeply important to the population. Perhaps most critically, Japanese culture is not wired for bowing to international pressure.

Nissan executives winced at the idea of combining their firm, with its literal name of "Japanese industry," with an outsider, especially from a position of weakness. Nor was the relationship between GM and Toyota any balm; in that case, both companies were of similar size and capability, the partnership essentially one of equals. Nissan had little choice—it needed a savior, not a partner. Having exhausted all possible avenues, including high-interest bank loans and government bailouts, the company went in search of a rescuer.

Enter Renault. Like Nissan, the French brand had once been a point of pride in its homeland. Slow sales had plunged the marque to the brink of bankruptcy by the mid-1990s, but by the end of the decade, things were on the uptick. The correction had come courtesy of a brash young executive with sharply raked eyebrows and a reputation for slashing budgets. He was known as "Le Cost Killer."

This was Carlos Ghosn. Born in Brazil, raised in Lebanon,

educated in the U.K., and just 42 years old when hired to save Renault in 1996, the multi-lingual Ghosn considered himself a citizen of the world. He had been the financial whiz behind a turnaround at the Michelin tire company, and his restructuring of Renault had been widely hailed. For Nissan, one of the greatest appeals of partnering with the French manufacturer, a firm not known for strong engineering or global savvy, was the inclusion of Ghosn's services in the deal.

Not that Nissan had much choice in the matter. By now, the company was hanging by a thread. The calculating and ruthless Ghosn knew he could ask for the moon, and he did. What he really wanted was to stay at Renault, where he was mooted as next in line for CEO. In sealing the Nissan deal, Ghosn requested to maintain his position at Renault, effectively serving as a top executive at both companies simultaneously. He also asked for a salary of $1 million, paid solely from the Nissan side, as well as 10 million shares of the company, a stock grant worth some $30 million. Nissan executives were so flabbergasted by the request, they asked their counterparts at Renault if Le Cost Killer had added an extra zero by mistake.

No, the French representatives said. There was no mistake.

Back in Japan, executives took a deep breath and confirmed the deal. They were backed into a corner, and one of the sharpest weapons in the business was headed their way.

IN MODEST SUBURBAN NEIGHBORHOOD, in a quiet part of the San Gabriel Valley, I pulled into a steep and hidden driveway that pointed almost straight up. The incline twisted right and then left, eventually plateauing beside a single-story house and garage, where I was directed around the side to a second, larger garage. It looked like a professional race shop. Inside lay a spackled floor, high-strength lifts holding cars high in the air, and corners stuffed with tools. The walls were adorned with racing posters and iconic motorsport photos. In the drive sat a modded Toyota Supra, a Toyota 86 stuffed with HKS customizations, and a bright-orange Nissan 240Z that Larry Chen had bought on his 21st birthday for $3,000. Parked just in front of that was a car he had once promised himself: a GT-R, an R32, Red Pearl Metallic.

Chen came out to greet me, popping through a gate in a fence before shuffling us into the backyard and inviting me into his studio. Inside, beneath prints of some of his most famous images, two assistants stared intently into massive monitors, editing images and videos to be published on one of Chen's many outlets. They could have been working on media for his YouTube show on the Hagerty channel, for his personal Instagram page of more than 800,000 followers, or for one of the many motorsport clients that pay Chen to photograph their cars on the track.

The team, he said, was on a tight deadline—we were smack in the middle of the 2023 motorsport calendar, and there was still a lot of travel left in the year. On the day I visited, Chen had just returned from Japan on assignment for Hagerty, and his factory-commissioned photos commemorating the launch of a new color on the Nissan R35 GT-R were set to go public at any moment. There was a lot to do, but Chen seemed unbothered by the rush, waved it off. He was happy, he said, to sit and discuss the teenage obsession that had led to all this.

Like many Skyline fans, Chen had marked his calendar for 2014, the year when the R32 GT-R would become legal for U.S. import. But that year came and went for him, as it had for so many, with no Skyline brought home. Just another four seasons of Maximas.

The market was different then. Like every car in the Skyline Trinity, the R32 is desirable and pedigreed, but when the feds opened the gates, the bidding wars and the feverish transpacific shipping never really happened. Maybe it was as simple as the state of the American economy at the time, still rebuilding from the 2008 crash, or maybe, like Chen, everyone else who had grown up idolizing the Drift King simply didn't have the cash. For whatever reason, the demand wasn't there yet, and so 2014 brought none of the fervor or the clamoring that would come with the legalization of newer GT-R models.

What Chen did have at that point was a healthy career and A-list status in his industry. He had become a staple on the sidelines of Formula Drift events, easily recognized by the trademark bucket hat and neck gaiter that he wore to protect his skin from the sun. His photos were everywhere in the sport and second to none. By 2018, after four more years of hustling and near-constant travel, he had saved enough to land a GT-R, so he drove across town and paid Toprank a visit.

The company had plenty of stock. He wanted a red one, and there were three red R32s on the lot. "Back then the inventory was so good because it wasn't hot yet," he said. "I don't know why."

Chen picked his favorite, paying what he now considers a steal. It was easy-peasy: The car was in the U.S. legally and had already been certified for California emissions. He drove it home the same day.

GHOSN DID what he came to do. Once in the door at Nissan, the "citizen of the world" gathered his team and set about reviewing the books. They were looking for easy wins, places where no-brainer decisions to lower costs or sell off assets would ease the company's financial load. But none of them were prepared for what they discovered.

Nissan was mired in a host of bizarre business practices. For a start, the company had been giving its Japanese-market customers special favor: In addition to selling products like the Silvia and Skyline only in Japan, management had been delaying vehicle launches in other markets by as much as 18 months in order to give domestic buyers an advantage. Those two choices alone cost the company untold millions in sales, especially in the United States, then the world's largest car market. An unintended consequence was the distrust those moves had fostered between Nissan's U.S. operations and its Japanese headquarters. Resentful executives in America had gone so far as to withhold information, and even money, from the home office. The accountants found hundreds of millions of dollars in accumulated profits that should have returned to Japan but never did.

Ghosn also discovered something called *keiretsu*. Coined in World War II, the term is best translated as a long-term relationship between multiple partner companies. That relationship is structured like a pyramid, with one large corporation at the top and a supporting base of suppliers beneath. What makes a keiretsu unique is how the companies involved all hold shares in each other, effectively tying the whole group together and compelling it to do business with itself indefinitely. The large corporation effectively owns the suppliers as subsidiaries, calling the shots and dictating terms. In return, the suppliers can charge whatever prices they want without fear of competition.

If you're in the lower tier of a keiretsu, there's a good chance you'll get on well with the corporation at the top. And if you aren't in a keiretsu at all, there's virtually no chance of gaining new business with any company that is. Quality and profitability barely matter.

If all that sounds suspiciously close to a monopoly, rife with potential for price-fixing, that's probably because it is. Keiretsu is no longer widely practiced, not least because it's generally despised by economists and prone to the kind of outcome you'd expect. (An example from a 1989 report by the United States Department of Commerce: "a Japanese electronics firm declined to use a U.S.-built microprocessor in an application for a U.S customer, despite functional equivalence and a 66-percent lower price than the Japanese 'in-house' version." Another report from the same year named the keiretsu as two of the six primary barriers to U.S.-Japan trade.)

Regardless, the system had undeniable benefits. Many Japanese companies depended on its stability for survival, and the practice had helped lift Japanese industry from the rubble of a world war. The U.S. Department of Commerce even theorized that American and European companies "would probably engage in [keiretsu] themselves, if the laws and policies... permitted them to."

When the depth and complexity of Nissan's keiretsu came to light, Ghosn and his team were shocked. In total, the automaker owned stakes in 1,394 other companies. Nissan was locked into deals without the ability to negotiate pricing, and suppliers were charging exorbitantly, far above market average. Those ownership stakes were effectively cash, waiting to be tapped, as Nissan employees were taking the stairs in high-rise buildings and working in hot and humid offices to shave overhead. There was no question: the keiretsu needed to go.

Ghosn had never promised an easy transition, and he had warned employees early on that he wasn't concerned with "being culturally sensitive." That hit a nerve. The Japanese can be especially prideful regarding their ability to handle their own issues internally. Immigrants comprise just 1.9-percent of the country's population, far lower than the global average, and while that homogeneity has been framed by some as a painful cause of the 1990s growth recession, many Japanese view it as a strength.

In short, handing a proud national brand to a Brazilian-born Lebanese executive from a French company caused Nissan employees, and the Japanese at large, to feel on edge. They saw Ghosn and Renault as invaders. Conflictingly, there was a simultaneous understanding that the country was receiving a necessary dose of medicine, as it had under General MacArthur. The recession had been especially hard on the middle class, which had become accustomed to an abundant lifestyle and could feel that lifestyle slipping away. Even as the workers at Nissan factories and dealerships knew the likelihood of layoffs increased with each passing day, most believed Ghosn represented the right path for the good of the company. "Our cars are boring," one salesperson said at the time. "Who would want to buy them?"

Ghosn did commence layoffs. He closed factories, consolidated teams, and eliminated entire departments. Thousands of Nissan employees, and their counterparts at the company's suppliers, lost their jobs as a result. The keiretsu also got the axe: By the end of 2003, Ghosn and his team had sold off the company's positions in all but four of those 1,394 firms.

Slowly, steadily, things turned around. Cash began to flow. The air-conditioning and the elevators were turned on again. Factory volumes increased. Renault and Nissan began buying bulk raw materials together to reduce production costs. Dismantling the keiretsu played a large role in helping Nissan achieve Ghosn's targeted 20-percent cost reduction one full year ahead of schedule. And Ghosn authorized new investment in research and development, using it to create competitive new models.

The company needed a new source of pride, and he knew it. Nissan had built the R34 GT-R for only three years, 1999 to 2002, producing only 11,578 vehicles – the lowest volume by far of the three Skyline GT-R models. The next step would require a fresh start. Crafting a new GT-R from the same old bones was not an option—the result would have been hopelessly uncompetitive against modern rivals from BMW and Porsche.

Nissan, and Japan, needed a hero.

"THE FUNNY THING about the R32, R33, and R34—you know, the trio—is, if you're not a car person, they just look like regular cars."

That's Larry Chen. He was right, of course; that sentiment echoes often outside the Skyline community. One automotive journalist I know described driving an R32 GT-R as "kind of like a Buick Grand National, but slower."

That assessment can sound harsh, but then, that individual also drove a dead-stock, unmodified GT-R. And it makes sense. Unless you're willing to hammer on the engine and throw the gearbox through fast, dramatic shifts, the Skyline GT-R "trio" doesn't always live up to its reputation. Their power is modest by modern standards, and less impressive still if you drive the car at anything below full steam. It helps to remember that all three models were designed to work best at the highest possible speeds: agility on the world's toughest and fastest circuits; 180 mph on the Wangan. Handled sedately, they can feel heavy and leaden.

That fact is just fine with Chen. "I own GT-Rs not because of the way they perform," he said. "They're 1990s cars, they're a time capsule. And of course, with modern massaging, you can get good performance, but it's so much more about the aura, the look, the feeling it gives me about textures, and the smell, and—what's a good way to put it? It has this nostalgia to it. It was from an era where Nissan... money was no object, to build something so ahead of its time."

The Skyline GT-R might be the ultimate "if you know, you know" car. Chen and others repeatedly described to me how it can be a production even to visit a gas station with a Skyline, where the driver is sure to be stopped by other customers, or by random passers-by who screech into the parking lot and sprint up, eyes wide and jaws agape. Chen has even seen GT-R chasers block traffic to get a better look, or chase him for miles to hear the engine up close. They simply can't believe they're seeing the car on U.S. soil.

"I have faster cars," Chen said. "They don't give me the same feeling. You don't have to be driving fast to enjoy a GT-R... [it's even in] looking back after you park. It's even more special in America, because it's a novelty to have right-hand drive. It reminds you, every moment you pull up to a spotlight, shift your gears, make a turn—you're in something different and very special."

The R32 clearly owns a special place in his heart; the license plate on his red car reads "WOWKEWL." In many ways, Chen treats the car like a toy. In other ways, it literally is a toy. Chen has a strong relationship with Hot Wheels, and the toymaker replicated his exact GT-R as a diecast model, packaging it with an HKS R32 GT-R racecar. The photographs of each car on the cardboard backing were shot by Chen. (He gifted me one of those sets when I arrived, signing it.) Chen declined to reveal what he paid Toprank for his mostly stock car, but he recently had it appraised by an expert on a *Hagerty* YouTube video. The photographer's shock is visible in the scene—the announced value was around $85,000.

"Humans don't need music to survive," Chen said. "We don't need our favorite songs, our favorite artists. We can live fine without music. But we choose to enjoy this thing that's become such a big part of our lives. It's the same way with engine sounds. The RB is so distinctive. If you take out the noise, if you're driving a Skyline and don't hear the engine, you're essentially taking out half of the [sensation].

"When you're watching a film, if there's no sound, you're only watching 50-percent of it. Good luck trying to enjoy a movie without sound. It's the same with cars… there's so many different variations. There's smaller displacement, there's single-turbo, you can even look at going naturally aspirated. Keep it more on the stock side or add a big turbo, top-mount, bottom-mount, whatever. There's so many ways to build this thing. And there's no right or wrong way."

IN JANUARY OF 2020, Chen began to think about adding to his collection. While in Japan to photograph the Tokyo Auto Salon, he paid a visit to the Toprank booth to say hello to old friends. Yaska Kosuge, the Toprank CEO, was there, and talk quickly turned to cars on-hand. Chen had marked off the R32's 25-year date in his mind, but it was the R34 GT-R that had hung on his wall as a kid, that was listed on his high-school graduation card as his life's goal. He asked Kosuge what a lightly used model would cost.

Kosuge shrugged, pointing to an R34 in Toprank's show booth. "You can have that one for $50k." Chen thought it over. It was a lot of money for a nonlegal car he would have to store in Japan. Besides, it was white, it was a little scruffy, and the color that mattered was Bayside Blue. He knew that. He had written it down, that was what High School Larry wanted, and that guy was worth listening to. He passed.

White paint or no, R34 values shot up as the model's 25th birthday inched closer. Two years later, that slightly dinged-up $50,000 car from the Tokyo show was easily worth two, maybe three times as much. Chen thought about that car a lot, imagined visiting it in Japan. The idea, quite literally, haunted him. He began to pay more attention to the value of the Japanese yen. As the summer dragged on, the exchange rate to a dollar grew better and better: ¥1.40 to a dollar. One-forty-five. When it reached 1.48, Chen called Kosuge: "I think this is the time."

On a car uncommon to begin with, Bayside Blue is easily the most coveted color. Hoping to keep his cost down, Chen asked Kosuge to find an example with front and rear body damage. Still drivable, just not top-of-market. A few months later, the two spoke again. Toprank had located plenty of suitable cars, but Kosuge didn't feel right. He bristled at the idea of selling his friend a scarred GT-R. He told him of an undamaged, un-rusted, clean-title Bayside example they had available. Then he told him the price. It was high.

Chen had already let one R34 slip through his fingers. The white car would have been a financial stretch, and this one would be an even greater reach. He wrestled with the idea for more than a week. The same money would have purchased a brand-new R35 GT-R, with more power and zero-mile everything. Chen could have popped across town and driven one off a dealer's lot that day. If he went with the R34, he would pay more in the end, with storage and eventual shipping, and the car still wouldn't see the spackled garage for at least 18 months.

Chen closed his eyes for a moment. He imagined seeing the car in Japan for the first time. He thought of keys being dropped into his palm. He imagined his family piling inside, young kids squeezing into the back seats, then pointing an RB26 at Mount Fuji. He might never get another chance.

He sent Kosuge a text message: "Yes, just do it."

THE WEAPON in a suit was a national celebrity. Yes, Nissan's new COO had laid off more than 20,000 employees in his first three years. But the company was also profitable again, having pulled itself up from financial depths that once seemed inescapable. Ghosn was booked on Japanese talk shows and stopped on the street by fans. A bestselling manga series depicted his life story.

Ghosn was promoted to president of Nissan in 2000, and to CEO in 2001. In just two years, he had accomplished exactly what he had promised from the start, and he had landed what he had privately coveted, the top job at a major global automaker. His next move was to loosen the company's purse strings and allow engineers to begin work on a next-generation, show-stopping sports car.

Nissan unveiled the first R35 show car that October, at the 2001 Tokyo Motor Show. Though basically a full-size model, with no engine or interior, the effort gave an accurate portrait of things to come: smooth edges and dramatic hips, lines like nothing in Nissan showrooms. This GT-R, the company announced, would be the first aimed at global markets, which meant the GT-R was finally coming to the U.S. for real. Tamura posed for photos on the show floor, well-tailored as always.

Ghosn could be a notorious micro-manager, but to his credit, he chose to trust his people in the GT-R development process and stay out of the way. And while Tamura played an important role in the car's marketing, the R35 GT-R truly belonged to a talented engineer named Kazutoshi Mizuno.

Mizuno had worked on each of the Trinity Skyline GT-Rs; within the halls of Nissan R&D, he was widely seen as the obvious choice to spearhead a successor. In an unprecedented move, Ghosn gave him sweeping control, including complete sign-off on the final product and three separate job titles: program director, chief product specialist, and chief vehicle engineer. Bringing the R35 to market took six years, but in late 2007, the car met Japanese dealers. Half a year later, for the first time in its four-decade history, the GT-R badge made its official debut in the American market.

The car was an immediate sensation. It was still all-wheel drive. It wore a twin-turbo V-6, an engine layout that Nissan engineers had been pushing for more than a decade. With 480 hp and a slick six-speed dual-clutch automatic, it could hurtle to 60 mph from a stop in less than four seconds. Some media testers saw an astonishing 3.2 seconds. The electronically controlled driveline and trick "launch control" programming helped make the car a drag-racing superstar right out of the box.

Even more astonishing, in the United States, the GT-R retailed for just $69,850. At that price, nothing from Japan could touch it. It was faster off the line than competitive efforts from BMW and Mercedes-Benz, and cheaper and faster than comparable machines from Aston Martin and Ferrari. In terms of all-round ability, raw speed, and lack of compromise, only the Porsche 911 Turbo really matched up—in a *Car and Driver* test conducted when both cars were new, the Porsche accelerated to 60 mph in 3.5 seconds, but it cost a whopping $127,060 before options, roughly twice as much as the Nissan.

Mizuno and Tamura had landed a triumph. In England, their work was named Performance Car of the Year. It won the World Performance Car award in the U.S. and the Most Advanced Technology Award in Japan. Articles and videos from around the world touted the R35's supercar performance while trumpeting the everyperson pricing long a GT-R calling card.

Yes, it was expensive. But it wasn't Porsche expensive, and a middle-class person could find a way to own one. It was a faster, cheaper Porsche beater. It was the return to glory that Nissan, and Japan, desperately needed.

CHAPTER 12

Like Larry Chen, William Sudbrock had dreamed of owning a Skyline GT-R. Instead of picking up a camera, Sudbrock joined the military, where he found himself stationed in Okinawa in the early 2000s. Once there, he became immersed in the sports-car scene, not least because he was surrounded by vehicles with Y-plates, models not found back home.

Servicemembers were among the first Americans to catch the Skyline bug. As the NASCAR driver Jesse Iwuji, a Navy veteran, suggested, it might have something to do with how those drawn to serve are often naturally inclined toward working with their hands. "A lot of military people are car people as well," he said. "The ones stationed in Japan were probably thinking, 'Now's my chance.'"

In 2003, Sudbrock decided to join the club. He found a blue R32 Skyline GT-R on the Japanese mainland and paid $20,000 for it. Shortly after, however, he received orders saying he would soon be shipped back to the United States. Having just bought the car, he chose to take it along.

Sudbrock needed a way to bring his Skyline into the country and into compliance, and he needed it quick. After tracking down a California company that could help, he was soon communicating with one of its representatives, a man named Hiroaki.

At the time, MotoRex enjoyed a reputation as the only company handling Japanese imports, especially GT-Rs, the right way. Because Sudbrock's GT-R was modified, Nanahoshi advised him to buy a second, stock GT-R, shipping both cars to America so MotoRex would have access to additional parts if needed. Sudbrock agreed, acquiring another R32, a white one, for $12,500. The two men reached a deal, and though MotoRex couldn't provide an estimate for the total cost, Nanahoshi promised to "keep the number low."

A short while after, MotoRex sent Sudbrock a bill, requesting $17,325 for shipping, storage, and federal-conversion work. Days later, on September 3rd, 2003, Sudbrock sent MotoRex an $8,000 deposit in the form of a money transfer. He also authorized the company to inspect both vehicles and handle certain modifications and maintenance on the blue car, including the installation of GReddy performance parts, upgrading the head gasket, checking the exhaust manifold for cracks, and relocating the battery to the trunk.

Sudbrock paid a further $3,000 to have the cars packed up and shipped to California, where they were unloaded in San Pedro and trailered a few miles north to the MotoRex offices in Gardena. Then he transferred to his new assignment, a military installation on the East Coast. By this point, he had given MotoRex $19,000 and even visited the Gardena facility, where he had been told that sorting and legalizing his cars would take about six months.

Sudbrock began making plans to have his Skylines trucked across the country to his new home. That shipment would never happen.

SUDBROCK WAS GETTING FRUSTRATED. He had been back in U.S. for months and MotoRex representatives weren't returning his calls. The company still held both of his GT-Rs. When he finally did get ahold of someone, they assured him that his cars would be ready to drive in "weeks, not months." After hearing nothing for too long after, he asked for further update, receiving only more silence. When he finally did get a response, it was platitudes, how his Skylines were up next and would surely be completed soon.

On November 12th, 2003, Sudbrock sent one more email inquiring after the project's status. He had multiple reasons to be concerned. Two weeks later, having heard nothing further from MotoRex, he shipped to the Middle East on combat duty. In early 2004, after returning to America, Sudbrock learned he would be flying across an ocean again, to serve in Afghanistan. He continued lobbing queries to his contacts at MotoRex.

In May of that year, while stationed in a warzone, Sudbrock finally got an email from Nanahoshi: "Oh, you are alive!!" (For anyone who lived through the so-called War On Terror, and remembers the venerable respect given to soldiers at the time, this could only be described as an unimaginable faux pas.)

Nahahoshi likely hadn't meant to offend. In his email, he wished Sudbrock well, wishing him that "you get paid a lot for what you do for this country!! (JK)." Still, he didn't bear good news: The cars were still sitting untouched. Because he knew Sudbrock was on an extended tour overseas, Nanahoshi said, he had moved other customers' cars to the front of the line. Soon, he promised, Sudbrock's GT-R would be taken to a conversion company up the coast in Ventura, where it would have work done to satisfy emissions requirements. Sudbrock's cars were now estimated to be ready in July of 2004.

Sudbrock heard from Nanahoshi again in August. This time, the MotoRex owner claimed that NHTSA had changed its requirements; in order for Sudbrock's cars to be legal, they would need to have airbags installed. The work would take one month. Nanahoshi must have thought the lie would buy him some time. It would have ripple effects he couldn't possibly have foreseen.

LANCE CORPORAL JERAMIE JORDAN was also a car enthusiast, and worked as a mechanic before joining the forces. He learned about

Sudbrock's cars through an Internet forum and, stationed just a two-hour's drive from Gardena at Camp Pendleton near San Diego, wanted to buy the blue 1991 GT-R to drive around the base—just like so many servicemembers running around with "Y-plate" cars in Okinawa.

In fall of 2004, Sudbrock arranged for him to visit MotoRex for an inspection.

Jordan really wanted to buy Sudbrock's car. When he and five other Marines traveled to the MotoRex office, they found it in the back lot, out in the open and covered in a thick layer of dust. When Jordan lifted the hood, he saw that Nanahoshi had done none of the promised work. The car had never gone up the coast to the Ventura conversion company. In all likelihood, it had arrived from the Port of San Pedro and not moved since. Jordan sent a note to Sudbrock documenting what he'd seen.

Sudbrock, furious, tried for months to reach Nanahoshi in vain. In the summer of 2005, he decided to take legal action. The civil lawsuit he filed against both MotoRex and Nanahoshi described the company as Nanahoshi's "alter ego." Sudbrock's attorney, Zachary Weschler, hired one of the founders of Formula Drift to assess the value of both GT-Rs, and he tracked down another U.S. servicemember, Andrew Wall, who had paid nearly $9,000 for MotoRex work three years earlier but still not received his car.

Sudbrock sought more than $155,000 in damages and alleged that Nanahoshi was guilty of fraud and racketeering. In the suit, Wechsler blasted Nanahoshi and MotoRex for a "pattern and practice of targeting vulnerable members of the United States military" and for two years of "evasive tactics better suited to an enemy combatant." He added, for good measure, that Sudbrock had sent final approval to file the suit while "on a troop ship and heading to a combat zone half a world away."

Court cases against "Hiro" were piling up. Multiple customer cars now sat in that Gardena lot, untouched and awaiting conversion, the company unable to keep up with demand. People were starting to demand their money back. MotoRex ceased importing cars, and Nanahoshi all but stopped showing up to work.

WHILE PREPARING SUDBROCK'S SUIT, Weschler dove into the rules for vehicle importing. In the process, he discovered that, when MotoRex commissioned its original crash tests, the only Skylines it had submitted for NHTSA approval were those where the company had replaced the driver's-side airbag with a unit modified to government standards. Any shop that wished to federalize GT-Rs would have to do the same.

But not all Skyline GT-Rs came with a driver's airbag. Weschler contacted NHTSA, where investigator and automotive-enforcement specialist Clint Lindsay confirmed his assessment: If the airbag wasn't there from the factory, then it couldn't be replaced with a government-approved version. Such a GT-R couldn't be made legal at all.

Neither of Sudbrock's cars had a driver's-side airbag. Therefore, Weschler alleged, MotoRex should never have taken payment or agreed to do conversion work on them in the first place. The company had never submitted an application for NHTSA to consider whether non-airbag Skyline GT-Rs could be modified to meet approval. Had Sudbrock known that, Weschler wrote, he never would have brought his cars to the U.S., let alone paid MotoRex thousands of dollars for conversion work that ended up being worthless. Furthermore, Wechsler alleged, MotoRex had known since 2000 that non-airbag cars couldn't be approved. The company had taken Sudbrock's money "knowing all along they could not and would not conform those vehicles... Surely, this is fraud."

Because Nanahoshi had mentioned the airbag work to Sudbrock, and because Weschler had called NHTSA looking to clarify the rule, NHTSA took a closer look at its own requirements.

Five years earlier, in 2000, the agency had issued VCP-17, the eligibility number that made 1990-1999 Skyline GT-Rs legal for import after conversion. But now Lindsay, the enforcement specialist, realized that MotoRex had lied, or at least left out critical details, on its original application. His research led to three declarations:

- MotoRex had only crash-tested R33 Skylines, yet the company was importing and converting R32 and R34 versions;
- NHTSA regulations falsely identified the R32, R33, and R34 as versions of the same model, instead of three different cars;
- NHTSA had no way of determining which R32 GT-Rs like Sudbrock's came equipped with a driver's-side airbag, and therefore, must assume that none of them did, making all R32 GT-R ineligible for conversion.

(Sean Morris asserts that the last two declarations are false, and the result of "a little conspiring" between Nissan and NHTSA to thwart Skyline importers, he told me. His position is the Trinity Skylines are similar enough to be lumped together under crash testing regulations, and that it is possible to verify through model codes which vehicles have airbags and which do not.)

In the wake of these decisions, on March 1st, 2006, Lindsay and NHTSA rescinded VCP-17, replacing it with an updated number, VCP-32. The change shrunk down importation eligibility to only R33 GT-Rs, model years 1996-1998, that had undergone the necessary conversions. This shut the door on importing and converting the R32 and R34, period, until those cars were 25 years old.

Shortly after the institution of VCP-32, Sudbrock had a conversation with Lindsay. Under the new rules, Lindsay told him, neither of his R32 GT-Rs were eligible for import or conversion, and NHTSA was legally within its rights to seize both cars. Internally, however, the agency's regulators had come to an "informal" decision to waive the regulations for those who owned 1990-1995 GT-Rs already in the country—"so as to avoid penalizing the innocent purchasers of nonconformable" cars, Lindsay said.

Essentially, the agency decided to give Sudbrock and other MotoRex Skyline owners a free pass. Those cars, even if they never received any of the federally mandated crash or emissions conversion work, could stay in the U.S.

Weschler, the attorney, decided he deserved special credit for this.

In the MotoRex case, he asked the judge to approve "extraordinary attorney fees" to levy against Hiro. The fees, Wechsler said, were compensation for convincing Lindsay and NHTSA to allow his client to keep his cars. "I consider my effort and the result extraordinary," Wechsler wrote to the judge, "because it is not often that federal agencies waive application of their rules on equitable principles on behalf of a small group of victims."

There was more. NHTSA didn't only give Sudbrock a get-out-of-jail-free card. Lindsay, the NHTSA investigator, also had the authority to permit Sudbrock to physically repossess his vehicles away from MotoRex. The very next day, Sudbrock arrived in Gardena with a group of friends and two trailers. He presented papers to MotoRex employees that showed him as the rightful owner of the two GT-Rs. With his friends' help, Sudbrock loaded the cars onto the trailers, towed them two hours away to the desert city of Barstow, and locked them in a storage unit. He was finally through with MotoRex.

It was February of 2006. Hiroaki Nanahoshi had lost his cars, he'd lost the federal exemption that allowed him to import and convert cars in the first place, and he was personally facing at least three civil lawsuits from members of the U.S. military alone. It got worse. Two weeks after Sudbrock hauled up to Barstow, NHTSA revoked MotoRex's coveted status as a registered importer.

The company was imploding. Confusion reigned. Owners showed up demanding their cars, but it wasn't always clear who owned what. MotoRex employees eventually sold off Big Bird, the yellow R33 GT-R used in the first *Fast & Furious* film, to a private owner in Wisconsin who didn't have appropriate documentation. After all, the car was imported through the TIB, or Temporary Importation under Bond, and never intended for everyday street driving. The car, a surefire high-dollar collector's item, was seized in 2010 and eventually met the crusher.

There would be no more shipping of Skylines, and MotoRex was required to either conform all vehicles in its inventory within 120 days or export them out of the country. The MotoRex empire had fallen and crumbled, reduced to ashes. But Nanahoshi still hadn't hit rock bottom.

IN DECEMBER OF 2005, Tadahoshi Wakita noticed that two of his cars were missing.

Wakita owned Blast Racing, a performance shop specializing in Japanese sports cars. He had recently moved from Japan to the United States and brought his business with him. More specifically, he brought it to Gardena. Even more specifically, he chose a location directly next door to MotoRex.

The missing cars, a Honda S2000 and a Mazda RX-8, belonged to customers. Wakita began asking around, trying to find information on where they might have gone. He started by asking his neighbor, Hiro.

By the end of 2005, Nanahoshi was deep in the throes of multiple lawsuits and facing serious penalties. He'd also incurred a backlog of Skylines, some of which, associates would later allege, had been sold to more than one buyer at once. MotoRex's garage and parking spaces were clogged with Nissans. It was getting difficult to keep up the appearance of running a competent business.

According to documents later filed in the County of Los Angeles Superior Court, when Wakita asked Nanahoshi if he knew where to find the missing cars, Nanahoshi said he would help. All he wanted in exchange was $35,000. Understandably, Wakita balked. Still new to the country, he didn't speak English well. He asked a friend, Hirofumi Fukamoto, to help him talk to the police. Fukamoto agreed, and the two began working with a detective in the Los Angeles Sheriff's Department to bring down the man they thought was involved —Hiro.

Wakita and Fukamoto traded information with detective Raymond Serna for weeks. One night, in mid-January, Fukamoto took a break, accepting an invitation for a night out with a friend. They went downtown, to a bar called Tee-Off. Fukamoto spent a couple of hours there. His friend, he noticed, seemed to be acting strangely, fidgeting and frequently stepping away to take phone calls. Finally, Fukamoto left, walking out into the night. A car quickly pulled up to the curb and four men jumped out. Two of them pushed Fukamoto to the ground, battering him with punches and kicks. The second two joined in a moment later, pulling out stun guns and tasing him before helping continue the beating.

Fukamoto would later identify the second pair as Nanahoshi and a friend of his named Hiroki Miyake, 25. After beating him into submission, the four men tried to force Fukamoto into their car. When witnesses intervened, the attackers sped off. Bystanders called an ambulance for Fukamoto, who was treated at a nearby hospital for what court filings called "severe bruises and lacerations."

When police brought Miyake into custody, he was said to have had an empty stun-gun box in his apartment. It took weeks to locate Nanahoshi, who was reportedly hiding out at his girlfriend's place in Reno, Nevada. Bail for Miyake was set at $500,000. Nanahoshi's bail was $1 million. (A judge later amended those amounts to $200,000 and $500,000, respectively, but the seriousness of the situation had been established.) Both men were charged with threatening a witness, assault with a stun gun, assault with a deadly weapon, and attempted kidnapping. With Nanahoshi, prosecutors tacked on attempted extortion, for that $35,000 offer to help.

Proceedings dragged on for four years. Each side would repeatedly agree to a trial date, only to request postponement as the date drew closer. At one point in late 2009, Michael Levin, the lawyer representing Nanahoshi and Miyake, requested to be taken off the case due to "irremediable breakdown of the attorney/client relationship." He informed his clients of this through both mail and email, sending the letters to separate addresses in Japan: Nanahoshi's, just outside Osaka, and Miyake's, near Yokohama. (Miyake used the email username "skylinegtr80.") A few months later, he rescinded the request and was allowed to return to the case.

In February of 2010, more than four years after the attack on Fukamoto, and with the trial again scheduled to start in just a few weeks, the defense sent a notification to the judge and plaintiff that Hiro's father had fallen ill and been hospitalized back in Japan. The letter was to notify the court that the younger Nanahoshi might request a continuance of the upcoming trial. As it turned out, though, that wasn't necessary. On April 1st, 2010, the judge granted Fukamoto's request for dismissal "of all parties and all causes of action."

Had Fukamoto grown tired of the whole ordeal? Had it become clear that Nanahoshi and Miyake were already back in Japan, with no plans to return? Had the attorney fees racked up to unbearable heights? In later reports, the police officer who worked with Fukamoto and shop owner Wakita early on, Detective Serna, would say that he thought Fukamoto was somehow involved in the crimes himself. Would a trial have brought those allegations to light sooner, and if so, would they have made a difference?

Whatever the case, it was the final act in a saga that had begun, more than a decade earlier, with a push to legally import Skylines. The one person who finally managed to budge the federal government, who successfully led the charge, was brought down by his own actions. No one has heard from "Hiro" since.

CHAPTER 13

The launch of the R35 GT-R met worldwide acclaim. Still, it wasn't perfect. The GT-R's accomplishments were overshadowed by poor timing. In the U.S., the collapse of the Lehman Brothers investment bank set in motion a financial calamity that wiped out billions in consumer spending power. After selling 1,730 R35 GT-Rs in the second six months of 2008, Nissan moved just 1,534 in all of 2009. The company's worldwide sales fell by 9.5-percent from 2008 to 2009. Ghosn predicted that Nissan would continue to be in good shape but admitted it was operating in "crisis mode."

Internally, the R35 had been a point of contention. Kazutoshi Mizuno, the program lead, took a purist viewpoint. He believed the GT-R could and should be everything an owner needed at once: a sports car, a luxury car, a family car. After all, he thought, it was relatively affordable, it was blazingly fast on a track, and it had four seats and a sizeable trunk. In his mind, the job was done.

The tuning community disagreed. They had patiently waited more than five years for a new GT-R, salivating over the chance to integrate high-tech modifications and welcome a new era. Nissan had squashed those fantasies without so much as a conversation. In Japan, the company strictly warned against modifying the R35, threatening to void the warranty if aftermarket parts or software were used to increase performance. Moreover, as the owner's manual noted, you could nix the warranty simply by turning off the car's standard electronic stability control or using its factory-installed launch-control system.

The increased-performance part is common practice at many automakers. The stability- and launch-control parts were not. Either way, for tuners, both were a slap in the face. Their passion and enthusiasm in the 1980s and 1990s had helped turn the GT-R into an icon. The factory package offered so much potential, they said. It was what had set the car apart. It was the whole reason that many owners had bought a GT-R over a Supra or an NSX in the first place. And the tuners, like HKS, Mine's and Top Secret, were the ones who showed what was possible.

At aftermarket shops, the warranty approach hurt feelings. The R35's arrival was supposed to have been a boon amid a global recession. Instead, customers were now hesitant to bring their cars in for upgrades, afraid to risk losing their investment over something like a turbo swap. The tone of Nissan's approach bordered on the comical. "There was a waiver you had to sign when you bought the car," Kenji Sumino, the longtime U.S. boss at GReddy, told me. "It said you acknowledge the adjustable traction-control settings could not be used to launch the car, but were to get out of snow, or whatever, and can't be tampered with."

"We signed the waiver, but we were always going to mess with it."

Mizuno, the project lead, had also ruffled feathers with his approach to special versions. The Trinity Skyline GT-Rs had thrived on a series of limited-edition variants that kept the car fresh in people's minds, gave passionate owners a way to separate themselves, and offered Nissan a chance to roll out new technology. The R34 GT-R alone had the V-Spec, the V-Spec II, the M-Spec, the Nür, and the Z-Tune. Tamura had spearheaded the introduction of the M-Spec, a luxurious version with leather seats, which he publicly called the "M for Mature" GT-R. (Privately, many at Nissan assumed the name was an homage to Mizuno.)

Mizuno felt the R35 stood on its own, variations unnecessary. He relented only for the 110-unit R35 Spec-V and the 150-unit R35 Track Pack Edition, neither of which were sold in the US. By 2013, the only GT-R variant for American buyers was the Black Edition, a cosmetic package with no speed upgrades whatsoever. The R35 GT-R had been out for five full model years, and U.S. owners were still walled off from performance modifications and mechanical improvements.

The car was a monster out of the box, but the beast remained leashed. Mizuno and Tamura engaged in intense boardroom battles. Multiple sources confirmed to me that the disagreements were heated and left both men simmering. One Nissan associate described the rivalry as "Godzilla vs. Mothra."

In early 2013, Mizuno announced he was leaving. He had joined the company in 1972 as a parts designer, at just 20 years old, and after 41 years worked his way up to one of the most sacred seats in the building. Many Japanese companies have an unwritten rule that executives must retire at the age of 60, though they can choose to stick around for a short while after. Mizuno had become a legend among JDM fans, but it didn't mean he could stay forever.

(Carlos Ghosn also departed, though in far less respectable fashion. After reports of his questionable compensation package were made public, he was arrested by Japanese regulators in 2018 and faced the possibility of decades in federal prison. Allegations included that he had established a shell company in order to funnel money directly from Nissan to pay for a 120-foot private yacht in the Mediterranean. Fearing a biased trial, Ghosn avoided charges by hiring an American military-extraction team to pose as musicians and smuggle him out of Japan on a private jet. He hid in their drum kit. The man they called "Le Cost Killer" is now an international fugitive and has lived in his native Lebanon since 2019. Just before press time, he sued Nissan for $1 billion in damages.)

In the wake of Mizuno's departure, Tamura was named chief product specialist, as well as NISMO "brand guardian," for both the Z and the GT-R. The move effectively put him in charge of Nissan's highest-performance models, and he quickly instituted changes. Nissan revised its warranty claims, allowing more leeway for owners who wanted to tune or customize their cars. Tamura also led the charge to release a 545-hp version called the GT-R Track Edition, followed by an all-out Nismo GT-R with an even more impressive 600 hp. Both models came to America.

Armed with those new variants, Tamura embarked on an aggressive media campaign. He led the effort to set a Nürburgring lap time with a Nismo GT-R of just 7 minutes and 8 seconds, crushing the times of more expensive models from Lamborghini and Porsche. In 2016, he organized a successful attempt to set a Guinness World Record for fastest drift, using an R35 GT-R modded by Trust/GReddy to more than 1300 hp. The car was held at more than 30 degrees of steering angle at 190 mph. And in late 2019, a GT-R Nismo set a new lap record around Japan's storied Tsukuba Circuit, 59.3 seconds, unseating a Porsche 911 GT3 for the win.

Inside a Nissan boardroom at the NTC offices, Tamura told me the story of each of those records from beginning to end. He left out no detail, gesticulating wildly and standing up to move around at some points, lowering his voice to a whisper in others. He will jump around or pantomime running a marathon—whatever it takes to make you feel what he feels.

Sitting there, it occurred to me that, above all, the man is a master storyteller. He is now paid to travel the world and express the value in becoming part of GT-R culture. To explain or show why a cash-strapped company would go to such great lengths to keep a story alive and growing. He travels to pay homage to the fans – those who want to see that the automaker they love so much, understands why they're so passionate.

Tamura doesn't like being referred to as "Father of GT-R," he told me, doesn't like the term itself. There are many fathers of the GT-R over its 50-year history, he said, and besides, who wants to be in a father-son relationship? He prefers something more... like big brother, he said. "A father you cannot escape. But brother you can fight."

We don't get to choose how people see us, though. GT-R people want Tamura to see who they are and how the car makes them feel, and they want his approval. And like a good father, he will go to great lengths to share their stories with the world.

"This kind of crazy behavior is not only for Tamura," he says. "It's for everybody."

BY THE TIME our meeting at the Nissan Technical Center ended, it was dark. Tamura and I had plans for dinner. At that point I had driven to Mount Fuji and back, experienced the most singular shotgun ride of my life, and conducted multiple hour-long interviews, all in one day. I was tired, and I needed a change of clothes.

I swung the GT-R over to my hotel, rushing upstairs to switch into a clean shirt and jacket. When I walked back out onto the street, the clouds overhead were threatening to drizzle. The restaurant was a couple of blocks away, but I was so exhausted that even the thought of rain felt refreshing.

Tamura had selected an upscale yakitori restaurant. The streets of Atsugi are lined with nondescript restaurants, but this one was so hidden that it had no sign of serving food at all. (When I tried to locate it on Google Maps weeks later, it didn't appear on any listings and the name Tamura gave me returned no results.) I walked inside and found Tamura waiting at his favorite booth in the heart of the bustling joint, so I removed my shoes at the door, squeezed past the hostess and hurried back to meet him. It was noisy, and the booth cushions were soft. A half-dozen plates of meats and vegetables were already on the table, either speared on skewers or soaking in sauce. We ate and they kept coming and then we ate more. It was perfect.

Over delectable rice balls and grilled chicken skin, Tamura and I discussed children and family. We talked about our favorite cuisines and countries to visit. We talked about work, and everything it asks of us, and the rewards of chasing dreams, and about why we do what we do.

I told him that I've faced a lot of hardship in my career. Journalism is full of reporters who have been overworked and underpaid for many, many years. During the Great Recession, every media outlet in America began to internally use the phrase "more with less." Meaning, if you wanted to keep your job, you were going to have to get used to increasing your output year after year, doing more and more. All with longer hours and less time to be careful with the details, maybe even adding a laid-off colleague's responsibilities to your own, while watching your pay stagnate or decrease.

I've had a good career. I've had moments of thrilling success, and I've achieved most of my ambitions. I've also gone on unemployment benefits on five separate occasions. That kind of precariousness would be hard on anyone. It's made me resentful and unceasingly nervous. It's not a healthy career path. But I do it, I told him, because of the chance to do something special.

Journalism has given me the opportunity to reach people. To provide them with information they might find helpful in their lives or a distraction that makes them smile or giggle or think. It's gifted me the opportunity to meet incredible people, visit amazing places, and learn some of the astonishing things we are each capable of accomplishing. It gives me moments I'll remember for the rest of my life. Moments that make it all worth it.

I had one of those experiences, I told Tamura, only a few hours earlier.

THERE ARE 65 miles of road between the HKS headquarters in Fujinomiya and the Nissan Technical Center campus in Atsugi. Once my interviews at HKS were done in the early afternoon, and to reach the NTC in time for my 4:00 p.m. meeting with Tamura, I needed to drive around Fujisan and its surrounding forests, hustle down the Tōmei Expressway, then beat the rush of heavy traffic heading back to the city after a hard day's work.

Sixty-five miles doesn't sound like a lot. But after my run up the mountain and the visit to HKS, I had only two hours. Google Maps estimated it would take 20 minutes more than that.

By now, I had put hundreds of miles on the GT-R. None of it had been while listening to music on the R35's stereo. All my driving had been in complete silence, in order to focus as much as possible. I was nervous—more accurately, I was scared shitless.

Laugh if you want. It was my first time driving in a country that uses the other side of the road. I was in an expensive, high-profile supercar that wasn't mine. The possibility of so much as curbing a wheel terrified me, much less anything more serious, like a head-on collision because the gaijin forgot which side of the road to use. I thought deliberately about every move, repeating to myself a mantra my therapist had told me days earlier: "No one can make you speed up or slow down," she said. "You go when you're ready. You make your own intentions."

This strategy had worked for two days. As I left HKS, I was feeling more confident—in the car, in the rules of the road, and in myself. I pulled onto the Tōmei. I smiled, turned on the stereo, and entered the open highway.

It was my first real chance to dive into the GT-R's engine. I wanted to see where it led. The on-ramp arced that jade-green cruise missile into the highway's slow lane, faster cars to the right. But there were two turbochargers just shoveling air into that 3.8-liter V6, and hundreds of horses went to all four wheels. I took a deep breath and smashed the gas. In an instant, the cars to the right were gone. Poof.

The hashiriya swear by Eurobeat. Think hyper-fast disco or house music, with high-pitched, sped-up backup singers, like The Chipmunks. They say the quick tempo and interwoven grooves mimic driving at speed, blurring surroundings and helping you focus. Eurobeat, basically, simulates street racing. Many believe that it literally improves your driving.

I settled into the far-right lane, the fast lane in Japan. It wasn't quite the Autobahn, but regular commuters stayed out of the way. The speed limit on the Tōmei is 100 kph, or about 60 mph. The highway was elevated above lush-green forests that stretched in all directions, its gentle curves visible for a mile or more in advance. You could see everything coming. The sun was out. The road was as smooth as porcelain. I exceeded the limit gleefully.

When the Tōmei was completed in 1968—when the hashiriya were just getting started—it looked something like this. No one really street races there anymore, at least not officially. The Wangan opened in the late 1980s and became the new ground zero. Gaijin take pilgrimages there now.

EuroBeat isn't my thing. I can appreciate the syncing drums and intoxicating synths. But I'm a '90s hip-hop kid who grew up on 2Pac and the Wu-Tang Clan. I need an edge—even when the occasion calls for pulsing bpm and go-go beats. There was really only one album that came to mind. I opened the Spotify app on the GT-R's Apple CarPlay and scrolled over to *Kiss Land*, by The Weeknd, an album I hadn't listened to in years. But I remembered its odd, up-tempo, falsetto choruses and spooky, echoing claps. I could feel myself digging deeper into the gas pedal.

The R35 GT-R doesn't have Super HICAS rear-wheel steering like its Skyline forebears, but the car felt more invincible the faster it went. The car was now different from earlier. Lighter, less cumbersome. The steering that had been so heavy and annoying around town was now natural and light. I kept losing my body in each turn, leaning my shoulders from side to side. The clunking and slamming transmission, the one that had shifted in the city as if it were trying to take the car apart, now clicked off downshifts with an intoxicating blip of the throttle. Where the tires had once shouted out every crack in the pavement, they now sent humming little telegrams of the road's pitch and angle. The gentle curves and elevation changes were like riding a jet stream. The car had been yelling and cursing at me throughout the trip. Now it was singing.

I had clicked off a good chunk of the trip when I noticed the Mercedes. Behind, in the mirror, coming up fast. I was in the right-hand lane, following some late-model sedan, and then we were moving to the left together, past slower traffic. The Mercedes slotted in behind, three cars in a train. After half a mile or so, the sedan moved out of the way.

At the first break in traffic, the Mercedes popped out and pulled alongside. I caught a glimpse of "AMG" badges on the front fenders, symbols from Mercedes's high-performance division. The throaty V-8 crackled and the car shot past, pulling into my lane to lead. We whistled along as if tethered to one another.

It hit me that *Kiss Land* is basically dark, Americanized Eurobeat. The album cover is plastered with Japanese characters that look like hidden meanings but probably mean nothing at all. As our speed increased, the lyrics kept slamming into my chest.

> "I'm not a fool...
> I just love that you're dead inside..."

The Mercedes whisked into a tunnel. The Tōmei cuts through so many mountains; they appear in the distance, one after the other, as if on a conveyor belt. Japanese tunnels are insanely well-lit. They have this soothing simplicity, they always feel open, there's always a long view ahead, sometimes miles long, you can see a curve before it's time to do anything about it.

> "I'm not a fool...
> I'm just lifeless, too..."

But the best part is the symmetry. Some have a railing extending the full length of the tunnel, the support posts equally spaced. Others have yellow markers that give a soothing glow from the lights above; in rare cases, there are small signs that give an audible whoosh as you pass. Each tunnel has a different rhythm.

The overhead lights were the bumping percussion, the railings were the swooping synths, and the signs were those trashcan-banging claps.

> "Honey-honey-honey-honey-honey honey
> pleeeeeeeeease..."

Daylight again. We were whipping toward the opening, and then the tunnel ended in a flash and I was free. I slammed on the gas and the GT-R surged, singing along as if finally given permission to perform. The Mercedes was still glued to the front bumper.

This, I thought, must be what the car is meant to do. Like following notes on sheet music. I started to picture the GT-R stretching its legs, unfurling and hitting its stride, its shape changing and getting longer, morphing with every kilometer. On a bright and sunny weekday afternoon, I was blasting across the Honshu mainland, across the eastbound Tōmei, not a care in the world, and the R35 GT-R just plain went *Super Saiyan*.

This car could do this for hundreds of miles, I thought. I could feel all the bullshit melting away. All of the pressure, and the expectations, and the imposter syndrome. I was no longer stressed about making a mistake on the road. I let go of the frustration about my career problems that otherwise follow me around everywhere. If I let this car keep going it would drive straight off the edge of Japan. Maybe even take to the sky.

I wasn't anxious any more. The trip had just become worth every second of stress. There was no way I could lose. I had already won.

I told all this to Tamura. He just kept grinning.

IN MY RESEARCH on Hiromu Naruse, the late Toyota test driver, I had encountered the phrase genchi genbutsu—"go and see for yourself." It's what kept Naruse-san in sweltering Toyota workshops, beneath dirty and leaking cars, instead of his air-conditioned office. It's what kept him outside in winter, in freezing snow, watching young drivers work on lap times. In his mind, that was the only way to land constant improvement, to go out into the world and experience it. It was less a mantra and more an imperative.

At that yakitori restaurant, as we made a meal of skewered hearts and livers, Tamura told me about a similar concept. For him, the top priority is *gemba*. The literal translation is "the actual place," usually in the context of where something is made or created. But what it's really about is people.

The phrasing is different, but the ideas are the same. The whole point of gemba is that you need to get your hands dirty. No one ever got the full picture from a cubicle or a laptop screen. Tamura mentioned the idea of driving a GT-R in *Gran Turismo* versus driving one in real life. To truly understand something, he suggested, you need to be in its physical presence. You need to feel the love and culture that people put into it. You need to get off your ass.

It was nearly 11:00 p.m. by the time we wrapped our meal. I was already thinking about the hotel bed. Tamura had other ideas. "How would you feel about going to a car show?" he said. "There is one not far. Do you know Daikoku?"

Do I know Daikoku? If it's not the most famous car meet in the world, it's damn close.

They call it Daikoku because it's in the Daikoku Parking Area, a rest stop for truckers coming into or out of the Yokohama port, so they can grab a shower or a nap. Though it was built to handle 18-wheelers and smelly drivers who've been on the road for days at a time, the Daikoku P.A. has been reclaimed by the hashiriya and curious car-spotters. Daikoku sits smack in the middle of Yokohama's web of elevated highways, with quick access west to Atsugi, south to the Miura Peninsula, or east to Tokyo. It is a perfect central location for enthusiasts from all directions.

I was beyond exhausted. I knew from the outset that a trip to Daikoku was possible—a contact at Nissan had told me, "Going to Daikoku with Tamura-san is like going with a god"—but, given the time, had decided to not broach the subject. The window of opportunity had closed, I figured, and I had already made peace with it.

But since it was Tamura who had brought up the idea, something changed. Saying "no thank you" was not an option. I tried my best to enthusiastically accept, to make it clear that I appreciated his willingness to stay out so late. The Father of GT-R as my personal tour guide at one of the most iconic car meets on earth? Who could resist?

Rolling into Daikoku is an experience in itself. A lattice of elevated highway ramps surrounds the parking area, looping around it, hundreds of feet off the ground, like concrete soba noodles. Coming in, you can look down and take in the whole meet in at once. It was a weeknight, and nearly midnight when we arrived, but the lot was still stuffed with cars.

We crept in slowly, through a side entrance, no one giving us a second glance. Plenty of R35s were already there. The lot was huge, most cars concentrated toward the middle, some flashing multicolored lights or neon-green underbody glow, like automotive peacocking. In the back, I spied an open space between a black Silvia S14 and a grey 240SX. I figured it was far enough out of the way.

Stock cars like my loaner R35 tend to blend into the woodwork at Daikoku because there are so many fascinating homebuilt versions to check out. Still, it's hard to remain inconspicuous in a jade-green GT-R. We drew a crowd immediately, before I had even fully backed into the spot.

"Yooooo," came a voice. "Yo yo yo yo." Phones were pulled out. "Gotta be... it's gotta be a 2023 model. R35 GT-R T-Spec."

The crowd grew larger with every second. I waited for what I knew was coming. Exiting the car, I heard gasps as I closed the door.

"Holy shit," someone said in English. "It's Tamura-san."

The voice belonged to Drew Mowery, a 25-year-old mustachioed Pennsylvanian with checkered slip-on Vans and holes in the knees of his jeans. The only white face in the crowd, besides myself, curly brown hair poofed out the back of his trucker hat. Mowery and his friends had come to Daikoku during a once-in-a-lifetime trip to Japan, hoping to catch a bit of the magic they'd heard and read about for decades. As our R35 came rolling into the lot with Tamura, he realized they had found it.

Mowery approached cautiously. He greeted Tamura in Japanese, introducing himself and complimenting the car. Then he asked politely for a picture, to which Tamura responded affirmatively. Mowery's face lit up. I offered to take the photo, snapping off a couple of shots with his phone from different angles. One image was on his Instagram within hours, showing Mowery on one side of

Tamura, throwing up a peace sign, as his friend Devon smiled on the other.

"Somehow, japan just keeps giving," Mowery wrote, under the (frankly hilarious) username @osakaflackaflame. "Meeting @mid_night_new_wave was just an insane, unbelievable dream that I didn't think could ever happen. The new TSPEC is sick... No GTR, No Life."

On his account of 650 followers, it got 127 likes, a huge rate of engagement.

Tamura waved a thanks to the crowd and we set off to see the rest of the show. It was a relatively small gathering by Daikoku standards, he told me—"Friday nights, you have to see it when you come back someday"—but the eye candy was still astounding. Off to the side, a pair of white twin-turbo Toyota Soarers slammed to the ground. Feet away, a right-hand-drive NSX in black, then a bright-yellow Honda S660 convertible. There was a purple Corvette with Lamborghini-style scissor doors next to a white Maserati sedan whose flashing multi-colored lights looked like a four-door Christmas tree. A young woman in a white dress climbed from a rose-gold Camaro with purple underglow. (You have to love Japan.) There were Mazda Miatas, Toyota 86s, and Honda S2000s of every type and variation and in every state of mod. It was all backlit by the breathtaking city lights and framed by shadows cast on the pavement by the freeway overpasses.

We came upon the GT-Rs. A grey R32, a stark white R33. Tamura found an R35 painted a brilliant crystal blue, grabbing his phone to snap a picture.

The next GT-R over was a bit of a Frankenstein. At first, seeing the vented carbon-fiber Z-Tune hood and the massive front bumper scraping the ground, I mistook it for an R34. In reality, it was an R32 with an extreme body kit. There were enormous side scoops, and the interior held a roll cage. The gold five-spoke wheels held fat tires that looked built for drag racing, but the car's real purpose couldn't be mistaken.

A pink sticker had been slapped onto the front at a crooked angle.

And though the bumper was missing paint in spots, battered by debris over the years, the words "Mid Night Car Speciall" were clear as day.

BACK HOME IN PENNSYLVANIA, Mowery is a delivery-truck driver near the town of Hershey. We caught up by phone a few weeks after each of us had returned to the States. He described himself as "obsessed" with Japanese cars. He fell hard for the scene in high school, he said, watching old clips of high-speed testing at Yatabe, devouring whatever copies of *Option*, or *Autoworks*, a French-language magazine about JDM culture, he could find. "I've always been this way," he said.

Mowery bought a GT-R of his own, a gold-painted R32, in early 2020, just before prices skyrocketed. Though it has spots of rust and is often disassembled for work, he hasn't regretted the choice for a minute. "Once I get into something, I really dive into researching and figuring it out. I like to know what's cool and what's not—who were [the real] the contributors back in the day that led to the culture now, and who was doing the big power moves."

When we met at Daikoku, Mowery and his friend Devon were in the middle of their trip. The two had spent more than a year planning and saving, motivated to the extreme after the coronavirus pandemic had kept them penned inside a town of "mostly farmland," he called it. Once the vaccines arrived and Japan reopened to foreign visitors, Mowery decided it was time. He and Devon still had to wait a few months, however, because they had to apply for and receive passports. It was their first time leaving the United States.

The trip lasted nearly a month. The two visited one tuning shop after another, traveling around day after day to see the shops they had read about or seen on video. They saw wild RX-7s at RE Amiriya, then a collection of Fairladys and Toyotas and German muscle at Revolfe SA. They visited the famous builder Akira Nakai and his custom widebody Porsches at RWB, and they browsed the legendary halls at Mine's. Of course, they went to Top Secret. Smokey Nagata invited them inside for tea.

"It was amazing to meet such massive figures," he said. Still, the chance encounter with Tamura stuck out. Under those bright lights, for the only time on his trip, Mowery was starstruck.

"He was the first person we met where I really had to collect myself. I had to step outside of my head and think, 'Okay, take a deep breath.' Talking with him for a few moments and getting to shake his hand was incredible. He's probably very used to it. Obviously, that man is a superstar… he was so genuine and so polite. He asked me how I was doing, he asked me where I'm from—those little things really make a difference. I really look up to him. And he was so nice."

BACK AT DAIKOKU, Tamura and I left the widebody GT-R with the Mid Night sticker and continued exploring the meet. As the clock ticked past midnight, people were realizing it was time to go home. A parade of Silvias and Toyota Crowns burbled past us on their way to the on-ramps.

Off in a back corner, I noticed one remaining crew. A dozen or so men and women in their 20s huddled around a pair of new Nissan Zs.

Along with his role as GT-R brand guardian, Tamura does the same job for the Z. And just as the GT-R community sees him as a hero for keeping their cars' spirit alive, Z fans feel the same way. The current model, launched in 2022, simply wouldn't exist without him. In the late 2010s, that car's predecessor, the 370Z, faced dwindling demand. It had been in production since 2009 but was based on a platform then nearly 20 years old. After Ghosn bailed out, Nissan, once again strapped for funding, had considered ending the model for good.

Tamura had spurred his team to convince upper brass that Nissan needed a new Z. He can be a hard driver. (One U.S. associate told me that it wasn't unusual for him to call at 3:00 a.m. and ask for a written proposal full of innovative ideas to be on his desk the next morning.) One evening in 2019, after most employees had left for the evening, Tamura appeared at the office door of Makoto Uchida, the executive who took over from Ghosn. The CEO was finishing up his day and preparing to go home. Tamura made a proposal—*I know it's late, but come to Daikoku with me.* If reports couldn't get executives on his side, maybe gemba would.

Uchida had inherited an unenviable task: clean up the mess left by Ghosn and find a new path forward for the tangled Nissan-Renault-Mitsubishi partnership known in Japan as the "unequal treaty," all while keeping the automaker in black ink. The head job at any car company is stressful enough to turn your hair white; at that point, Uchida's job wasn't so much stressful as a living nightmare. But it was there in Daikoku, Tamura told me, that Uchida saw the fruits of his hard work. Freed from the paperwork and market reports that filled his days, he looked around and saw genuine passion. At the parking area, the vehicles he was responsible for weren't numbers on a sheet but real steel and glass, lovingly cared for and celebrated years after their maker had moved on to other things.

Here, Uchida thought, was his company's lasting impact. And a place of opportunity. A chance to write his legacy.

Months later, Nissan officially confirmed the development of a new Z sports car.

On my own trip to Daikoku, I gestured to Tamura, nodding to the group of Z owners in the corner, but he was hesitant. Either he knew what would happen or he didn't want to interrupt their moment. Or both. But I eventually talked him into it, and we ambled toward the two Zs in the corner. Sure enough, one of the men gasped. He came rushing up and bowed, introducing himself and inviting Tamura to sit in his car. Then the whole group realized who was among them.

Tamura estimates he's signed at least 3,000 autographs in his career. Of those requests, he said, maybe a third were to sign someone's car. For a Z or GT-R owner, a Tamura autograph on your dash carries the same weight as a Carroll Shelby signature on your 427 Cobra. Or a Ken Griffey autograph on your copy of his rookie card.

I stood by and watched as each member of the group approached, one at a time, to greet him and thank him for his work. He politely sat in both cars, complimenting choices in spec and modification. And, of course, there were the photos. At one point, three iPhone photographers took the same picture from different angles, so the owner of one of the Zs could have options for Instagram later.

This was the man in his element. The celebrity aspect makes him uncomfortable, but once a fan returns to earth and begins to talk cars, he lights up. Deep down, Tamura is still that hard-headed teenager, consumed by making things faster and more alive. "I can't help it," he said. "I'm a five-year-old child."

I asked Tamura how it felt to know that his reputation stretched around the world. That he was inspiring a generation to enjoy cars, whether in his backyard of Daikoku or all the way over in Hershey, Pennsylvania. It was very nice, he said.

"But this feeling, it's actually not for me. As you can see, GT-R is worldwide."

CHAPTER 14

During one of my meetings with Sean Lee, the Taiwanese-born businessman and GT-R collector who started GMR Touge and the Purist group, he took me to a restaurant in the San Gabriel Valley called Teddy's Tacos. It was his favorite, he said.

We hopped in his Toyota GR Corolla, an all-wheel-drive, manual-transmission, 300-hp hatchback that Lee had purchased just days earlier. The engine popped and burbled. From the outside, the Toyota looked like the stereotypical overdone-boy-racer wannabe car that most people Lee's age try to avoid. But he loves the thing.

On the day we visited, Teddy's was out of marlin tacos, Lee's recommendation. ("F***!" he said, a cross between a shout and a whisper. "I really wanted you to try those.") We made up for it by ordering everything else. I grabbed two shredded-chicken street tacos, a jalapeño taco stuffed with melted Monterey cheese, and an Azteca taco, with chorizo and Peruvian beans. They were delicious. Lee got four of his own concoctions, ingredient mixes of his own.

Between bites, he outlined his packed schedule. After meeting with me, Lee said, he was taking calls to plan the next Purist event, picking up his Nissan Z from the shop to get it ready for a track day, then making last-minute preparations for FuelFest.

FuelFest is a car-culture extravaganza, part colossal meet and part show business. There were seven FuelFest meets in 2023, six in America and one in Tokyo, but the L.A. one, the original, takes place each summer at Southern California's Irwindale Speedway. Lee helps organize the event with Cody Walker, the younger brother of the late *Fast & Furious* actor Paul Walker.

"Oh, yeah," I said. "I have a request in for media credentials. Was hoping to follow Cody around for an hour or two during the show. Watch him interact with fans, feel the energy, that sort of thing."

"No, no," Lee replied. "No, there's no way. The show is crazy, he won't have time."

I protested, trying to explain my case: I wasn't looking for a long, one-on-one interview, just the opportunity to shadow the guy, watch him move through the event. I could observe from afar, I said. But Lee was insistent. He was pulling out his phone.

"You won't get to him," he said. "If you want to meet Cody, you need to go tomorrow."

LEE HAD Walker on the phone within minutes. Shortly after that, I had an invitation to visit during load-in at Irwindale, the day before the event. FuelFest started out in 2019 as a tribute to Paul Walker, who died in a car accident in 2013. Years later, it's morphed into a traveling circus of car culture. There's a FuelFest in Palm Beach, Florida; in Dallas; in Las Vegas. In 2023, the one in Japan was held at Fuji Speedway. Each iteration brings a mixture of industry vendors and influential shops and media, combined with professional drifting and racing.

The underlying theme is a celebration of what is best called *Fast & Furious* Mania. Among the throngs of people who attend are many who have been in love with the films for years. They bring cars like Mitsubishi Eclipses or Toyota Supras that have been made into replicas of machines in the movies. They come dressed as their favorite characters or wearing T-shirts with the franchise's most quotable lines. Actors like Tyrese Gibson and Ludacris, who have played staple characters, often make in-person appearances. Vin Diesel came to the one in Miami.

Above all, though, the crowds adore Paul Walker. His portrayal of Brian O'Conner, the main *F&F* protagonist, set the tone for the series. On top of that, Walker was known for embracing fans of the franchise more than anyone else in the cast. He made sure O'Conner wasn't just driving fast and delivering quippy one-liners—he pushed to have the character spend screen time drooling over the coolest cars and the latest performance technologies, not least because he did the same.

Off the set, Walker made no secret of his enthusiasm for sports cars, especially JDM ones. In a 2011 video, currently at more than 33 million views on YouTube, Walker is seen visiting the famous tuning shop Mine's, in Japan. As he straps into a Mine's R35 GT-R, he says to the camera, "This is what dreams are made of, right here." On the screen, his face holds genuine joy, the kind many Hollywood stars try to fake around cars but never rarely pull off.

Yes, the movies became increasingly ridiculous. One *F&F* installment saw Vin Diesel drive his muscle car off a moving submarine to avoid a heat-seeking missile. In another, a car swung through the air on jungle vines. But to fans, the series has always been grounded in another kind of movie magic: the scenes that show Walker under the hood, turning wrenches and covered in grime, trying to squeeze every last drop of performance from his car. Just like they were.

When Walker was killed while leaving a Southern California car show, fans were left reeling. Few accidental deaths are less than shocking, but his was jarring and violent—a rare Porsche in which Walker was riding, driven by one of his friends, crashed in a business park and burst into flames. Car culture as a whole seemed to feel a loss, to say nothing of Walker's fans, who tended to feel a kinship to the actor, a degree of ownership in his career. He was also, by all accounts, remarkably generous. In the wake of a devastating 2010 earthquake in Haiti, Walker founded the disaster-relief nonprofit Reach Out Worldwide. The event he attended on the day he died was a fundraiser and toy drive for victims of a super typhoon in the

Philippines—Reach Out had sent around a dozen workers to the islands on an aid mission only days prior.

FuelFest has grown to be so popular, at least in part, because it offers fans a chance to connect with what Walker represented. From seeing on stage those he acted with and called friends, to the cars he built or drove or battled in their favorite chase scenes. At the core, FuelFest is just a car show, but it's also so much more: It's a way people can get one step closer to knowing modern car culture's fallen son.

THOUGH IT WAS 80 degrees out, a bright and sunny June afternoon in Los Angeles, Cody Walker wasn't wearing sunglasses. So when he hopped off a golf cart and extended a hand to greet me, his bright blue eyes were there in plain sight. My throat tightened a little at the resemblance. Cody looks much like his late brother, if slightly more boyish and less chiseled. But then, he is still only 35, five years younger than Paul was when he passed.

"Hey man!" he said. "I'm Cody."

We ducked into an air-conditioned RV and started to chat. Preparation for FuelFest had been hectic, he said, getting ready to welcome hundreds of show cars and tens of thousands of visitors the next morning. But when Sean Lee called on my behalf, Walker told me, that sealed our meeting. He considers Lee "a brother," and the two have spent untold hours at the track, sharing cars and talking about life.

Walker ran me through a list of the cars he's owned personally, starting with a charcoal-gray Infiniti G35 that Paul bought for him for his 16th birthday. (The G35, a luxury car built by Nissan, is badged as a Nissan Skyline in Japan.) Also on the list were a Mark VI Volkswagen Golf, a BMW 340i, and a Honda S2000 that he modified for track use and later regretted doing so. He had recently bought a new Nissan Z, he said, after the company flew him to Japan for the car's official reveal, snapping photos of him next to Lee and Tamura.

The Walker brothers didn't grow up wrenching on cars, but they bonded over them, and many of his favorite memories with Paul, Cody said, come from road trips. The younger Walker was still a teen when his parents divorced, and his older brother knew the split hit him hard. Paul, by then already a movie star, would sometimes swing by and scoop up Cody in the middle of a school week, scurrying him off to his home in Santa Barbara for a couple of days. When the boys' mother would return home and find her youngest son missing, she immediately knew who to call.

"Did you take Cody with you?" she would yell into the phone. "Paul, it's a school night!"

Cody remembers his brother's answer: "Mom, everything he needs to know, he's going to learn here with me."

CODY WALKER DOESN'T OWN a GT-R, but he said the model holds a special place in his heart. After the debut of the first *Fast & Furious* film, Cody, then just 14 years old, was hanging with his older brother when Paul turned to him and said, "Hey, I have this really dope car imported from Japan. I'm gonna go pick it up. And you're gonna come with me."

They set off. After winding through L.A.'s highway system for a bit, the Walker brothers arrived at the garage that stored the car. (Though Cody couldn't recall the exact location, it was likely the shop owned by Craig Lieberman, the Universal Pictures vehicle fixer.) There he saw the car in question: a boxy two-door with bright blue paint and the steering wheel on the wrong side.

The younger Walker walked up to it, admiring the lines. There was an enormous rear wing atop the trunk, and a shiny badge that said V-Spec II. He thought the Nissan was the coolest car he'd ever seen, but he didn't know what it was. When he asked, his brother simply pointed to the GT-R badge. Get in, he said.

Paul dropped into the driver's seat and started the car, winding his way back onto the freeway and toward the family home. "I'm thinking this is the coolest damn thing," Cody said. "I'm sitting on the left side, and it's so exotic. I don't realize what we're in, and the significance of being in a car that's not technically kosher. I just know it's awesome."

On the freeway, another car suddenly sped up to pass before pulling alongside. All the windows came down, and a mass of arms, torsos, and heads came clamoring out of the car, gawking at Cody, trying to get the closest look possible.

"I look at Paul, and I go, 'Bro, they recognize you.'" And then, Cody said, Paul turned his head and said words that could easily have been written for Brian O'Conner:

"Bro, it's not me. It's this car."

THE NEXT DAY, it was just after noon when I reached Irwindale, almost two hours early. FuelFest wouldn't open its doors to spectators until 2:00 p.m., but I still met gridlock. A line of cars waited to drive into the track, at first four lanes wide, then narrowing to one, and every car in the line was stopped. I escaped on the shoulder and went looking for another way in.

After locating an off-site parking lot where a tram was set to ferry attendees into the track, I took one look at the queue of people looping around the lot and started to walk. The two-mile hike to Irwindale's gates took about 30 minutes, but once there, I flashed a media pass and was waved past a general-admission line that easily held thousands. FuelFest had nearly broken me before it even opened, and I was one of the lucky ones.

Inside, I met with vendors, spoke with GT-R owners displaying their cars, and eventually watched the crowd pour in from all angles. After catching a monster-truck demo and filming some drift cars, I headed into the VIP area, where fans who paid extra were lined up around a water fixture and against a series of concrete safety barriers placed next to the track's surface. They were waiting to meet Walker.

It might seem odd that the lesser-known younger brother of a star actor who passed away 10 years ago served as the center of all this.

But Cody Walker has a form of niche stardom where he might not be exactly famous, but to some, he's extremely famous. The people that love him think Walker is a very big deal indeed—his Instagram account has 2.1 million followers—while everyone else on earth may not have any idea who he is.

Many *F&F* fans see Walker as having taken the mantle from his older brother. Since Paul passed, he's become a fixture of a certain part of the car community, a pillar for the *Fast & Furious* generation and a kind of avatar for automotive enthusiasm in general. For the sort of person who comes to FuelFest, Cody is both appealing in his own right, and as close as they'll ever get to Paul. And they're grateful for the opportunity.

The first VIP fans I met were Damian and Tyler, a pair of 20-something coworkers at a Massachusetts electrical company who had saved up their paychecks and traveled to California for the show. FuelFest holds events on the east coast, closer to their home, but the JDM scene there, they agreed, is "nonexistent." They wanted to experience it for themselves.

"It's an honor to meet Cody," said Damian, who came up with idea for the trip. "Overall, I just want to show support for his brother. It's going to be one of the great experiences of my life."

Near the front of the line I met a young woman, a SoCal local named Angelica, who called herself a dedicated *Fast & Furious* fan. Angelica had circled FuelFest on her calendar far in advance. "I really enjoy that this all goes to charity," she said. "And then the drifting, the loud cars, it's just amazing for me, as someone who loves muscle cars."

As we were talking, a murmur began to spread through the crowd. I turned to see spectators outside the VIP area gathering at the fence and pushing their way to the front. I couldn't see what the draw was, but the whispers were building, people alerting their friends. "Cody!" someone said. "That's seriously Cody Walker right there."

I told Angelica goodbye and walked to the front. When I got there, Cody was gradually making his way to the greeting area, protected by a small flock of stocky security guards. The going was slow, the guards having to elbow their way through the crowd virtually person-by-person. Finally, Walker leapt up a set of stairs and into a cleared area.

"What's *up*, guys?" he yelled. A nervous silence followed.

"What's up," a few brave souls finally mumbled. Then more silence.

You would think people in L.A. would be used to familiar faces, immune, at least to a degree, to being starstruck. But an anxious energy pulsed through the crowd. From the outside, it was like watching a large group of people meet a ghost. Cody Walker looks an awful lot like his brother, even as brothers go.

"Thank you for being here!" he yelled to the crowd. And with that, he began to meet folks.

I pressed my way to the front, flashing a media badge to an imposing man in a black polo with "SECURITY" stitched across the front and back. (If he wasn't a member of the L.A. Rams offensive line practice team, the coaches may want to consider it.) Then I was allowed through the guards' perimeter to snap photos of Cody and his fans. The first two I saw come up, a young couple, looked stunned to meet him; he, in turn, in his jeans and maroon FuelFest T-shirt, seemed genuinely happy to greet each of them with a smile and a handshake. They posed for pictures, handed him things to sign, and spent a few moments chatting.

FuelFest organizers told me that this is one of the greatest challenges in assembling the entire show: Cody tends to forge such a deep connection with fans, they say, it can be difficult to keep the line moving. "Sometimes we have to give him a little nudge," one told me. "And then, other times, it's a big nudge."

Finally, both parties said goodbye. I ran to catch the couple as they headed down the stairs. Daniel, the man, was completely flustered, a woozy grin on his face. He was holding an iPhone with one hand, FaceTiming a friend and trying to find words. His other hand was planted on the back of his head, as if to keep it from spinning off like a top.

While he wrapped up the call, I chatted with his fiancée, Kyra.

She told me it was Daniel's birthday. They had traveled from San Antonio, Texas, coming to L.A. specifically to attend the show as Daniel's surprise present, a gift she had bought and organized.

"I asked his friends if this was a good show, and if Daniel would like VIP tickets since I know how much he likes *Fast & Furious*, and of course Paul," she said. "They told me to do it."

Daniel put his cousin on hold and composed himself in time to hear the end of the story. "Best. Fiancée. Ever," he said. "Aw man, I'm sure everyone tells you this, but what influenced me in cars was the first movie, of course. Unfortunately, with Paul, he passed. But he brought so many people together. Look at all of these people here, together, loving cars."

With that, he returned to the phone, saying he was "still unable to believe" what had just happened. Kyra told me that it was no accident that they were first in line to meet Cody. It was important to them to be there, as a sign of support, she said, and as a public showing of their enthusiasm. She isn't naturally into cars. "I did it for him," she said. "I try to understand. And look at the crowd here. Wow."

THE FINAL POINT Daniel wanted to make—he told me to be sure I put it down in my notebook—was how he was blown away by Cody's attitude. Walker had asked where the couple was from and how their trip was going, and he had wished them a happy life together. "He was a lot more humble than I was expecting," Daniel said. "I'm sure it's different being famous."

That fame is a clearly a sore area for Cody. He is quick to say that meeting fans is his favorite part of the show, and that he knows what it means for them to form a connection with someone close to Paul. But he still isn't exactly comfortable with celebrity, or with the tangle of feelings his can prompt. "I have a hard time with it," he said. "I go through big bouts of feeling like an imposter. Because I'm not my brother, I'm not Brian O'Conner, I'm not responsible for this culture. I'm his youngest brother, you know?"

Universal was in the middle of shooting the latest *F&F* installment, *Furious 7*, when Walker died. Rather than cancel the release or cut the rest of Paul's scenes, the studio asked Cody and his older brother Caleb to stand in for him, then used CGI to make it appear as if Paul had acted throughout.

Predictably, for the Walker brothers, the process was not easy. Cody and Caleb, still in mourning, were on set for more than three months. Cody in particular felt an obligation to help Paul finish what he had started, an approach that didn't always pull him through difficult stages of grief. Paul had a tattoo on the inside of his forearm, and the crew affixed a replica to Cody's arm that stayed there for weeks. Sometimes he would just stare at it. "There were good days and bad days," he said.

Sometimes, Cody would finish his scenes and retreat to his trailer to be alone, emotionally taxed from the weight of pretending to be the brother he had just lost, and from playing the character that had propelled him to stardom. But other days, he'd stick around set, spurred on by members of the cast. The crew told him how Paul would hang and joke with them instead of acting like a Hollywood A-lister, how he would turn down the separate meals made for high-profile cast in favor of eating whatever craft services had prepared for the day.

When finished, the movie was mostly a typical *Fast & Furious* film, with fast-paced action and stunts only loosely based on the laws of physics. But it was also a tribute to Paul. There were scenes that linger on his smile longer they need to, and that showed his character spending time with his family. The final scene in particular was surprisingly graceful and tender. Rather than explain away Paul Walker's absence, or ignore it entirely, the film took a moment to let everyone involved—cast, crew, viewers—say goodbye.

Cody Walker started FuelFest as a way to raise money for Reach Out Worldwide, his brother's charity. But he also wanted it to be a way for fans to express their appreciation for the films and Paul's role in them.

"I get to engage with car lovers all over the place," he said. "They tell me, 'I'm into cars today because of your brother,' or 'I was in a dark place when *The Fast & the Furious* came out, and it saved my life.' It gives me chills. Total strangers will tell me the most intimate stories. It's cool to hear, because my brother is the reason I'm into cars, too. We have that in common."

I ask Walker what he thinks people feel when they meet him.

"They tell me they feel the connection. For whatever reason it's me, it's not Caleb, that the fans connect so hard with. Caleb's not a car guy, I guess that's what it is. I love the car stuff. I go to different events, I support the Purist group, I'm learning everything that I possibly can. I have a connection with the community, and I guess they feel that energy from me. I appreciate that so much. They've been so welcoming and so wonderful to me. I do wonder why, though."

It seemed obvious. Fans connected with Brian O'Conner, with Paul, because he made the effort. Like Tamura at Daikoku, like so many others around the GT-R, or in any part of the culture in which I'd become so immersed, he tried to make their passion feel seen, and justified, and respected.

It's probably very easy to come into a community of people who care deeply about something, especially when you're famous, and decide only to take. One of the great things about Paul, I told Cody, was that he did the opposite. He tried his best to give.

"Honestly," Cody replied, "what's the point otherwise?

ON MY LAST day in Japan, I hopped into the GT-R and left Atsugi. Gone were the high-speed stretches of the Tōmei Expressway and the swirling lights of the Daikoku meet. Now I was piloting the GT-R from one urban center to another, squeezing through tight streets, to Zama.

Roughly 25 miles southwest of Tokyo, Zama is home to around 130,000 people. It was once rural land, becoming the first training ground and barracks for the Imperial Japanese Army Academy in the lead-up to World War II. After the war, American troops took control of the facilities. The land is now Camp Zama, a U.S. Army post.

After a half-hour drive, I reached the Zama engine manufacturing plant. The facility was once a powerhouse of Nissan production, building more than 11 million vehicles between 1965 and 1995. During the Ghosn years, a 5-billion-yen injection modernized some of the factory's equipment. That funding also helped build the Nissan Heritage Collection, a museum of important models stretching from the company's earliest days all the way up to the present. Each of the 400-plus vehicles inside is lovingly cared for by former Nissan employees.

I was there for a private visit, approved personally by corporate higher-ups. VIP access or no, though, my time bumbling around Japan was not yet complete. When I arrived at the gate, security couldn't find my name on any list of approved visitors. Worse, none of the guards on duty spoke English. Maybe it was the late night at Daikoku or the waning adrenaline that had pushed my whirlwind trip along to that point, but I couldn't make any headway. My thumbs fumbled over my phone screen while attempting to pull up old emails. All those poor security guards could gather was that some strange American had arrived in a green GT-R expecting to be let inside. One of my last professional acts in Japan involved being called a gaijin to my face.

Mercifully, my contact arrived at the gate and waved me through. I parked the GT-R and we headed inside. The Nissan Heritage Collection—simply "Zama" to Nissan heads—only finished construction around 10 years ago, and the facility wasn't open to the public until 2018. Even then, a visit required online registration and patience to receive approval, and only around 20 people were allowed to visit Zama each day. Then, in late 2019, during the coronavirus outbreak, the museum was closed to the public. It's still invite-only.

We hurried inside, where I registered at a check-in desk to receive my nametag—a formality, as I was the only guest expected for the day. Then I was ushered around to the back of the room and through a set of double doors that opened into an expansive warehouse.

I stepped into the storage area. Its scale was astounding. My visit to Japan had been defined by outrageous spectacle, from the secret Toprank GT-R garage to the Skyline graveyard at Trust Kikaku. At Zama, the feeling was different. The room was a temple. Hundreds of cars were lined up neatly and with no room to spare between, yet they still filled an area the size of several airplane hangars. Each was clinically spotless, their paint shining, almost shimmering, under the room's intense LED lights.

The other destinations on my trip had been put on the list in order to learn. You come to Zama to pay homage.

My guide checked to make sure I was still breathing. Before leaving, he rattled off a couple of facts about the space and a request to please be respectful. As the double doors closed behind him, I was left, flat-footed and alone, to bask in a monument to Japanese engineering and production. Not a sound emanated from the room.

Well, I thought, might as well get started.

NISSAN HAS an eclectic history to say the least. Over the past century, the company has chased and abandoned different trends and tastes, sometimes leading from the cutting edge, sometimes following. The room held overwhelming variety.

There were mass-market, late-20th-century models with fantastic names like the Nissan Sunny, the Cherry and, my personal favorite, the Cedric—just like the one Hiroyashi Kato was forced, decades ago, to disassemble piece by piece and then reassemble in order to begin his career as a test driver. There were all manner of pickup trucks, vans and minivans, sports cars and luxury sedans and 4x4 off-roaders. There were multiple 1960s fire trucks with bubbly faces. A 240Z Fairlady police car that had covered more than 230,000 miles. The short kings were the bizarre but adorable Nissan Pao and the Nissan Figaro, part of the company's "Pike" family of microcars, rolling cartoons from the late 1980s and early 1990s built to draw buyers based solely on cuteness. Few people wanted them, but damn if they didn't nail the art-deco-cute part.

Want old-timers? A mustard-brown 1935 Datsun 14 Roadster looked straight out of a black-and-white mobster film. The adorable, cement-blue 1937 16 Coupe would have been similarly menacing if it weren't so deliciously small, barely larger than a golf cart. The oldest car in the room was a 1933 Datsun 12 Phaeton, the first car Nissan ever made. With its giant headlights and its massive, upright grille, the 12 Phaeton wants you to believe it is a big, serious machine. But all I could see was its charmingly tapering hood, as if someone had given it a sweet little pinch on the nose.

That was a common thread in so many rows—small and chipper cars, one after another, for a small island country, that seemed to take themselves seriously. They appeared to have been designed and built by people who didn't see a lack of dignity in a lack of scale, and even occasionally took humor in it. Down the line was the 1952 Datsun Sports, dense and tidy, its features hinting at the iconic Z cars to come. Then there was the Datsun Bluebird "Flower Car," delicately hand-painted to commemorate the 1959 wedding between Japan's Crown Prince and his Empress Michiko, a commoner—the day the country's royal family officially entered its modern era. The brushwork was astonishing. Such delicacy has no American equivalent, no parallel to what it represents in the history of its home nation. Laying eyes on it felt like an honor.

I walked through the 1960s and past a rush of invigorating new designs. The Prince merger passed, then the first Skylines. Their proportions were well-balanced—they worked visually, but the cars were still ungainly. The designers hadn't quite figured out how to make a fast car look fast.

That changed in 1969. A few steps later, in those silent halls, I met the first of the GT-Rs: a bright red PGC10 four-door sedan, a.k.a. the Skyline 2000GT-R—the Hakosuka. It was slim in the waist, with a flat hood, starkly purposeful lines, and less chrome than anything even remotely related that had come before it. The car looked light and sporty. The two-door model that followed in 1970 took the idea even further. The one at Zama boasted black wheels and menacing, fender-mounted side mirrors. The hairs on the back of my neck stood up.

Rumors persist that original Hakosukas are coveted by the yakuza. It was mentioned to me more than once on my trip that criminal enterprises don't take kindly to those who try to export Hakos from Japan; I heard stories of distinguished gentlemen who would show up at ports to firmly prevent certain examples from leaving. It is impossible to stare into the headlights of one of those cars without understanding that desire, even a little.

I was not fully prepared for the Kenmeri GT-R. The 1970s one, with the American styling, fewer than 200 made because of the oil crisis. In photos—previously the only place I had seen a real, honest-to-God Kenmeri—the model always seemed to be trying too hard, a kind of Camaro-Mustang Lite. The rear fender lines were off; the wide grille was a Dodge Challenger knockoff; the skinny tires were unconvincing. I largely wrote it off.

And then. The Zama car, painted in a bright cherry red that seemed to jump off the body under the room's soft lights, was a total smack in the face. So much presence! The wide Challenger grille in front of that long, flat hood was actually a strength, not a weakness—I couldn't stop staring at it, waiting for it to gulp me up if I got too close. Several distinctly Japanese elements breathed in regional flavor, like the black, hood-mounted mirrors and the large, curvy overfenders. The rear fender lines still didn't work for me, but who cares? The Kenmeri GT-R parties hard.

As I walked away, I thought about the low production—was it 197 made? One ninety-eight? The number was in my notes somewhere, I couldn't remember. Those cars, with so few made, so few people will get to see what I saw in person, how great they can be. The Kenmeri largely parties alone.

Further on, through the 1970s and into the 1980s, Nissan performance felt mostly like a dead zone. That period of fuel shortages and tightening emissions regulations, when producing exciting cars was a struggle. The 1987 R31 2000 GTS-R didn't go far enough. The one in

Zama, painted dark black, had all the makings of an interesting design, low-slung, with neat air intakes and a fat rear spoiler. It just... didn't connect. Something was missing.

I found that something a few cars down, in the Mid4-II on display. A sleek and silver sports-coupe bullet, this was the futuristic, mid-engine supercar concept created by Shinichiro Sakurai in his grand return after a lengthy illness. It was a departure from the rest of the room, a sea change, like absolutely nothing Nissan made before or since: exotic lines and curves, a low nose, flowing aerodynamic surfaces. Somehow the Mid4-II looks both glued to the ground and, simultaneously, ready to take flight.

That was what Sakurai and Nissan needed to bridge the gap between where the Skyline had been and where it needed to go. By shooting for the moon, they narrowed their focus, which let them firm up their goals. And then they went out and destroyed them.

PUT in context with the rest of Nissan's history, it's remarkable what the R32, R33, and R34 Skylines were able to do. In the grand scheme, they launched an embattled Japanese automaker onto the global stage and helped establish it as one of the world's great car companies. They inspired millions of fans on every continent and became the star of any media that featured them.

Over time the car, the company, and the fanbase grew together to create a triumvirate of passion, one that I don't believe has been matched by any competitor since. And it's not as if Skyline GT-Rs are exactly rare. Honda made only 18,000 NSXs over 15 years. Toyota made some 40,000 Mark IV Supras in a shorter span. Nissan made more than 60,000 examples of the Holy Trinity GT-Rs from 1989 to 2002. Yet the Nissans are easily the most widely coveted of the three.

The magic of the GT-R is what happened when people took them home and made them their own. Skyline GT-Rs are not especially impressive in stock form; even the biggest Nissan superfans will tell you the cars need tweaking to be just right. But whether you're street racing or drag racing, tackling the touge or building a *Fast & Furious* tribute, none of those tweaks would have been possible without the vision and ambition of those who built the car.

Real individuals dreamed up that potential. Real people wanted to create a car that reached new heights, that inspired in a way other Nissans had not. They created new technologies and tried new strategies, and when that didn't work, they built outrageous concept cars to clear their heads. The Trinity GT-Rs didn't appear out of thin air; they were born and raised in a Japan that had grown up inspired by how the first Hakosuka won races, that hoped and wished to recapture a magic it had once felt.

Out of everything that eventually became part of the Skyline GT-R story—the warehouse at Toprank or the parts cottage industry at Trust Kikaku, the mess at MotoRex or the seizures at Kaizo, the legends at Racing Team Mid Night or the famous scenes in *Fast & Furious*—none of it would have happened without the work that went in at the root, at the carmaker, at the company. The only reason we have epic showdowns at TX2K and a frenzied crowd at FuelFest is because a group of Nissan employees worked for years to make it all possible.

Admittedly, I'm simplifying the point here. Nissan is not the only company with a story like this. You could tell a similar tale about many performance cars. Yet standing in that museum at Zama, among decades of factory-fresh examples, only drove home to me how the importance of the those who cast and stamped the metals and turned the wrenches. They put the cars out into the world, hoping and praying someone would enjoy them.

Seeing stock Skyline GT-Rs on display at Zama isn't a particularly moving experience. They seemed a little too pure, newborn, like fresh blocks of clay that you're not allowed to play with. Zama doesn't show us what the world of Skylines and GT-Rs would ultimately become. It shows us what a small collection of passionate car people wished—that ultimately, the whole of what they had just built would be greater than the sum of the parts.

The miracle is that it actually worked. Ordinary people felt something. And in the end, those people took that feeling further than anyone would have thought.

It was the realized vision of Sakurai. The vowed redemption of Naganori Ito. The delicate testing of Hiroyoshi Kato. The finishing touches of Kazutoshi Mizuno and Hiroshi Tamura.

My greatest takeaway from seeing the Holy Trinity at Zama was their humanity.

THAT WAS my first hour at Zama. I spent the second hour absolutely losing my mind.

An entire wing of the Nissan Heritage Collection is dedicated to racing. Some of the most lustworthy racecars on the planet, all parked tightly together, as if laid out specifically to give you an aneurysm. It's an orgasm of GT-R track dominance.

There were three R32 GT-R racecars, parked together, that would blow the doors off any auction if they ever hit the market. The inspiration for countless imitators, except they were the real thing: the stunning blue Calsonic-liveried car that won the 1990 Japanese Touring Car Championship and forced the restructuring of the class rules around fairness; the white Zexel car that won the 24 Hours of Spa in 1991 by an incredible 21 laps; the red-and-black STP Taisan car that ran at the front of the pack throughout 1993 in the hands of the "Drift King" Keiichi Tsuchiya.

Titans. Immense monsters of image and story and 100-proof meaning, and they all appeared before me as a whole, a complete unit, as if I had chosen them to spawn in a video game.

The breadth of Nissan's motorsports legacy is stunning. The Pennzoil R33 and Xanavi R34 that people pay hundreds of dollars simply to buy plastic model kits of? There. Rear spoilers with their own spoilers, spoilers on spoilers, over there. Super Silhouette cars, a few feet away. There were more iconic R34 racers, extreme ground-effect Super GT machines with insane aerodynamics from the early 2000s, *Gran Turismo* favorites one after another. On this side of the room was an entire row of R390 GT1 prototypes intended to conquer the 24 Hours of Le Mans. On that side was a row of unhinged IMSA GTP Group C prototypes. *I've been entrusted with these vehicles... alone? No supervision? This is madness.*

There was so much more. Want the four-door Hakosuka that captured the first overall victory for the GT-R family in history? The Prince R380 that beat Porsches in 1966; another that set seven world records in top speed? There you go, there they are. Right there.

I was utterly overwhelmed, trying to capture as much video as I could, unable to process what I was seeing. I knew that, in a matter of hours, none of it would feel real, the memory fading. I had the whole room to myself, row after row of inspiration, and yet, when I held my pen and notepad and prepared for the words, they did not come. Those race cars meant something to people, and if you know, you know. Right?

It was too much.

Of course it was too much.

All that history, spinning around. It can be exhausting to hear, someone spouting off every single car and accomplishment, I know. That level of nerding-out can intimidate those who maybe don't know as much, or who can't remember it all, or who are simply into something different. It was too much for me, even. I get it. I'll stop now, I promise.

As my allotted time at Zama wound down, I didn't want to spend it chasing one last photo, or racing to spend more time with some little-known GT-R that I nearly missed and had all but forgotten about. Instead, I simply walked over to the car that had resonated with me the most, and I sat down, and I visited with it.

It was a 1995 R33 GT-R LM. The only one in the world. Basically, Nissan wanted to win Le Mans, but the class it wanted to enter required you to race a version of a car that people could buy for the road. You had to build only one of those cars, so Nissan did. I was standing next to it.

I don't know why this particular R33 gets me so bad. Maybe it's that rarity. There were 44 R33 400Rs made; there were 19 R33 Z-Tunes built; those were mass-produced by comparison. Maybe it was because the LM was a *Gran Turismo* fantasy for so many around the world. Maybe because Le Mans is my biggest motorsport-nerd weakness, the one subject in the space I cannot get enough of, and here was a GT-R designed for nothing but a back-alley entry into what I humbly suggest is the coolest race in the world.

I sat and stared at it for a few minutes. Not trying to answer the question, just wanting to... share its space, I suppose. How many opportunities like this do we get in life? To be allowed to simply occupy a moment with something important to us, without expectation or ROI? No one had sent me to Japan, or to Zama. There was no boss sending me directives. No one would flood my phone with calls or texts demanding that I edit or post, or like, comment, and subscribe.

I sat and stared at the R33 LM like you sit and stare at the ocean. Watching the reflections in its fenders as you watch a wave crash into the shore and retreat, eyes fixed on one particular spot in the hope it'll reveal some grand design. Here's the funny part: That car didn't even accomplish anything. The LM isn't key to the GT-R's street-racing or tuner lore. It never raced. It was never even really driven, just immediately socked away in a museum. I was standing next to piece of sculpture with a VIN.

That's enough, isn't it? A sculpture on wheels to represent the GT-R era. The media doesn't get to review it, write pithy quips about its pros and cons. No collector gets to examine it, pore over its flaws, assign it a number value. The car simply gets to be. Free of expectation. It exists for its own sake.

That was good enough for me. I was ready to go. I grabbed the notebook I had set on the floor, having written not one word, and turned and left through the double doors.

CHAPTER 15

Bill Gates lost his car to United States Customs for more than a decade because he felt compelled to own a Porsche 959 in his own country. Hiroaki Nanahoshi had to disappear because he had wanted the GT-R lifestyle more than he wanted a successful business. And Daryl Alison, an officer sworn to protect, was convicted of federal crimes because something drove him to bring Skylines into the country by any means necessary.

Those stories all seem to align with that "emotional arousal" arc described by those European researchers.

The story of Andres Diaz and Nicole Chiong, unsurprisingly, traces a similar path.

For the people who gave Diaz and Chiong money, the couple offered something more than mere wheels. The chance to own an R32 GT-R or a Japanese-market Civic Type R was a gateway, a door into a world they had only read about or seen on a screen. Soho Imports was selling cars, but its customers were buying fantasies.

The attempt to bring Diaz and Chiong to trial dragged on for over a year. I started tuning in to livestreams of their pretrial hearings in November of 2022. By July of 2023, I had watched five separate court appearances and five separate requests for postponement. Once, overwhelmed by Soho's sheer number of customers, the prosecution asked for more time to track down additional victims. In another hearing, Chiong's lawyer told the judge that his client had been "actively negotiating" with authorities since before charges were even filed. The only remaining issue standing between her and a plea bargain, he said, was the determination of how much the victims were owed in restitution.

"Well," the lawyer added, "I would say 'victims' in quotes. But how many are there? And how are we gonna evaluate that?"

I thought a lot about those customers while writing this book. They were not easy to get ahold of. Most had gone into hiding. Some appeared to have turned in their vehicles in exchange for a payout for their troubles. But what is a car that can't be driven, titled, or registered really worth?

That question, Chiong's lawyer said, was the only "sticky issue" left to sort out. He planned to interview an owner to determine a figure. One owner. Imagine trying to come up with an average value for nearly 90 cars, each of the same make and model but with different modifications, histories, years, and conditions. Who knows how many special editions, how many rare parts from places like HKS or Nismo, would have been overlooked or purposely hidden.

Unfazed, the judge ordered both sides to come to an agreement. "You guys seem to have narrowed it down to some fairly succinct issues," he said. "There's gotta be a car guy out there who can give you the answers."

One car guy? If my research taught me anything, it's that it's never, ever that simple.

And what of the owners who didn't turn in their cars? The ones who couldn't bear to part with them, even if that meant a title forever invalid, a life where a single parking or speeding ticket could mean seizure, the crusher, or arrest? Those cars are almost certainly under wraps. Maybe they're stored in secret garages, stuffed in the back of large collections, hidden under tarps and out of sight.

Those people probably won't try to unload those cars onto someone else. Nor, experts told me, are they likely to export them to somewhere they can be legally owned and driven. Because in the end, they hadn't purchased a car, or a GT-R, or a Nissan—they had bought themselves a tangible piece of a dream. They had been sold the opportunity to finally live their lives as they had always wanted. The 25-year law wasn't enough to kill that, and a revoked title wouldn't be enough to make them give it up, either. Maybe the people who ran Soho Imports, and the cars they imported, will one day meet a hefty sentence. Or maybe, like so many in the GT-R world, they'll find a loophole or a safe space to hide, and eventually, like a lone *sakura* flower lifted by a gentle breeze into the air, they'll simply float away. To disappear. And be all but forgotten.

YOU DON'T HAVE to be an owner to be an important part of the GT-R community. In my time researching this book, I met dozens of individuals who simply felt a need to be as close to Skylines and GT-Rs as possible, regardless of whether they could put one in their garage. Those folks scratched the itch by working on GT-Rs as mechanics, or by shooting photos and video of them, becoming historians, cataloging material to help it be saved and preserved. To make sure a story was remembered.

When you talk to those people about the roots of their passion, they invariably mention a respect and admiration for what the car represents. They tell you about those who created the machine, or who drove it to victory, or who wrote their own chapters in its history. But they will also tell you how the GT-R itself has an aura, a character all its own, different from other fast cars. They refer to Skylines as if they were living, breathing, endangered things. Something to be protected for future generations, sheltered for its own good.

In one source's garage, I turned a corner and was stunned to find myself face-to-face with an R34 GT-R. The source hadn't told me the car was there, but that big, blunt face was unmistakable, those squinting headlights staring deep into my chest. The R34 had been casually hidden under a thrown-together pile of towels, flags, and tarps, but the shape was unmistakable.

In my travels, I came across multiple people who felt drawn to the role of GT-R preservationist. Maybe it's because the car attracts poachers and scammers, those who would take advantage of a desire to get close to the beast. From Derek Allen Banks, pitching the promise of GT-R expertise, to the individual who sold Kelvin Malli his "rust is minimal" R32, to the dozens of fibbing sellers exposed by the Team Free Spirit Instagram account (look it up, it's fantastic), the world is rife with those looking to use the cars to squeeze a quick buck.

The preservationists see themselves as stewards. They work to expose the bad guys and call out nonbelievers. Their interactions on social media can turn sour, a crucifixion because a car was not modified in a widely approved fashion or not treated as it "should" be. Some will call the bona fides of an owner into question, wondering whether that person bought the car because they understand and love it, or because ownership carries outsize weight online. ("Doing it for the clout," the phrase goes.)

Lastly, there are those who pay attention to whether widening GT-R appreciation attracts the right kind of customer. In those cases, I'm immediately reminded of the buyer of a particular R33 400R, one of the rarest GT-R models, with only a handful of examples in the U.S. It was at Toprank to be sold, and the company had reportedly received multiple offers of more than $2 million. Rather than chase the largest check, Toprank selected an individual who already owned multiple Skyline GT-Rs. One who had expressed a passion for the species, and who promised to share the car with the public.

Yes, that buyer paid handsomely. More than seven figures, by his own admission. But Toprank was looking for someone who would actively give back. What GT-R enthusiasts—sorry, preservationists—want is not for the cars to simply find good homes. They want them to find sanctuary.

THREE DAYS DOWN. After returning to Nissan's headquarters and pulling back into that same underground parking garage, I stepped out of the Millennium Jade car and collected my things. I'd been traveling around Japan with only a laptop bag and a backpack of clothes, and it was time to slog back across an ocean. After a quick walkaround of the R35 and a few words of thanks, I handed over the keys and watched someone else drive "my" car around the corner and out of sight. *Sayonara*, my friend.

Nissan's global H.Q. is just a few minutes' walk from the Yokohama train station, so I floated over there, light on my feet and feeling peaceful, and I caught a train. But I wasn't headed to the airport just yet. Instead, I took the Shohan-Shinjuku Line for 30 minutes, hopping off at Shinagawa Station and transferring onto the Rinkai Line. Fifteen minutes after that, I walked off the platform at Shin-Kiba Station and into the Tokyo ward of Kōtō City.

Outside, waiting at the curb, was a white minivan with a smiling woman at the wheel. She popped out and rushed to greet me, black bangs covering her forehead and curling to frame wire-thin glasses, accompanying a stylish puffy yellow blouse under brown overalls. This was Mamina Inada, daughter of Daijiro Inada, the *Option* magazine founder and high-speed-testing king. We were off to meet the master himself.

Mamina invited me into the van. I tossed my bags on the floor and headed for the left-side passenger seat. The van's interior was littered with auto magazines and racing DVDs. A screen mounted on the dash of the car played commercials on a loop, even as she drove. When I pointed out the copies of Video Option in her DVD stack, Mamina smiled and laughed. She likes to watch them on long drives, she said.

It took only minutes to drive to the offices, a compact three-story building on a man-made strip of land in Tokyo Bay. Both of the brand's magazines, *Option* and *Option 2*, live there, along with the staff of Video Option—roughly 30 staffers in total. But you wouldn't know it from the outside. When we pulled up, the only indication that we had arrived at the most influential automotive publication in Japan was a sole R32 GT-R parked out front.

Mamina led me inside and up the stairs, past decades of past *Option* issues in stacks up to my waist, to the second floor. There we found the root of it all, Dai Inada himself. He tottered over in a slim-fitting grey V-neck sweater, his famously spiky wild-orange hair now a closely cropped salt-and-pepper style. With a friendly welcome, he motioned me and Mamina to a conference room where we could chat, and pointed me toward a seat with a waiting green tea.

Inada is older now, well into his 70s. He's accumulated five decades of publishing experience under his belt. But he is fit and virile, with round forearm muscles shaping the sleeves of his cardigan. When he speaks, it's with the vigorous and forceful tone of someone who's seen it all.

He would not have come this far without this bold self-assuredness. Inada never studied journalism or writing, and he launched *Option*, in the early 1980s, as a self-proclaimed bad driver. But he was passionate about the burgeoning customization-and-tuning scene. "The theme of *Option* was to have the world recognize the excellence of tuning," he said. The very first issue issued a call for a public "cannonball run," a loosely organized, high-speed, point-to-point race on public roads that soon became a reality. The staff became active players in the scene, modifying magazine cars with their own hands and documenting the work in each issue. The publicity was a boon to tuning companies, who reacted to the newfound demand by expanding their businesses and capabilities.

But at the time, tuning and customizing was largely still illegal. Even changing the fenders on your car, then a pretty basic and time-honored modification in the US, could land you a fine in Japan. In the eyes of police and inspectors, performing any mods on your personal car lumped you in with the trouble-making bosozoku. *Option*, led by Inada, proposed the idea that tuning and even fast driving were enjoyed by upstanding citizens. "The bosozoku, his car is not a tuning car—only sound," Inada said. "Japanese tuning people want to drive fast. Not POP-POP-POP-POP-POP! They are very different from bosozoku. Option is not bosozoku."

Option encouraged its readers to rally around the cause. They petitioned and called the phone lines of local vehicle inspectors to plead their case, and eventually, slowly, the laws began to change. Around 1990, as *Option* closed in on its first decade in print, the restrictions lifted on custom bodywork and some tuning regulations. The mission had been a success. What happened, Inada said, was that the people in government realized they liked cars, too.

"Japanese policemen are very kind," he said. "Our modifying culture is very progressed, and they mix enforcement with kindness. In the United States, people with tuned and custom cars are typically young. So policemen are very strict. But here in Japan, tuning it not young. It's just normal people that like cars. Policemen like cars too, and they say, 'Nice car, now slow down or go home.'"

At this, Mamina turns to face me. "Policemen love Dai," she says. "It's because he is famous."

Inada lets out a quick chuckle. It's more of a nod of acknowledgement that, hey, it is what it is. The man has seen it all. It was Inada who pushed cars to their limit and beyond on the Yatabe High Speed oval. It was Inada who brought D1 GP to California for its iconic exhibition. It was Inada who sent cameras to the UK for Smokey Nagata's 200-mph attempt on public roads, that turned the shy mechanic into a global superstar.

After getting bailed out of jail, Nagata called Inada and gave him the news. "You got arrested?" the *Option* boss said over the phone. "Well, of course you did!"

These days, he still wants to go fast. For his daily errands Inada drives a Nissan Sunny pickup truck adorned with red, white, and blue stripes. The design was made famous by Datsuns raced in America during the 1970s, and it holds special significance to the *Option* founder. But he still considers the R32 GT-R a cornerstone of the tuning movement, and a masterstroke of Japanese engineering. From its first arrival at the Nurburgring as a development mule in the late 1980s, Inada said, the speed and ease of the GT-R around the track's famously treacherous curves made Porsche engineers sit up and take notice. "They could see the GT-R is more easy to drive," he said. "Easier than Porsche."

Like many in Japan, the idea of normal people bring priced out of GT-R ownership saddens him. Attainability is, after all, supposed to be the whole point of the car. "They're more expensive in the US than in Japan," Inada noted. "And the R34 will become the most expensive because it's limited. China and the United Arab Emirates love to buy 34s, too. Honestly, loving cars is okay. But this is not in best interest. Now rich people buy them for investment. That's sad."

What hits him most is just how Japanese the GT-R is, at its core. He describes with reverence the classic Japanese shape, smooth but boxy styling, with a long hood. But when I ask Inada what truly makes the GT-R stand apart from its rivals, he has an interesting perspective. It's not the RB26 motor. It's the four-wheel drive system.

"ATTESA is the character," he said, noting that lots of cars are capable of making big power, but the GT-R offered stability and capable handling at speed. "Everybody can drive fast. Since GT-R are so safe, even children can go fast."

Safety is the top priority for Inada these days. He's seen colleagues perish at the Yatabe high-speed course in the early *Option* days. He's endured ghastly collisions of his own during record attempts in New Zealand and Australia. Many times he's raced the Bonneville salt flats, in Utah, where the fastest land-speed machines in human history entered their names into the record books. If he can find the right car, Inada would like to return for another shot at topping 300 mph. "I want to be champion of Unlimited class," the septugenarian said.

In the meantime, he's happy to serve as chief steward of worldwide tuning culture. The market has seen a lot of change in his 40-plus years, and he predicts more is on the way. "In the future, tuning culture will be like hot rod culture," he said. "Old body and new engine." Inada sees electric vehicles merging with older body styles, like those of the Holy Trinity Skylines, pumping them full of electric juice that can be controlled by computers. Ripe for tuning. He's a purist at heart, and prefers a traditional gas engine to electric vehicles. But they are "useful," he said, and besides, an RB26 may one day be too valuable to risk driving on public roads—just like his beloved Hakosuka.

Times change, and Inada and *Option* will change with them. But after my meeting with the tuning master, it's clear his appreciation for the GT-R will remain the same.

"The good thing is, they look slow," he said. "Not like a Ferrari. But with tuning, they can be faster than a Ferrari."

I let out a laugh, and Inada-san sent a knowing glance.

"It's the *Option* way," he said.

OUR INTERVIEW WRAPPED, Mamina dropped me back at the train station. I boarded the line for the airport—happy, but exhausted. My three days were officially up. It was time to go home.

When the plane lifted into the air, I was ready to sit back and knock out. Then, out the window, I caught one last glimpse of the city and bay below. It seemed impossible that there, in those same waters, Commodore Perry had first stormed in and changed the course of Japan forever. And that somewhere below, in one of those jutting jawbones of docks and highways, was the *Option* offices. Further down was the Nissan Global Headquarters, and the Daikoku Parking Area. Within the past 24 hours I had visited all three, speaking with legends and wandering the world's most famous car meet "with a god," as my friend had predicted. Time with Tamura-san on a private tour of hallowed ground? Had that really happened? Had any of it really happened at all?

My eyes felt heavy. I was beginning to fade, mercifully, from consciousness. The lights below grew tinier and blurred together. It seemed impossible that one place, so densely packed, could have produced so many dedicated people, so much culture that dented the rest of the world.

When you got high enough above it, you could almost see it, all of it, all the history at once.

I wondered how it felt to hit those roads at night, and approach the soaring Bay Bridge at in the dark. Passing over Yokohama, attacking the curving highway Wangan ramps as they glowed soft orange from the lights overhead. As the red-and-white arrows on their concrete walls lead you forward, moving faster and faster until they seem animated, blinking in sync and egging you on.

I wondered how it felt to hear the turbos spool and the engine scream as the arrows speed up, as the road straightens out and you fly into the night as if shot from a cannon. Maybe you're in an R32 GT-R, that legendary stalker of the Wangan, the engine so stuffed with aftermarket parts that the hood all but bursts at the seams. Crack the window; take it all in.

I imagined dancing through traffic stable and calm. Maybe you touch the wheel with only three fingers from each hand, or maybe you turn off the headlights for "stealth mode," as the old Mid Night drivers did. Maybe, as speeds creep higher, your spine pins deeper and deeper into a Nismo or Bride or Recaro bucket seat. As the speedometer reaches the 300-kph mark you hold it there, engine full-bore and exhaust howling, for a full minute. Or five. Maybe 10. Is it really possible that, back in the day, they did this on public roads for 20 minutes straight?

I wondered how it felt to see the headlights of a competitor—running alongside at first, then drifting back and falling behind. You keep pushing, and they can't keep up. In the rearview, the dots of light gradually fade, then flicker, and finally disappear.

And that's it. You have the highway to yourself. You're all alone, in a piece of the story, in its homeland, the night stretching out before you, endlessly. You've won. You are free; you are alive; you have a soul. You lived the dream.

ACKNOWLEDGMENTS

From the outset, this easily became the most challenging work of my career. Not only for the breadth of its scope, spanning multiple countries and languages and incorporating several centuries' worth of history into a (hopefully) entertaining package, but also in the potential for letting people down. There is a sanctity to the Skyline GT-R and its culture that means a great deal to its most ardent enthusiasts. This is not lost on me. I would like to sincerely thank those who accepted me among their ranks and deemed me worthy of hearing their stories. Without their openness and willingness to participate, this book would simply not be possible.

Similarly, I would also like to issue my sincere gratitude to my contacts in Japan, who received me with warmth, grace and understanding, and helped keep me from bumbling around their country too much in my effort to learn their stories and understand their passion. In particular, I am grateful for the time spent with Hiroshi Tamura, both in the U.S. and in Japan, and for his belief that I could do justice to his story. I believe the book is significantly enhanced because of his trust in me, and I hope he feels the same.

I was floored by the support offered to me by Caryn Baird, of Flat Rate Research, and the Poynter Institute. Her willingness to look over mountains of documents and seek out additional sources was so validating at a time when I needed it most. People like Caryn and organizations like Poynter are the reason journalism has remained alive and kicking as long as it has.

Any positive sentiments for this book should be directed toward my incredible editors. My deepest, deepest thanks to my friend Sarah Bennett for her keen early insights into structure and pacing. Your reporting instincts are surpassed only by your ability to instill joy in journalism students and the writing community at large. It was an absolute pleasure to team up again with Sam Smith, who has now guided both of what I consider my greatest achievements in writing, and who is for my money the most jealousy-inducing automotive journalist of our generation. Thank you both, sincerely.

I would be remiss not to thank my marketing and business advisors, Geoffrey Kutnick and Michael Chiavetta, for the many coffees, lunches and impromptu brainstorming sessions that I sprung on them whenever I became fixated on an idea or hit a dead end. The value of their steadfast confidence in me, and willingness to provide a jolt of needed inspiration at a moment's notice, cannot be overstated.

My brothers for life, Aaron Sanchez, Andrew Veis, Brian Roberts and Allan Lagomarsino, made themselves available anytime I asked. A few times they dropped in just to check on me, before I even realized how badly I needed someone to reach out and do just that, and graciously let me catch them up on all the twists and turns of the GT-R world, no matter how maniacal I must have sounded after the fifth or sixth time. I will always remember your support throughout this journey.

To my family, who one again agreed to put up with missed calls, booked weekends, rearranged dinner plans and all manner of other inconveniences so that I may pursue this endeavor, thank you. You never failed to show genuine interest, help me keep things in perspective, and make sure I remembered to eat a snack and take a nap. To my sister Leigh, my bonus sisters Melissa and Stephanie, my brother-in-law Keith, my parents-in-law Ellis and Gabriela, my stepfather Todd, my mother Dana, and my father Dave – there simply aren't words to express thanks for the strength you make sure I receive.

Finally, for my girls, Claire and Nikol, you are my world and moon and stars. Over the years I have asked so much of you, and every single time, you've shown up in all the ways I needed and more. Thank you for placing your trust in me, and for being willing to walk blindly into the unknown by my side. Thank you for believing in my excitement, and matching my energy when I need a cheerleader. It is my main purpose in life and work to make you proud. I know I am forever in awe of your heart, your spirit, and the way you love me. I know I am proud of us.

NOTES

This book is based on firsthand accounts, painstaking review of rare materials and never-before-reported documents, and hundreds of interviews conducted between late 2022 and the Fall of 2023.

The world of Skyline GT-Rs and JDM imports is murky and full of accusations, rumor and hearsay. I made the decision to omit many unconfirmed stories shared with me, and if a story is included but could not be independently verified, it is noted as such.

Events in the narrative are provided by primary sources, or told to the author and corroborated through additional research. Dialogue was taken from video recordings, audio files or transcripts. Emails and text messages were viewed by or described to the author.

Thank you to those who opened doors, offered their time and pointed me in the right direction. This project would not exist without your generosity, passion, and contributions to the culture.

Chapter 1
Based on the author's firsthand experiences, interviews and perspective gleaned from 10-plus years of reporting.

Chapter 2
...900-hp R34 GT-R: Mario Christou, "Foreign Exchange: A Well

Traveled R34 GT-R," SpeedHunters, June 16, 2020, http://www.speedhunters.com/2020/06/foreign-exchange-well-travelled-r34-gt-r/.
...track-focused R34: Trevor Ryan, "Five of the Best From R's Day," SpeedHunters, December 31, 2017, http://www.speedhunters.com/2017/12/five-of-the-best-from-rs-day/.

Chapter 3

...known as the Tokugawa: George Feifer, *Breaking Open Japan* (Smithsonian Books, 2006).
...Europeans had stormed ashore: "The United States and the Opening to Japan, 1853," Office of the Historian, https://history.state.gov/milestones/1830-1860/opening-to-japan.
...Perry stayed in the bay: "Brief Summary of the Perry Expedition to Japan, 1853," Naval History and Heritage Command, https://www.history.navy.mil/research/library/online-reading-room/title-list-alphabetically/b/brief-summary-perry-expedition-japan-1853.html.
...Japan promised to protect: "The Treaty of Kanagawa," National Archives, https://www.archives.gov/exhibits/featured-documents/treaty-of-kanagawa.
...typical junior high textbook: Norimitsu Onishi, "Ripples From Perry's Ships Are Still Felt in Japan," *New York Times*, August 11, 2003, https://www.nytimes.com/2003/08/11/world/yokosuka-journal-ripples-from-perry-s-ships-are-still-felt-in-japan.html.
Born in 1880: "Nissan Legend 1 Yoshisuke Aikawa: A Modern Man With Insight," Nissan Motor Corporation, October 8, 2023, https://usa.nissannews.com/en-US/releases/nissan-legend-1-yoshisuke-aikawa-a-modern-man-with-insight.
...found work as a mechanic: Kenji Kato, "The Men who Aided Manufacturing," Hitachi Review, February, 2021, https://www.hitachi.com/rev/column/gf/vol10/pdf/GlobalForesights.pdf.
...produced railyard machinery: Susan J. Eck, "The Gould Coupler Strike of 1914," Western New York History, https://www.wnyhistory.com/portfolios/businessindustry/gould_coupler_1914/gould_coupler_1914.htm.
...1934 shareholder's meeting: Shizuo Takashima, "Nissan Started

With Attitude," Nissan Motor Corporation, https://asean.nissannews.com/en/NissanStartedWithAttitude.

..."If you have strong belief": Nicolaus Li, "Nissan Unveils Redesigned Logo Badge to Match Digital World," Hypebeast, July 16, 2020, https://hypebeast.com/2020/7/nissan-new-2020-redesigned-logo-badge-unveil-info.

...pattern its business methods: Evelyn Anderson, "Nissan's Keiretsu, 1956-1970," Business History Conference, 2007, https://thebhc.org/sites/default/files/anderson.pdf.

...effort to establish a Southeast Asian empire: "The Japanese Wartime Empire, 1931-1945," Princeton University Press, https://press.princeton.edu/books/paperback/9780691145068/the-japanese-wartime-empire-1931-1945.

...pivoted to making trucks and airplanes: History.com Editors, "Nissan Motor Company founded," HISTORY, May 28, 2020, https://www.history.com/this-day-in-history/nissan-motor-company-founded.

...lost more than two million people: The Editors of Encyclopaedia Britannica, "How many people died during World War II?" Britannica, https://www.britannica.com/question/How-many-people-died-during-World-War-II.

...established military posts: John W. Dower, *Embracing Defeat: Japan in the Wake of World War II* (W. W. Norton & Company, 1999).

..."endure the unendurable": Feifer, ibid.

...in a 1951 Congressional hearing: Mieko Endo, "Douglas MacArthur's occupation of Japan | Building the foundation of U.S.-Japan relationship," University of Montana, 2006, https://scholarworks.umt.edu/cgi/viewcontent.cgi?article=3123&context=etd.

...sharing his concerns privately: Kato, ibid.

...very first car made: Informational placards at Nissan Heritage Collection in Zama, Japan.

...established a stronghold in Korea: "Korean War," Eisenhower Library, https://www.eisenhowerlibrary.gov/research/online-documents/korean-war.

...the Japanese cheered privately: Dower, ibid.

…**customs like bureaucracy:** "History of METI," METI, https://www.meti.go.jp/english/aboutmeti/data/ahistory.html.

…**"low, humble posture"**: Lee Kuan Yew, *From Third World to First: The Singapore Story, 1965-2000* (Harper, 2000).

…**shocked Allied pilots:** Russ Lee, "Nakajima Ki-43-IIb Hayabusa (Peregrine Falcon) OSCAR, Smithsonian, August 1, 2013, https://www.si.edu/object/nakajima-ki-43-iib-hayabusa-peregrine-falcon-oscar%3Anasm_A19600098000.

…**flew in Italian craftsmen:** "Prince Skyline Sport," Nissan Motor Corporation, https://www.nissan-global.com/EN/HERITAGE/302_prince_skyline_sport.html.

…**six-cylinder S20 engine:** "Infiniti to show Prince R380 at 2017 Amelia Island Concours d'Elegance," Infiniti Motor Company, https://usa.infinitinews.com/en-US/releases/release-847653c927c5437a80a375001633de8a-infiniti-to-show-prince-r380-at-2017-amelia-island-concours-d-elegance.

…**merging of two terms:** "From Skyline to GT-R," Nissan Motor Corporation, September 21, 2021, https://usa.nissanstories.com/en-US/releases/from-skyline-to-gt-r.

…**adopt shorter production timelines:** Brendan McAleer, "The Hakosuka Nissan Skyline GT-R was a legend well before it was named "Godzilla," Hagerty, February 12, 2019, https://www.hagerty.com/media/archived/hakosuka-nissan-gt-r-is-legendary/.

…**skyrocketing fuel prices:** "1973 Nissan Skyline H/T 2000GT-R 'Kenmeri,'" RM Sotheby's, 2015, https://rmsothebys.com/en/auctions/mo15/monterey/lots/r155-1973-nissan-skyline-ht-2000gt-r-kenmeri/180548.

…**first entered the U.S. market:** Jeff Koch, "Front-Drive, Funky, Fun, First! - 1970-1972 Honda N600," Hemmings, September 24, 2018, https://www.hemmings.com/stories/article/front-drive-funky-fun-first-1970-1972-honda-n600.

…**first model stateside:** "Company History," Toyota Motor Corporation, 2023, https://pressroom.toyota.com/company-history/.

…**typical Japanese automaker:** Tim Larimer, "Japan, Nissan and the Ghosn Revolution," Columbia Business School, 2003.

..."strong anticommunist bastion": Paul Krugman, *The Return of Depression Economics and the Crisis of 2008* (W. W. Norton, 2008).

...world's second largest economy: "Japan's Economy," Asialink Business, https://asialinkbusiness.com.au/japan/getting-started-in-japan/japans-economy?doNothing=1.

...To Western astonishment: Krugman, *The Return of Depression Economics*, ibid.

...Nissan followed up: Chris Bruce, "13 Generations Of Nissan Skyline Reveal Godzilla's Evolution," Motor1, September 30, 2020, https://www.motor1.com/news/446562/nissan-skyline-13-generations-evolution/.

...Skyline had lost something: Ben Hsu, "50 YEAR CLUB: Nissan Skyline GT-R," Japanese Nostalgic Car, February 21, 2019, https://japanesenostalgiccar.com/50-year-club-nissan-skyline-gt-r-hakosuka/.

...started with Prince: "The Real Face of Mr. Skyline," Nissan Motor Corporation, https://www.nissan-global.com/EN/HERITAGE/LEGENDS/LEGEND_04/.

...run-up to the launch: Rowan Horncastle, "Dark tourism: the Nissan Skyline graveyard," Top Gear, August 26, 2019, https://www.topgear.com/car-news/tgs-guide-japan/dark-tourism-nissan-skyline-graveyard

...trounced by competitors: Adam Ismail, "The MID4 Concept Was This Close To Being Nissan's Flagship Supercar," Jalopnik, August 18, 2021, https://jalopnik.com/the-mid4-concept-was-this-close-to-being-nissans-flagsh-1847502580.

..."The Skyline is my alter ego": Dennis Gorodji, *Nissan GT-R Supercar: Born to Race* (Veloce, 2009).

Gorodji ibid.

...Ito instructed his engineers: "Nissan Legend Hiroyoshi Kato: The Man Who Found His Calling," Nissan Motor Corporation, October 8, 2013, https://usa.nissannews.com/en-US/releases/nissan-legend-hiroyoshi-kato-the-man-who-found-his-calling.

...Nissan limited sales: Andy Butler, *Skyline: The Ultimate Japanese Supercar* (Haynes, 2005).

..."most advanced touring car": "Sky's the Limit," *Motor Australia*, August 1989, retrieved via compilation from R.M. Clark, *Nissan Skyline GT-R – 1989-2002 Road Test Book* (Brooklands Books Ltd., 2003).

..."flatters your driving": Kevin Radley, "The World's Most Advanced Road Car," *Car*, February 1990, retrieved via compilation from R.M. Clark, *Nissan Skyline GT-R – 1989-2002 Road Test Book* (Brooklands Books Ltd., 2003).

...massive $110,000 base price: Andy Enright, "Five facts even the biggest GT-R nerd probably didn't know," Which Car, April 1, 2020, https://www.whichcar.com.au/features/five-facts-even-the-biggest-gt-r-nerd-probably-didnt-know.

Chapter 4

...more than $2 billion: Mike Stachura, "Ripple Effect: How Hideki Matsuyama's Masters win could revive golf's popularity in Japan," *Golf Digest*, April 14, 2021, https://www.golfdigest.com/story/hideki-matsuyama-masters-win-japan-golf-popularity-participation-equipment-sales

...eight Toprank facilities: "Locations," Top Rank Global, https://toprankglobal.jp/about_us/#_japan.

...not sold in America: Matt Robinson, "This Honda Accord Euro R Is A Hard-To-Find Slice Of JDM Cool," Car Throttle, September 13, 2021, https://www.carthrottle.com/post/this-honda-accord-euro-r-is-a-hard-to-find-slice-of-jdm-cool/.

...comprise a large portion: "How do you buy a JDM car in Japan as a US military member?" Top Rank Global, https://toprankglobal.jp/y-plate/.

...reputation for causing accidents: Masanori Hirakawa, "'Beware of Y license plates': Okinawans struggle for justice over US soldiers' accidents," Mainichi, July 17, 2020, https://mainichi.jp/english/articles/20200717/p2a/00m/0na/004000c.

Chapter 5

...old dairy farm shed: "About," HKS USA, https://www.hksusa.com/about.

Ben Hsu, "Hiroyuki Hasegawa, 1945 — 2016," Japanese Nostalgic Car, November 10, 2016, https://japanesenostalgiccar.com/hiroyuki-hasegawa-1945-2016/.

...young Yamaha motorcycle engineer: "History," HKS Global, https://www.hks-global.com/en/history/index.html.

...first to Hawaii: "Building Tracks to New Beginnings: Japanese Railroad Workers in the West," University of Utah, April 20, 2016, https://blog.lib.utah.edu/building-tracks-new-beginnings-japanese-railroad-workers-west/.

...the area would become home: Akiko Fujita, "Toyota built Torrance into the second-largest home of Japanese Americans. Now, it's leaving," The World, May 16, 2014, https://theworld.org/stories/2014-05-16/toyota-built-torrance-second-largest-home-japanese-americans-now-its-leaving.

...made it to 197: "Smokey nagata VS U.K.police," YouTube, September 10, 2006, https://www.youtube.com/watch?v=uWUslYuZ9k4.

...president of GReddy traveled: Interview with Kenji Sumino, conducted May 10, 2023.

...grown fewer and fewer: Caroline Brady, "Robinson may get TI spot for track," *San Pedro News-Pilot*, September 23, 1993, https://www.newspapers.com/image/608250316/?terms=torrance%20%22street%20racing%22&match=1.

..."sheer audacity of their operations": Michael Gougis, "Law puts brakes on drag racing," *San Pedro News-Pilot*, February 4, 1997, https://www.newspapers.com/image/608399179/?terms=torrance%20%22street%20racing%22&match=1.

...marketing unhealthy foods: Alice Binder, Brigitte Naderer, Jörg Matthes, "A "Forbidden Fruit Effect": An Eye-Tracking Study on Children's Visual Attention to Food Marketing," *International Journal of Environmental Research and Public Health*, March 13, 2020, https://www.ncbi.nlm.nih.gov/pmc/articles/PMC7142814/.

...authorized notary public: Complaint/Arrest Affidavit, Circuit and

County Courts, Miami-Dade County, Florida, obtained via public records request, received on April 25, 2023.

…**2015 and 2020 alone:** Michael Satterfield, "Florida Cracks Down Revoking Nearly 400 Titles," The Gentleman Racer, March 18, 2022, https://www.thegentlemanracer.com/2022/03/florida-cracks-down-on-illegally.html.

…**"an immediate serious danger":** Order of Emergency Suspension of License, State of Florida, Department of Highway Safety and Motor Vehicles, downloaded via "400 JDM Imported Cars Lose their Titles in the USA," JDM Buy Sell, July 27, 2021, https://www.jdmbuysell.com/jdm-lifestyle/400-jdm-cars-that-were-imported-by-jdm-importers/.

…**two-year extended prison sentence:** Sam Fosness, "Davison County felony court cases for April 25," *Mitchell Republic*, April 27, 2023, https://www.mitchellrepublic.com/news/local/davison-county-felony-court-cases-for-april-25.

Chapter 6

…**in 1979, a local optomestrist:** "WHITTAKER, Robert Russell," Biographical Directory of the United States Congress, https://bioguide.congress.gov/search/bio/W000426.

…**a flashbulb smile:** "Representative Bob Whittaker," Congress.gov, https://www.congress.gov/member/robert-whittaker/W000426?q=%7B%22sponsorship%22%3A%22sponsored%22%2C%22bill-status%22%3A%5B%22introduced%22%5D%7D.

…**43 bills and resolutions:** "Rep. Robert Whittaker," GovTrack, https://www.govtrack.us/congress/members/robert_whittaker/411585.

…**Americans wanted new cars:** John B. Hege, *The Automotive Gray Market: An Inside History* (McFarland & Company, 2022).

…**"virtual tidal wave":** Nancy L. Ross, "U.S. Preparing to Curb Importers Of Highly Discounted Luxury Cars," *Washington Post*, December 16, 1984, https://www.washingtonpost.com/archive/business/1984/12/16/us-preparing-to-curb-importers-of-highly-discounted-luxury-cars/1d32c739-08ba-4c5b-b495-b556ea12f3b2/.

…**notorious gray-market character:** Paul Dean, "Wheeling-Dealing

Gray Market Hits the Skids," *Los Angeles Times*, July 11, 1986, https://www.latimes.com/archives/la-xpm-1986-07-11-vw-19912-story.html.

...34 cars converted: Jane Applegate, "Newport Beach: Car Dealer Sentenced for Smog Test Fakery," *Los Angeles Times*, November 26, 1985, https://www.latimes.com/archives/la-xpm-1985-11-26-me-2039-story.html.

...suddenly careened off the road: "Highway Patrol seeks witnesses to Saturday's fatal auto crash," *Napa Valley Register*, June 13, 1984, retrieved via https://www.newspapers.com/image/565154791/?terms=%22suzanne%20zelonis%22&match=1.

...Prosecutors threw the book: "San Francisco man charged with vehicular manslaughter," *Napa Valley Register*, August 15, 1984, retrieved via https://www.newspapers.com/image/565256256/?terms=%22suzanne%20zelonis%22&match=1.

...To bolster his case: Sean Silverthorne, "Star witness swayed Walker jury," *Napa Valley Register*, February 8, 1986, retrieved via https://www.newspapers.com/image/565025055/?terms="suzanne zelonis"&match=1.

...conveniently couldn't recall: Sean Silverthorne," *Napa Valley Register*, February 4, 1986, retrieved via https://www.newspapers.com/image/565024637/?terms=%22suzanne%20zelonis%22&match=1.

...preparing for a diplomatic event: "Official OKs Deaver's Discount on BMW but Bans Future Deals," *Los Angeles Times*, March 12, 1985, https://www.latimes.com/archives/la-xpm-1985-03-12-mn-34208-story.html.

..."This rapid change in the market": Jared A. Rosenholtz, "Elite Theory, Individual Autonomy and Interest Groups: An Examination of America's Rules on Imported Vehicles," University of Central Florida, 2005.

Chapter 7

...Japan's Forestry Agency: "Tanzawa Recreation Forest," Ministry of Agriculture, Forestry and Fisheries, https://www.rinya.maff.go.jp/e/national_forest/recreation_forest/tanzawa.html.

...It told of Minis: David Barry, "Street Racing Mulholland Drive in

1978," Edmunds, July 4, 2011, https://www.edmunds.com/car-reviews/features/street-racing-mulholland-drive-in-1978.html.

…89 PRP-branded products: "Platinum Racing Products for RB26," Platinum Racing Products, https://www.platinumracingproducts.com/en-us/pages/search-results-page?q=rb26&page=1&rb_filter_ptag_7623bb393d9a9572e14f73411610e29b=Platinum%20Racing%20Products.

Chapter 8

…Gates wanted one: Andrew G., "The Porsche 959: a Story of Baur, Bott, Boost, and Bill Gates," Car Throttle, November 21, 2016, https://www.carthrottle.com/post/nr7vere/.

…group known for causing trouble: "Japan cops to classify bosozoku gangs as 'semi-yakuza'," *Tokyo Reporter*, March 7, 2013, https://www.tokyoreporter.com/crime/yakuza/japan-cops-to-classify-bosozoku-gangs-as-semi-yakuza/.

…still largely criminalized: Dai Inada, "The World of 300+ km/h," *JDM Option International*, May 2008, http://www.jdm-option.com/eng/column/05_08/inada.html.

…In October 1981: Ben Hsu, "We'll Always Have Yatabe," Japanese Nostalgic Car, March 28, 2008, https://japanesenostalgiccar.com/well-always-have-yatabe/.

…"the guy everyone wants": Dino Dalle Carbonare, "Nissans Take Over Sodegaura," SpeedHunters, October 8, 2015, http://www.speedhunters.com/2015/10/nissans-take-over-sodegaura/.

…The fastest car overall: "Yatabe: The Proving Grounds," Auto Team Retro, Facebook post, December 17, 2017, https://www.facebook.com/autoteamretro/posts/yatabe-the-proving-groundsive-spoken-at-length-about-yatabe-before-and-i-will-co/140766749974079/.

…when HKS turned up: Ben Hsu, "TBT: HKS M300 Toyota Celica XX," Japanese Nostalgic Car, October 22, 2015, https://japanesenostalgiccar.com/tbt-hks-m300-toyota-celica-xx/.

…posting a final top speed: HKS Japan, Instagram post, February 9, 2020, https://www.instagram.com/p/B8V97D4gt1k/.

…headed by Trust founder: Karl Aleksander Kivimägi, "The Yoshida specials 930 Turbo (Blackbird Porsche) and Mid Night Club member's cars," Atelier Eau Rouge, August 4, 2021, https://ateliereaurouge.com/yoshida-specials-930-mid-night-club-members/.

...**flooded with callers:** Peter McKay, "Monster in demand," *Sydney Morning Herald*, August 26, 1989, retrieved via https://www.newspapers.com/image/121004567/?terms=nissan%20skyline%20gt-r&match=1.

...**one local racing champion:** Peter McKay, "Maybe, maybe..." *Sydney Morning Herald*, October 14, 1989, retrieved via https://www.newspapers.com/image/123459329/?terms=nissan%20skyline%20gt-r&match=1.

...**spawning a film adaptation:** "Black Statement Book," IMDB listing, https://www.imdb.com/title/tt0228498/.

...**"deeply engaging and unrelenting experience":** Adam Symchuk, "Film Review: Black Test Car (1962) by Yasuzo Masumura," Asian Movie Plus, August 26, 2020, https://asianmoviepulse.com/2020/08/film-review-black-test-car-1962-by-yasuzo-masumura/.

...**In Japan in 1990:** Karl Aleksander Kivimägi, "Blackbird Porsche 911 and Devil Z: The legends of wangan Midnight," Atelier Eau Rouge, September 27, 2021, https://ateliereaurouge.com/blackbird-porsche-and-devil-z-wangan-midnight/.

...**Japanese characters on its doors:** Joe Terrell, "Ultimate Initial D AE86 Guide," Drifted, June 30, 2023, https://www.drifted.com/initial-d-ae86/#specs.

...**Born in Hong Kong:** Matthew Kang, "Fans of Japanese Drift Car Series 'Initial D' Are Blowing Up This San Gabriel Valley Tofu Café," Eater, February 2, 2022, https://la.eater.com/2022/2/2/22914685/fujiwara-tofu-cafe-initial-d-theme-san-gabriel-valley-boba-car-drift-culture.

...**Bill Gates was growing impatient:** David Colman, "At Long Last: Federalizing the Porsche 959 has been a long road. Now, at least, it can be traversed," *Autoweek*, September 14, 2003, https://www.autoweek.com/news/a2102531/long-last-federalizing-porsche-959-has-been-long-road-now-least-it-can-be-traversed/

Chapter 9

...blog post in 2014: Sean Morris, "Forged Entry Documents From SOHO Imports in Florida on a Nissan Silvia S15," Import A Vehicle, January 1, 2014, https://www.importavehicle.info/2014/01/forged-entry-documents-from-soho.html.

...responsible for policing Dade County: "MOTOR VEHICLE FIELD OPERATIONS - REGIONAL OFFICES," Florida Independent Automobile Dealers Association, January 21, 2020, https://cdn.ymaws.com/www.fiada.com/resource/collection/921A39C0-769A-4695-8F5F-B50C3326D04F/Regional_Office_Locations.pdf.

...wasn't even listed: "Registered Importers," NHTSA, August 2, 2018, https://www.nhtsa.gov/sites/nhtsa.gov/files/documents/active_ri_list_as_of_august_2_2018.pdf.

...approved by the state of Vermont: Complaint/Arrest Affidavit, ibid.

...3.7-percent of containers: "Container Inspection: An Unsolved Need," American Journal of Transportation, July 8, 2021, https://ajot.com/insights/full/ai-container-inspection-an-unsolved-need.

...containers inspected globally: Rose George, *Ninety Percent of Everything*, (Picador, 2014).

...lax vehicle-registration laws: Rob Siegel, "The end of 'The Vermont Loophole,'" *Hagerty*, July 24, 2023, https://www.hagerty.com/media/opinion/the-hack-mechanic/the-end-of-the-vermont-loophole/.

...morning of March 7th: Complaint/Arrest Affidavit, ibid.

...closed after officials seized: David Tracy and Ryan Felton, "Cops Seize $130,000 Nissan Skyline GT-R At Florida Car Show And The Story Is Wild (Updated)," Jalopnik, April 26, 2018, https://jalopnik.com/cops-seize-130-000-nissan-skyline-gt-r-at-florida-car-1825542919.

...abruptly left town: Ryan Felton, "Lost Nissan Skylines, A $335,000 Lawsuit, An Empty Warehouse: Has A Well-Known JDM Importer Skipped Town?," Jalopnik, June 19, 2018, https://jalopnik.com/lost-nissan-skylines-a-335-000-lawsuit-an-empty-ware-1826873554.

...another way in: "Temporary Importation under Bond (TIB)," U.S. Customs and Border Protection, June 1, 2023, https://www.cbp.gov/

document/guidance/temporary-importation-under-bond-duty-free-entry-goods-be-re-exported.

...he joined forces: Richard S. Chang, "Access Denied," *0-60 Magazine,* Summer 2008, http://skylinegt-r.wikidot.com/0-60mrex.

...forming a company: "Motorex, Inc.," Open Corporates, January 7, 2023, https://opencorporates.com/companies/us_ca/2054912.

...bright blue R32: "GReddy BNR32 Quick Reference Guide," GReddy, http://www.greddy.com/featured/68.

...His first project: Instagram post by user @greddykenji, February 27, 2022, https://www.instagram.com/p/CaeVMW1LFXf/?img_index=4.

...both JK and G&K: Colman, "At Long Last," ibid.

...imported and federalized: Sean Morris, "How Many MotoRex Nissan Skyline GT-R?" GT-R USA Blog, February 1, 2017, https://www.gtrusablog.com/2017/02/how-many-motorex-nissan-skyline-gt-r.html.

...adding as much as $25,000: "The INSANE true story of the MotoRex scandal," VINwiki, YouTube video, April 30, 2021, https://www.youtube.com/watch?v=i-lir9E7hyA.

...Sachs who assigned: "Decision that Nonconforming 1990-1999 Nissan GTS and GTR Passenger Cars Are Eligible for Importation," Federal Register, January 19, 2000, https://www.federalregister.gov/documents/2000/01/19/00-1125/decision-that-nonconforming-1990-1999-nissan-gts-and-gtr-passenger-cars-are-eligible-for-importation.

..."epic of fast cars": "Godzilla Versus The Banhammer: The Sad Tale of Motorex and The Legal Status of R33s and 34s," 23GT, September 13, 2015, http://www.23gt.net/2015/09/godzilla-versus-banhammer-sad-tale-of.html.

...set a new course record: "NISSAN SKYLINE VICTORIOUS AT PIKES PEAK HILL CLIMB," Motorsport, July 8, 1999, https://us.motorsport.com/hillclimb/news/pikes-peak-nissan-skyline-update/1758484/.

...when Lieberman called: Brian Silvestro, "The Yellow R33 GT-R From Fast and Furious Was an Original Motorex Import That Got Crushed," *Road & Track,* February 19, 2020, https://www.

roadandtrack.com/car-culture/entertainment/a30986918/fast-and-furious-yellow-r33-gt-r-explained/.

...**"doesn't have a brain in its head"**: Roger Ebert, "The Fast and the Furious," RogerEbert.com, June 22, 2001, https://www.rogerebert.com/reviews/the-fast-and-the-furious-2001.

...**an importing authority:** Preston Lerner, "Tuning Japanese," *Popular Mechanics*, February 2003 issue. Printed edition retrieved May 25, 2023.

...**A 2005 story:** John Pearley Huffman, "How to Get One of the Most Desirable Sports Cars in the World," Edmunds, May 19, 2005. Printed edition retrieved May 25, 2023.

...**an EPA exception:** "Kit Car Policy," United States Environmental Protection Agency, July 8, 1994, https://www.epa.gov/importing-vehicles-and-engines/kit-car-policy.

...**"strengthened seatbelt mounts":** "2000 Nissan Skyline R34 GT-R by Kaizo Industries," Bonhams, https://cars.bonhams.com/auction/29008/lot/1P/2000-nissan-skyline-r34-gt-r-by-kaizo-industries/.

...**"The chassis can be registered":** "Kaizo Industries Skyline R34," forum post on GT-R Life, https://www.gtrlife.com/threads/kaizo-industries-skyline-r34.21388/.

...**Widely panned by critics:** "Fast & Furious Reviews," Rotten Tomatoes, https://www.rottentomatoes.com/m/fast_and_furious/reviews?type=top_critics.

...**just three months:** Sean Morris, "UPDATED: ICE, DOT - CARB Serving Search Warrants Today," GT-R USA Blog, June 4, 2009, https://www.gtrusablog.com/2009/06/ice-dot-carb-serving-search-warrants.html.

...**make the paperwork line up:** "United States v. One Nissan Skyline," United States District Court, Ninth Circuit, California, June 3, 2014.

...**dissolved as a corporate entity:** "Kaizo Industries, Inc.," Open Corporates, January 6, 2023, https://opencorporates.com/companies/us_ca/2963385.

...**federal agents had visited:** "United States v. One Nissan Skyline," ibid.

…JDM enthusiasts were warning: Sean Morris, "What's Going On With Kaizo?" Import A Vehicle, August 2, 2009, https://www.importavehicle.info/2009/08/whats-going-on-with-kaizo.html.

…some owners reported: Sean Morris, "The Kaizo Drama Thus Far," GT-R USA Blog, October 3, 2009, https://www.gtrusablog.com/2009/10/kaizo-drama-thus-far.html.

…the government charged: "Summary of Criminal Prosecutions," United States Environmental Protection Agency, March 7, 2011, https://cfpub.epa.gov/compliance/criminal_prosecution/index.cfm?action=3&prosecution_summary_id=2157&searchParams=M5%2C%3A%2FXT%2A%5CCYZ%40JZ%5DIWY45%3DXBI%3EX%3A%29M%3B%5CSK%25%29%3F%5F%5B%202%2CEZ6B8%276%5FCUOD9VHJ308%0AM7%25K9%26UQ%28%27%29J%23.

…conspiracy charge: "18 U.S. Code § 371 - Conspiracy to commit offense or to defraud United States," Cornell Law School, https://www.law.cornell.edu/uscode/text/18/371.

…false statements charge: "18 U.S. Code § 1001 - Statements or entries generally," Cornell Law School, https://www.law.cornell.edu/uscode/text/18/1001.

…smuggling and laundering charges: "18 U.S. Code § 545 - Smuggling goods into the United States," Cornell Law School, https://www.law.cornell.edu/uscode/text/18/545.

…smuggling and laundering charges: "2182. Jury Instruction -- 18 U.S.C. 1956 -- Laundering Of Monetary Instruments," Department of Justice Archives, January 17, 2020, https://www.justice.gov/archives/jm/criminal-resource-manual-2182-jury-instruction-18-usc-1956-laundering-monetary-instruments.

…Alison plead guilty: "Clean Air Act Vehicle and Engine Enforcement Case Resolutions," United States Environmental Protection Agency, January 31, 2023, https://www.epa.gov/enforcement/clean-air-act-vehicle-and-engine-enforcement-case-resolutions.

…"While many car buffs": David Zimmerle, "Resident Charged with Illegally Importing Muscle Cars," *San Clemente Times*, November 4, 2010, https://www.sanclementetimes.com/resident-charged-with-illegally-importing-muscle-cars/.

...**Forced to leave the country:** Brian Silvestro, "Buy Paul Walker's Skyline R34 GT-R From Fast & Furious," *Road & Track*, March 30, 2023, https://www.roadandtrack.com/news/a43465935/paul-walker-skyline-r34-gt-r-fast-and-furious-for-sale/.

...**previous record-holder:** Bogdan Bebeselea, "This Nissan Skyline R34 GT-R V-SPEC II Driven by Paul Walker Just Sold for $577,000," Auto Evolution, August 21, 2022, https://www.autoevolution.com/news/this-nissan-skyline-r34-gt-r-v-spec-ii-driven-by-paul-walker-just-sold-for-577000-196510.html.

Chapter X

...**"more focused on building cars":** Nick Kostov and Sean McLain, *Boundless: The Rise, Fall, and Escape of Carlos Ghosn* (HarperCollins, 2022).

...**driven by overvalued real estate:** Kostov and McLain, *Boundless*, ibid.

...**2.5 times its gross domestic product:** Jared Diamond, *Upheaval: How Nations Cope with Crisis and Change*, (Little, Brown, 2019).

...**Nissan materials researcher:** "GT-R Executive Profile: Hiroshi Tamura," Nissan Motor Corporation, November 16, 2013, https://global.nissannews.com/en/releases/release-633f5fc2dac265a06b78fdb8490b1345-gt-r-executive-profile-hiroshi-tamura.

...**"to save money":** Angus MacKenzie and Peter Nunn, "Killer Godzilla!" *Wheels*, March 1995, retrieved via compilation from R.M. Clark, *Nissan Skyline GT-R – 1989-2002 Road Test Book* (Brooklands Books Ltd., 2003).

...**"growth recession":** Krugman, *Return of Depression Economics*, ibid.

Chapter XI

...**two movies grossing:** "Franchise: The Fast and the Furious," Box Office Mojo, https://www.boxofficemojo.com/franchise/fr3628568325/.

...**wanted to expand:** Moto Miwa, "Flashback Archive: GT Live 2004, a Japanese Motorsports Extravaganza in America," Club4AG, June 7,

2015, https://club4ag.com/gtlive2004-a-japanese-motorsports-extravaganza/.

…**The weekend drew:** Chris Rosales, "Remembering the Only Time Japan's Super GT Racing Series Came to America," The Drive, September 4, 2023, https://www.thedrive.com/news/remembering-the-only-time-japans-super-gt-racing-series-came-to-america.

…**California winter day:** "Ontario, CA Weather History – December 17, 2004," Weather Underground, https://www.wunderground.com/history/daily/us/ca/fontana/KONT/date/2004-12-17.

…**All over the world:** Nick Kostov and Sean McLain, *Boundless*, ibid.

…**"a Japanese electronics firm":** "Japan's Keiretsu as a Strategic Relationship with Suppliers," CAPS: Center for Strategic Supply Research, 2005, https://comexitape.files.wordpress.com/2012/02/caso-5-keiretsu2005caps.pdf.

…**Ghosn had never promised:** Larimer, "Japan, Nissan and the Ghosn Revolution," ibid.

…**Immigrant comprise just 1.9-percent:** Diamond, *Upheaval*, ibid.

…**appraised by an expert:** Henry Kelsall, "Here's Why Larry Chen Did Not Expect The True Value Of His Nissan R32 GT-R," Hot Cars, August 24, 2022, https://www.hotcars.com/larry-chen-nissan-r32-gt-r-true-value/.

…**first R35 show car:** Adam Ismail, "The 2001 Nissan GT-R Concept Was The First Stop On The Long Road To The R35," Jalopnik, June 30, 2021, https://jalopnik.com/the-2001-nissan-gt-r-concept-was-the-first-stop-on-the-1847195619.

…**Even more astonishing:** Evan McCausland, "Prices for 2009 Nissan GT R Jump Almost $6000," *Motor Trend*, September 5, 2008, https://www.motortrend.com/news/prices-for-2009-nissan-gtr-jump-almost-6000-134755/.

…**Only the Porsche 911 Turbo:** Tony Quiroga, "2009 Nissan GT-R vs. BMW M3 and Porsche 911 Turbo," *Car And Driver*, July 2008, https://www.caranddriver.com/reviews/comparison-test/a15142828/2008-bmw-m3-vs-2009-nissan-gt-r-vs-2008-porsche-911-turbo-comparison-tests/.

…**Performance Car of the Year:** "Managing Through the Global

Crisis," Nissan Annual Report 2009, https://www.nissan-global.com/EN/DOCUMENT/PDF/AR/2009/AR09E_P18_Sales_Performance.pdf.

Chapter 12

...found a blue R32: "Case No. YC051290 - William D. Sudbrock vs. MotoRex, Inc. et al," Superior Court of California, County of Los Angeles, September 8, 2006, retrieved via public records request at Los Angeles County Superior Court on May 25, 2023.

...Two weeks after Sudbrock: "Registered Importers Whose Registrations Have Been Revoked - Fiscal Years 2006 – 2016," NHTSA, June 1, 2016, https://www.nhtsa.gov/sites/nhtsa.gov/files/revoked_suspended_ris_june012016.pdf.

...private owner in Wisconsin: "Quick fix: De Pere man avoids prison, but loses 'Fast and Furious' car," *Milwaukee Journal Sentinel*, https://archive.jsonline.com/news/crime/quick-fix-de-pere-man-avoids-prison-but-loses-fast-and-furious-car-me5is5s-154790445.html.

...December of 2005: "Case No. BC356922 - Hirofumi Fukamoto v. Hiroaki Nanahoshi et al," Superior Court of California, County of Los Angeles, April 1, 2010, retrieved via public records request at Los Angeles County Superior Court on May 25, 2023.

Chapter 13

...selling 1,730 R35 GT-Rs: "Nissan GT-R US Sales Figures," Car Figures, July 6, 2023, https://carfigures.com/us-market-brand/nissan/gt-r.

...worldwide sales fell: Carlos Ghosn and Toshiyuki Shiga, "Fiscal Year 2009 Financial Results," Nissan Motor Corporation, May 12, 2010, https://www.nissan-global.com/EN/DOCUMENT/HTML/FINANCIAL/SPEECH/2009/2009results_speech_437_e.html.

...point of contention: Based on interviews with GT-R enthusiasts and insiders, confirmed by former and current Nissan employees with knowledge of the situation who spoke on the condition of anonymity.

...thrived on a series: Vlad Radu, "20 Years Ago, Nissan Said Goodbye to the R34 GT-R With Two Badass Limited Editions," Auto Evolution, April 6, 2022, https://www.autoevolution.com/news/20-years-ago-nissan-said-goodbye-to-the-r34-gt-r-with-two-badass-limited-editions-185767.html.

…had joined the company: "Top Gear chats to Mizuno-san: Mr GT-R," *Top Gear*, February 23, 2012, https://www.topgear.com/car-news/top-gear-magazine/top-gear-chats-mizuno-san-mr-gt-r.

…established a shell company: *Boundless*, ibid.

…he sued Nissan: Nico Demattia, "Carlos Ghosn Sues Nissan for $1 Billion, Vows a 'Fight to the End,'" June 20, 2023, https://www.thedrive.com/news/carlos-ghosn-sues-nissan-for-1-billion-vows-a-fight-to-the-end.

…led the effort: "Nissan GT-R breaks the Guinness World Records title for fastest drift," Nissan Motor Corporation, April 7, 2016, https://global.nissannews.com/en/releases/release-2eab3328f5bf96b6dc5b97649100bb41-nissan-gt-r-breaks-the-guinness-world-records-title-for-fastest-drift.

…set a new lap record: "Nissan GT-R NISMO breaks lap time record on Tsukuba Circuit," Nissan Motor Corporation, January 28, 2020, https://uk.nissannews.com/en-GB/releases/release-cff9d88d82d639c6ae57480cf200399d-nissan-gt-r-nismo-breaks-lap-time-record-on-tsukuba-circuit.

…completed in 1968: "Shin Tomei Expressway Project," International Bridge, Tunnel and Turnpike Association, https://www.ibtta.org/awards/shin-tomei-expressway-project.

…find a new path: "Nissan keeps annual profit forecasts and cuts unit sales target," Japan Times, February 9, 2023, https://www.japantimes.co.jp/news/2023/02/09/business/corporate-business/nissan-annual-profit-forecast-same/.

Chapter 14

…fundraiser and toy drive: "Philippines Typhoon 2013," Reach Out World Wide, November 22, 2013, https://roww.org/project/philippines-typhoon-2013/.

…once rural land: "My Camp Zama," U.S. Army, https://home.army.

mil/japan/index.php/my-fort#:~:text=Camp%20Zama%20also%20-houses%20an,the%20U.S.%20Army%20Garrison%20Japan.

…once a powerhouse: "Nissan to Build Global Production Engineering Center in Zama-- 350 new jobs to be created," Nissan Motor Corporation, September 25, 2005, https://global.nissannews.com/en/releases/050926-01-e?source=nng&year=2005.

…5-billion-yen injection: "NISMO Nirvana," Nissan Motor Company, December 5, 2017, https://global.nissannews.com/en/releases/release-2f7966f516e271fc4ea0f79a9a040e36-nismo-nirvana.

…400-plus vehicles: "Nissan CEO Ghosn Visits the Zama Heritage Garage," Nissan Motor Corporation, April 19, 2012, https://usa.nissannews.com/en-US/releases/nissan-ceo-ghosn-visits-the-zama-heritage-garage?selectedTabId=releases.

…240Z Fairlady police car: "Fairlady 240ZG Highway Police car," Nissan Motor Corporation, https://www.nissan-global.com/EN/HERITAGE/fairlady_240z_g.html.

…Rumors persist: Isaac Mion, "'71 Nissan Skyline 2000GT - Old School Flavor," *Motor Trend*, March 14, 2011, https://www.motortrend.com/features/modp-1103-1971-nissan-skyline-2000gt/.

…Rumors persist: Peter Kelly, "A Hakosuka In The Hills," SpeedHunters, July 12, 2014, http://www.speedhunters.com/2014/07/a-hakosuka-skyline-in-the-hills/.

…Rumors persist: Shamsul Yunos, "Original Hakosuka GT-R spotted in KL ," *New Straits Times*, July 10, 2017, https://www.nst.com.my/cbt/2017/07/256140/original-hakosuka-gt-r-spotted-kl.

Chapter 15
Based on the author's firsthand experiences and interviews.

ABOUT THE AUTHOR

Photo by Forest Casey.

Ryan ZumMallen is an automotive journalist and video host, and the founder of Carrara Media. He has served as Senior Writer for both *Trucks.com* and *Edmunds.com*, and his debut book *Slow Car Fast* received critical acclaim. Further work has appeared in *Road & Track*, *The Verge*, *Autoweek*, *SLAM Magazine*, and other publications. He holds a degree in Print Journalism from California State University, Long Beach and is a former fellow of the California Endowment Health Journalism program at the University of Southern California. He lives in Long Beach with his wife and daughter.

Carrara Media, LLC.

Cover art by Aaron Sanchez.

To learn more about Carrara Media and its products, events and newsletters, visit CarraraBooks.com or follow us at @CarraraBooks.

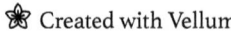 Created with Vellum

Printed in the USA
CPSIA information can be obtained
at www.ICGtesting.com
LVHW010351231223
767218LV00092B/4140